Cultural Resource Laws and Practice
An Introductory Guide

Heritage Resources Management Series

Series Editor: DON FOWLER, *University of Nevada, Reno*

*Sponsored by the Heritage Resources Management Program,
Division of Continuing Education, University of Nevada, Reno*

Books in this series are practical guides designed to help those who work in cultural resources management, environmental management, heritage preservation, and related subjects. Based on a series of successful workshops sponsored by the University of Nevada, Reno, the books are designed to be "workshops between book covers" on important strategic, legal, and practical issues faced by those who work in this field. Books are replete with examples, checklists, worksheets, and worldly advice offered by experienced practitioners in the field. Future titles in this series will deal with assessing historical significance, management of archeological sites, working with native communities, and other topics.

Volumes in this series:

1. **Cultural Resource Laws and Practice: An Introductory Guide,**
   Thomas F. King

2. **Federal Planning and Historic Places: The Section 106 Process,**
   Thomas F. King

Cultural Resource Laws and Practice
An Introductory Guide

Thomas F. King

ALTAMIRA
PRESS

A Division of
ROWMAN & LITTLEFIELD PUBLISHERS, INC.
Walnut Creek • Lanham • New York • Oxford

ALTAMIRA PRESS
A Division of Rowman & Littlefield Publishers, Inc.
1630 North Main Street, Suite 367
Walnut Creek, CA 94596
www.altamirapress.com

Rowman & Littlefield Publishers, Inc.
4720 Boston Way
Lanham, MD 20706

12 Hid's Copse Road
Cumnor Hill, Oxford OX2 9JJ, England

British Library Cataloguing in Publication Information Available

Library of Congress Cataloging-in-Publication Data

King, Thomas F., 1942–
    Cultural resource laws and practice : an introductory guide / Thomas F. King
      p. cm.
    (Heritage resources management series; v. 1)
    Includes bibliographical references and index.
    ISBN 0-7619-9043-7 (cloth : alk. paper)
    ISBN 0-7619-9044-5 (pbk. : alk. paper)
    1. Historic preservation—Law and legislation—United States.
    2. Cultural property—Protection—Law and legislation—United States.
    I. Title. II. Series.
    KF4310 .K56 1998
    344.73'094—ddc21
                                    98-25397
                                       CIP

Printed in the United States of America

♾™ The paper used in this publication meets the minimum requirements of American
National Standard for Information Sciences—Permanence of Paper for Printed Library
Materials, ANSI/NISO Z39.48–1992.

Production management by Pamela Lucas
Illustrations by Nick Del Cioppo and Thomas F. King
Production and editorial services by Katherine Nickerson
Cover design by Joanna Ebenstein

Dedication

To the memory of Robert R. Garvey, Jr.,
who taught me that preservation is about live people.

Contents

Figures

Series Editor Introduction

by Don Fowler

In 1987, at the request of numerous colleagues working under the rubric of "Cultural Resources Management" (CRM), we began a program of continuing education at the University of Nevada, Reno (UNR) for CRM professionals, land managers, tribal officials, agency administrators and others who wished to learn about and keep current in this rapidly expanding and changing field. By 1995 it was clear that we needed courses as well in natural resource management and in areas where the cultural and natural realms overlap, as they often do in land managing agencies. Hence, we changed the name of our program to "Heritage Resources Management Program." By whatever name, the aims and purposes of the program from the beginning have been to provide state-of-the-art, practice-oriented workshops, seminars and short courses in scientific, technical, legal, administrative, and public exhibit aspects of heritage resources management. Our efforts have been enhanced by formal cooperative agreements with the Advisory Council on Historic Preservation, the National Park Service, and various other federal, state and private groups. Our first goal was to find and hire the best qualified experts on any given topic, who could also teach, and teach well, in a continuing education setting—a very difficult thing to do successfully. Our second goal was to then give these individuals their heads in the development of the courses. We have drawn our instructors from state and federal agencies, research institutes, the judiciary, consulting firms, universities, museums, and the private sector. We regard all our instructors and all those who take our courses as members of an informal, interactive advisory board, giving us ongoing feedback on how we can improve the program, suggestions for new courses and instructors, and so on. It has been a highly successful experiment, and one we expect to continue. By 1996, the need for a series of textbooks and manuals to accompany the courses became clear, rather than the UNR Continuing Education Division continually enhancing the value of Xerox Corporation stock with all those copies. Through the vision of Mitch Allen, of AltaMira Press, this need has been satisfied. The present volume is the premier work in the series.

One of the first persons we sought for our program was Thomas F. King, the author of the present volume. Tom and I have grown older and grayer since we first met at the now-legendary CRM conference in Denver in 1974. Tom was then, as now, dedicated, acerbic, articulate, eminently rational, and at the same time passionate about issues that matter. Over the years, as a bemused but never detached participant-observer of and in CRM, agency, congressional, administrative and researcher tribes, he has come to understand, as well or better than anyone in the country, the nuances, limits, and meanings of laws and related rules which inform cultural resource management practice. He has given fully of this wry wisdom in dozens of teaching and consulting situations for our program and others around the country—to the benefit of the hundreds of persons who have attended and learned much from his courses, and his counsel. He has, at the same, been a major participant in the ongoing discussions about what our program should be and how we get there. Hence, it is with a great deal of both pride and pleasure that we inaugurate our new publication series with Tom King's *Cultural Resource Laws and Practice.* We could not get off to a better start.

Don Fowler,
Director
August 5, 1998

Acknowledgements

No one but me is to blame for this book, but I want to thank AltaMira Press, especially Mitch Allen for his understanding, patience, and thoughtful advice, and Pam Lucas and Kathy Nickerson for riding herd on me during its production. I'm also grateful to Dr. Constance W. Ramirez and Mary Pierce, for reading and commenting on a draft. Thanks also to series editor Don Fowler for encouraging me to do this volume, and for his unfailing support and encouragement during its preparation.

In addition, I'm grateful to all those who've worked with me over the years in developing and presenting courses in historic preservation, environmental review, and related topics, to all those who've taken my classes as active and often critical participants, and to all those who've challenged me and my premises in negotiations, consultations, conversations, publications, and internet debates. For better or worse, without you all, this book would not have come to be.

Finally, I'm grateful to Nick Del Cioppo for his illustrations, without which I would remain mired in the mud.

Tom King
Silver Spring, Maryland
June 1998

The historical and cultural foundations of the Nation should be preserved as a living part of our community life and development in order to give a sense of orientation to the American people.

—National Historic Preservation Act
(16 USC 470 et seq.) Section 1(b)(2)

Part One

Background and Overview

Chapter 1

Introduction

The Voice of the People

Chitaro William's house sat on a rocky ledge overlooking the mouth of Pou Bay. Midden—dark soil charged with marine shells and animal bones, detritus of thousands of meals consumed over countless generations, the stuff archeologists excavate—streamed down the face of the ledge. Chitaro was the current political chief of Mechchitiw Village, and his house, a green, tin-roofed plywood bungalow overlooking the bulk of the village, reflected it. My wife—cultural anthropologist Patricia Parker—and I had come to pay our respects to him and Teruio, Mechchitiw's traditional high chief and senior elder. It was 1979. We were leaving the islands of Chuuk ("Truk"), in Micronesia, after two eventful years.

Pat had finished her dissertation research in nearby Iras Village. I had finished my two-year contract as "Consultant to the High Commissioner of the Trust Territory of the Pacific Islands: Archeology and Historic Preservation"—a contract the HiCom would have been happy to have terminated a year earlier had not the National Park Service forced him to rethink his position. Together we had mediated a major dispute between the Trust Territory Government and the villages of Iras and Mechitiw over construction of an airport on the fringes of their sacred mountain, Tonaachaw. Now we were leaving, great with child, experience, and dissertation data, ready to move on to other challenges.

We chatted over instant coffee laced with sweetened canned milk—a contemporary Chuukese tradition. Then Teruio reached into a dusty corner and pulled out a magnificent conch shell. We knew that conches, in Micronesia as throughout the Pacific, are traditionally used as trumpets. The chief blows into the conch to produce a piercing, wailing moan that summons the people to the *wuut*—the meetinghouse—to ponder grave issues or respond to urgent threats, to mobilize for war.

With trembling hands (he drank a lot of coffee), Teruio presented me with the conch. Pat translated as he told me what he meant by this:

> "When you are back in Washington, in that White House, keep this to remember the voice of the people."

We've not made it to the White House, except as tourists and to a reception or two, but Pat and I keep the conch in a prominent place, still specked with the green paint of Chitaro's house, to remind us of what we're about. Every now and then I pick it up and think about Teruio's words. It helps provide a measure of focus.

Over the years—particularly since the 1960s—the United States Congress has enacted a number of laws aimed at controlling the impacts of federal government actions on aspects of the environment. Among these aspects are those that are "cultural"—that is, those parts of the environment to which people ascribe significance because of the roles they play in their community life and history. In analyzing impacts on these "cultural resources," and in figuring out what to do about them, it is of course particularly important to listen to, and understand, "the voice of the people."

This book is about the federal laws that require consideration of cultural resources, and about the regulations, standards, and guidelines that have flowed from them. It is about practice under those laws, regulations, standards and guidelines, as I understand such practice. It deals in only the most slanting, peripheral way with local ordinances, state laws, and international law. This doesn't reflect a belief on my part that those aspects of practice aren't important; it just reflects the fact that I don't know very much about them. My practice has been mostly in and around the federal government, and that's what I'm qualified to write about.

Pretty dry stuff? It can be, at times, but not necessarily, and not always. The laws have made a difference, and they continue to do so. They have stopped federal projects that would otherwise have done violence to places people hold dear. They have caused major changes in such projects, to reduce or mitigate damage. They have been the subjects of lawsuits and congressional hearings, and they have had impacts on the careers of civil servants, military personnel, and political leaders. On the other hand, they have often worked smoothly to ensure that cultural concerns are integrated into project planning, creating situations that these days are referred to as "win-win," by allowing important projects to proceed while treasured aspects of the cultural environment are respected. One of the purposes of this book is to help people, organizations, and agencies achieve the latter happy condition in responsible, cost-effective ways.

More and more people are earning their livings working with the federal "cultural resource" laws—as attorneys, as government, Indian tribal, and corporate officials, as consultants, as field researchers. Such work can be professionally challenging and satisfying. It can also be frustrating—in large part because the laws, regulations, standards and guidelines have been developed with little reference to any overall vision, and with little coordination. They can appear to contradict one another, and they can be interpreted in a wide range of ways, some of which are little short of weird. They have spawned a number of governmental institutions whose goals are not always coincident with one another or, I believe, with the broad purposes of the laws, and whose procedures sometimes cross-cut and conflict with one another.

So, another thing this book will do is to elucidate some of these problems—as I see them from my own, admittedly biased, perspective—and where I can, to suggest ways of fixing them.

Who Should Read This Book?

Generally, this book is designed for use in college, university, and continuing education classes in historic preservation, environmental studies, social impact assessment, and "cultural resource management." It makes what might be called a good faith effort to present all the historical, legal, procedural, and policy stuff that a student practitioner of cultural resource management needs. It is also designed to replace a textbook that I co authored in the mid-70s with Pat Parker (then Hickman) and the late Gary Berg (King, Hickman, and Berg 1977), and to supplement such texts as Murtagh (1997), Fitch (1982), or Stipe and Lee (1987) on historic preservation, Cantor (1996) on environmental impact assessment, and Burdge and Colleagues (1994) on social impact assessment.

Much of this book is based on syllabi that I—or I with others—have developed over the last several years for short courses in historic preservation and "cultural resource management" sponsored by the Advisory Council on Historic Preservation (ACHP), the National Park Service (NPS), the University of Nevada, Reno, the National Preservation Institute, CEHP, Inc., the U.S. Navy, and others. As either the sole or principal author of such syllabi (which, fortunately, are also in the public domain), I have freely borrowed from them and adapted them to my needs. Thus another presumed readership comprises the people who frequent such courses or would do so if they could afford to—typically, environmental and historic preservation personnel in federal and state agencies, local governments, and Indian tribes, and consultants in environmental and historic preservation work.

Finally, parts of what follows are designed for colleagues who have expressed the desire to understand the laws and regulations, who value debate on the principles that underlie them, and some of whom flatter me by suggesting that I have something to contribute to such understanding and debate. My knowledge of all the legal authorities, and the theory underlying them, varies from authority to authority. I know a good deal about some of them, though, and can speculate about a good deal more. I have freely done so throughout the following chapters, and have expressed my opinions equally freely, in the hope of stimulating debate and discussion.

What are Cultural Resources?

The terms "cultural resource" and "cultural resource management" (CRM)—invented by archeologists in the 1970s to equate what they did with natural resource management—is variously taken to mean a number of different things (for definitions, see Appendix II). In publications, environmental documents, and agency guidelines, "cultural resource" is used:

- As a synonym for "historic property," defined in the National Historic Preservation Act;

- To mean known historic properties and properties that may be historic but whose historicity hasn't been established;

- To mean both historic properties and properties that are thought to be historic, but that someone nevertheless feels obligated to manage for some kind of cultural reason;

- To include any or all of the following:
  - Native American graves and cultural items
  - shipwrecks
  - museum collections
  - historical documents
  - religious sites
  - religious practices
  - cultural use of natural resources
  - folklife, tradition, other social institutions
  - theater groups, orchestras, and other community cultural amenities

- Without definition, on the assumption that everybody knows what it means.

The term "Cultural Resource Management"—which one might assume means managing cultural resources—is, in fact, used mostly by archeologists and much more occasionally by architectural historians and historical architects, to refer to managing historic places of archeological, architectural, and historical interest and to considering such places in compliance with environmental and historic preservation laws (cf. Lipe and Lindsay 1974; Johnson and Schene 1987).

In fact, the corpus of laws, executive orders, and regulations require, to some extent, that U.S. agencies and others pay attention to virtually all the kinds of "resources" listed above, and to the human cultural environment in general. The world of cultural resources can be thought of as a set of overlapping circles, no one of which (except the big, outermost circle) represents the whole (see Figure 1). The fact that different people mean different things by "cultural resource" and "cultural resource management" inevitably leads to communication problems, and this in turn means that whole classes of cultural resources can be inadvertently ignored in planning. This is a problem for project planners because it can

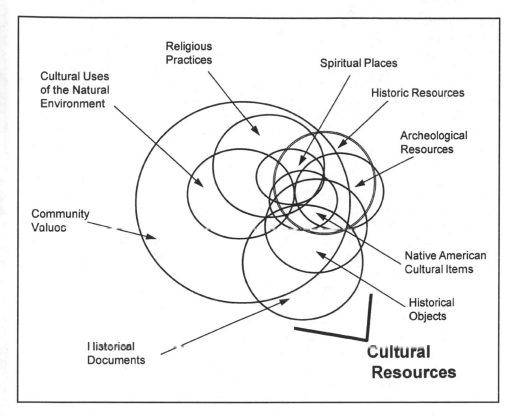

Figure 1. The world of cultural resources.

leave cultural resource issues unaddressed, waiting to cause trouble at the eleventh hour. Of broader concern is that the unaddressed issues are often those that are of deepest concern to affected communities—the things that the "voice of the people" would call upon us to consider, if that voice were only heard.

A classic example of how communication problems can lead to disaster is the case of the African Burial Ground in New York City.

In the late seventeenth and early eighteenth centuries, the African Burial Ground was a low area among the dunefields of Manhattan Island, a short distance outside the walls of New Amsterdam. Enslaved Africans—yes, there were slaves in New York then—and their equally enslaved descendants buried their dead there. Later, the area was buried as the dunes were leveled and New York spread north. The street called Broadway was built along the west side of the cemetery, which had been more or less forgotten.

In the late 1980s, the U.S. General Services Administration (GSA) was authorized and directed by Congress to construct a new federal office building on the "Broadway Block," a parcel of land east of Broadway adjacent to an existing major federal office tower. During the environmental assessment that preceded the work, an old map was found that noted the existence of a "Negro burial ground" on the site.

The environmental assessment was prepared by a planning firm under contract to the design and development firm that was under contract to GSA to design and build the new facility. This firm in turn subcontracted with an archeological firm to do the "cultural resource" work. All concerned perceived the "Negro burial ground" as an archeological site—a cultural manifestation buried in the ground that could be excavated and gotten out of the way by archeologists. No one seems to have perceived it as any other kind of "cultural resource." As a result, it was not seen to be a particular problem. Archeologists could be paid to excavate it, remove its contents to a laboratory somewhere, study and report on it, and that would be that. No one seems to have perceived a need to contact New York's African-American community and find out how they might feel about the place.

The results are history (cf. S. Wilson 1996). When the Burial Ground was encountered—and turned out to be bigger and more intact than anyone expected—all hell broke loose. African-Americans in New York and across the country—and around the world—protested vehemently against the desecration of their ancestors' remains. A congressional investigation ensued; the project had to be redesigned to preserve part of the Burial Ground while the remainder was subjected to extensive and expensive excavation and analysis preparatory to reburial. The construction contractor was able to claim massive penalty payments because of the delay, and, at this writing (although the office building is now up and occupied), a large chunk of the project site is vacant, occupied only by grass, a chain-link fence, and a sign identifying it as the African Burial Ground, where someday a memorial will be constructed to those who were buried there. GSA's lawyers used to refer to it as "our 46-million dollar lawn," because that's what the whole embarrassing mess had cost the agency, and the taxpayer, as of about 1994. It's doubtless close to fifty million dollars worth of lawn by the time of this writing.

There were lots of things that caused the African Burial Ground to bite GSA so hard, but one of the most important was that the value of the site was misperceived at the outset. The moment the map was found with "Negro Burial Ground" on it, somebody should have perceived that the place would have great emotional, cultural importance to African-Americans. Intensive consultation should have been undertaken, a cooperative program should have been developed with the African-American community, as was successfully done in a similar case in Philadelphia (McCarthy 1996). Dealing with the Burial Ground would still have been expensive, but it would have cost a lot less than fifty million dollars, and it could have been done in a calmer, more orderly, far less contentious manner. But the cultural value of the site was instead equated with archeological research value, and it was assumed that archeologists alone could realize and preserve that value. The notion of what a "cultural resource" is was too narrowly construed, and the results were costly.

I won't belabor examples. My point is really a simple one. The cultural environment, the corpus of "cultural resources," is a big, complex, intricate mosaic of things and institutions and values, beliefs and perceptions, customs and traditions, symbols and social structures. And it's integral to what makes people people and communities communities, so it's charged with a great deal of emotion. As a result, "cultural resource management" needs to be a great deal more than archeology, or architectural history, or folklife, or historic preservation. It needs to deal with management of the whole cultural environment, and the effects of contemporary plans and decisions on that environment in all its aspects.

By "cultural resources," then, I mean those parts of the physical environment—natural and built—that have cultural value of some kind to some sociocultural group (cf. Lynch 1972, Rapoport 1982). The "group" can be a community, a neighborhood, a tribe, or any of the scholarly and not-so-scholarly disciplines that documents and studies cultural things—archeologists, architectural historians, folklorists, cultural anthropologists. I also mean those non-material human social institutions that contribute so much to the "environment in our heads"—our social institutions, our beliefs, our accustomed practices, and our perceptions of what makes the environment culturally comfortable. "Cultural resource management" ought to embrace the management of all these kinds of resources, and all kinds of impacts on them. The need for compliance with the cultural resource laws is what drives CRM to occur.

Cultural Resources and Social Impacts

CRM as defined here is closely related to, and overlaps, another acronymous body of practice—"Social impact assessment," or SIA. SIA is the systematic effort:

> ...to assess or estimate, in advance, the social consequences that are likely to follow from specific policy actions (including programs, and the adoption of new policies), and specific government actions (including buildings, large projects, and leasing large tracts of land for resource extraction. (Interorganizational Committee 1993: NOAA 1994:1)

SIA is sometimes mixed and not very well matched with "socioeconomic impact assessment," whereupon it often takes on the dismal characteristics of economics and loses all sight of the sociocultural factors that are the subjects of this book. SIA has its own interesting history, and its own rules of practice; we'll discuss some of these in the chapters to come.

Cultural Resources and Historic Preservation

It is to the practice of historic preservation that CRM is most closely related. Like CRM, historic preservation means different things to different people, but I'll follow Congress and the National Historic Preservation Act (NHPA) in defining it to include:

...identification, evaluation, recordation, documentation, curation, acquisition, protection, management, rehabilitation, restoration, stabilization, maintenance, research, interpretation, (and) conservation (of historic properties), and education and training regarding the foregoing activities or any combination of the foregoing activities. (NHPA Sec. 301[8])

Nobody ever accused the U.S. Congress of elegant wordsmithing. "Historic property," by the way, is defined in the same statute as:

...any prehistoric or historic district, site, building, structure or object included in, or eligible for inclusion on the National Register (of Historic Places), including artifacts, records, and material remains related to such a property... (NHPA Sec. 301[5])

Historic preservation deals with one kind of cultural resource—the "historic property." Historic preservation has a highly developed (perhaps overdeveloped) body of procedure, operating at the federal and local levels and, to some extent, in international, regional, state, and Indian tribal contexts. The focus of this book is largely on the federal historic preservation system as it affects compliance with federal cultural resource legal requirements.

"Compliance" and Beyond

"Compliance" is another word that means different things to different people. To an environmental engineer, "compliance" means compliance with the Comprehensive Environmental Response, Compensation and Liability Act (CERCLA) and a few other laws that seek to control or clean up toxic and hazardous wastes. There's a vague sort of recognition that other laws must be "complied with," too, but it's only CERCLA and its toxic-tinted kin that are seen as "real" compliance subjects. This is probably because only these laws, as opposed to the environmental planning laws that will be discussed in this book, impose jail terms and fines on individual violators (cf. Rubenstein, Aroesty, and Thompsen 1992).

In historic preservation and other areas of cultural resource management, "compliance" is taken to mean doing what the various laws require an agency to do to manage its impacts on the cultural environment. One complies with Section 106 of the National Historic Preservation Act, and one goes "beyond compliance" when one does some sort of positive management—beyond the bare minima that people think Section 106 requires.

I think this distinction is silly, and rather sad.

Silly because positive management is the *reason* for compliance. Congress did not enact Section 106 and its ilk just to cause agencies to pass papers around. Compliance with the law is supposed to result in good, thoughtful, balanced management of cultural resources and impacts on them. Compliance ought not to be a minimalist sort of thing, and if it doesn't result in positive management, what earthly good is it?

Silly too because an agency that's encouraged to think that it's going "beyond compliance" when it manages a cultural resource well—that is, doing more than the law requires it to do—isn't going to keep doing it when faced with conflicting demands. Stuff that's "nice to do" but not required by law isn't going to get done when budgets shrink or demands grow. Those who turn up their noses at compliance and pat themselves on the back for getting their employers or clients to go "beyond" live in a fool's paradise.

And it's sad because it reflects acceptance of a notion of compliance-driven cultural resource work as largely irrelevant to real management, and hence to the public interest. If widely accepted, this notion would mean that most of the multi-million dollar business of CRM—which like it or not is compliance driven—is of no real worth. I don't think that's true, but if it is, and we want to be responsible citizens, we'd all better look for new careers.

So I believe that compliance and good management are essentially the same. Certainly compliance requires that we dot certain procedural "i's" and cross certain procedural "t's," but this no more makes it poor management than good architectural draftsmanship means bad building design. Properly done compliance should result in good management, and good management should put an agency in compliance with the law.

That said, I'll cheerfully acknowledge that this book is substantially about procedural, process matters. The substance of CRM—how, in a hands-on way, one manages an archeological site or a book or an old building or impacts on a lifeway—is a many-splendored thing; there are so many possibilities that I wouldn't even know where to begin. Process, the subject of this book, is how possibilities get explored, selected, and implemented; to me this is a fascinating subject, and I hope it can be to the reader as well. In any event, it's something that a cultural resource manager must know, if she or he is going to be effective.

"It Depends"

Two of the most common words you'll find in this book are: "it depends." However much people might want things to be otherwise, there are few, if any, hard and fast rules in cultural resource management. How do we identify cultural resources? In depends on the law with which we're trying to comply, the kinds of resources that may exist, the kind of thing we're planning (if anything) that may affect them, and other factors. How do we determine what's significant? It depends on the kind of resource, the values that people load on it, and so forth. How do we determine how to manage a resource? It depends on the resource, the management challenges, the public or private interests we're seeking to achieve or accommodate, and so forth.

Some people are frustrated by this sort of ambiguity; they want a cookbook. For such people I'd suggest culinary school rather than CRM, though I think you'll find that even the temperature at which water boils depends on the altitude. The fact is that everything in CRM *does* depend on something else.

There aren't any absolutes; everything is contingent. Absolutes are nice for lazy thinkers, but they have no place in creative management.

So I'll use "it depends" a lot. I'll try to explain what things depend on, and why, and how to get along without absolutes, but I won't apologize for their nonexistence. Actually, I think CRM would be a pretty dull enterprise if there *were* a lot of absolutes on which to rely. And CRM is *not* a dull enterprise.

Laws, Regulations, and Alphabet Soup

We'll be discussing a number of laws here—listed in Figure 2 and summarized in more detail in Appendix III. We'll also be using a lot of more or less odd terms, many of which are or employ acronyms. These are listed for quick reference in Appendix I and defined in Appendix II. Complete texts of laws, regulations, guidelines, and other relevant documents are available at a number of World Wide Web sites, some of which are listed at the end of the bibliography.

Authorities that deal with all types of cultural resources
  The National Environmental Policy Act (NEPA)
  Executive Order 12898 (Environmental Justice)

Historic preservation authorities
  The National Historic Preservation Act (NHPA)
  The Historic Sites Act (HSA)
  Executive Order 13006 (Priority to use of urban historic properties)
  Section 4(f) of the Department of Transportation Act
  The Federal tax code

Archeological authorities
  The Antiquities Act of 1906
  The Archeological Resources Protection Act (ARPA)
  The Archeological Data Preservation Act of 1974
  The Abandoned Shipwrecks Act (ASA)

Native American cultural resource authorities
  The American Indian Religious Freedom Act (AIRFA)
  Executive Order 13007 (Indian Sacred Sites)
  The Native American Graves Protection and Repatriation Act (NAGPRA)

Historical documents authorities
  The Federal Records Act (FRA)

Figure 2. Cultural resource authorities discussed in this book.

Chapter 2

A Brief History of Federal Cultural Resource Management

This book is about working with the cultural resource laws as they exist today, so we'll save any detailed examination of history for another day and another book. Other books for those who specialize in the historic preservation aspects of CRM include Hosmer (1965, 1981) and Glass (1990). But a passing acquaintance with the roots of the legal authorities is something every cultural resource manager should have. So here are some basics:

In the Beginning...

The U.S. Government first got involved in the management of cultural resources in 1800 when Congress appropriated $5,000 to purchase books and create the Library of Congress. After the Civil War, it began to conduct ethnographic and archeological research through the Smithsonian Institution and the Department of the Interior, and to acquire and preserve battlefields through the War Department. Historic buildings and structures were being preserved by private parties and local organizations, but government on the whole was not involved. Management of impacts on the social environment was not even a gleam in anybody's eye.

In the late nineteenth century, more or less chauvinistic concern over the removal of antiquities from ruins on federal land led to a number of legislative efforts to control the situation. These finally resulted in the nation's first general purpose cultural resource management statute, the Antiquities Act of 1906 (16 U.S.C. 431-433). This law prohibited the excavation of antiquities from public lands without a permit from the Secretary of the Interior.

In 1916 the National Park Service (NPS) was created, for the first time giving the nation an agency with conservation of natural and cultural resources at the heart of its mission. The management of historic battlefields was transferred from the War Department to NPS.

The Depression Years

The Great Depression led to the creation of "make work" programs with implications for cultural resource management. Out-of-work historians were hired to write local and regional histories; out-of-work architects were hired to prepare detailed drawings of historic buildings, and all manner of people were hired to work on archeological projects, mostly salvaging material and data in advance of construction by the Tennessee Valley Authority and other agencies. NPS gathered some of these programs under its wing, and explicitly or implicitly gave them continuing life. Authority to do so came in 1935, when the Historic Sites Act (16 U.S.C. 461-467) authorized NPS to carry on a continuing program of recording, documenting, acquiring and managing places important in the interpretation and commemoration of the nation's history.

As well, local government became increasingly involved in historic preservation during this period, and at this level the idea began to take hold that what should be preserved was not just individual great buildings, but whole neighborhoods. Thus the Old and Historic District in Charleston, South Carolina and the Vieux Carre in New Orleans were recognized as "historic districts." This represented an important departure for historic preservation, relating the idea of preservation to urban planning and making "every citizen's house, environment, and neighborhood the prime focus of concern and action" (Murtagh 1997:59).

World War II and Beyond

Arguably, the experience of in-depth contact with other cultures that came from World War II had an important impact on Americans' perception of themselves and their own cultural resources. Certainly, the rapid pace of socioeconomic change after the war caused Americans to begin to worry about what they were losing. When the Corps of Engineers marched home they were put to work building dams and reservoirs, while in the 1950s President Eisenhower launched construction of the Interstate Highway System, designed to permit the rapid deployment of troops across the country in the event of attack. Both these programs began to do alarming damage to historic neighborhoods, buildings, structures, and archeological sites, and the government responded—albeit rather haltingly. NPS and the Smithsonian Institution organized the River Basin Survey program to salvage archeological sites threatened by Corps reservoirs, and in 1960 Congress passed the Reservoir Salvage Act (16 U.S.C. 469) authorizing continuing appropriations to NPS for the purpose. NPS also helped spawn a private sector non-profit organization to promote historic preservation nationwide. The National Trust for Historic Preservation, originally conceived largely by NPS historians and architectural historians, was chartered in 1949.

The post-war period also saw a growing dichotomy between those who viewed historic preservation largely as the preservation of particular buildings as artifacts of their time, and those who wanted to emphasize buildings in their social and architectural contexts. A number of conferences explored the relationships of historic preservation to urban planning, and the notion of preservation as a quality of life issue for all citizens achieved widespread acceptance.

Post-war progress in cultural resource management was not limited to historic preservation and archeology. The environmental movement was stirring in response to some of the same challenges that stimulated the growth of historic preservation. While focused initially on the natural environment—to the exclusion of that which had seen the impact of people—environmentalism, like preservation, soon expanded beyond preoccupation with the greatest most pristine places, and became something that all people could claim as their own. In this context the human-affected environment achieved a new level of interest.

At the same time, the burgeoning of the federal government and its files had created the need for a more orderly approach to records management. The Federal Records Act became law in 1950, creating the basis for the contemporary system of archiving potentially significant historical documents.

Urban Renewal, the Great Society, and NHPA

The Kennedy administration increased the pace of destruction of natural and cultural resources by launching the Urban Renewal Program. Urban Renewal laid waste to historic center city "slums" with the expectation that cities of the future would rise from their ashes. The fact that Lee Harvey Oswald fired from the window of a historic building is probably coincidental, however. Urban renewal was not necessarily all bad from the standpoint of historic preservation; one veteran of the program has suggested that if nothing else, it forced communities to look at their places of cultural and aesthetic value (Constance W. Ramirez, personal communication 1998). The reaction to urban renewal was not limited to "mainstream" historic preservation. Communities began to be concerned about their overall quality of life, and the social and cultural characteristics that gave them their particular identity.

During the Johnson administration, as part of the beautification program coordinated by first lady, Lady Bird Johnson, a study was undertaken that led to a comprehensive report (U.S. Conference of Mayors 1967 [released as report in 1965]) recommending creation of a national historic preservation program and sketching out its broad outlines. This recommendation was transformed into legislation with lightning speed, and enacted as the National Historic Preservation Act (NHPA) in 1966. The same Congress enacted the Department of Transportation Act, including its conservationist Section 4(f) and other pieces of conservation-oriented legislation.

NHPA created a number of the institutions that are central to CRM today. Notably, it authorized NPS to "expand and maintain" a "National Register of Historic Places" including properties of local, state, and national historical, cultural, and architectural significance. It also created an "Advisory Council on Historic Preservation" to advise the President and Congress on historic preservation matters. It provided for grants in aid to states to assist them in historic preservation, with such grants administered by "State Liaison Officers" who later came to be known as "State Historic Preservation Officers." And it included, at Section 106, a requirement that agencies consider the effects of their plans and projects on places included in the Park Service's National Register.

The 1960s were also the heyday of the Civil Rights Movement, including what came to be known as the Indian Civil Rights Movement. During the 1950s, the government had gone through one of its periodic flirtations with destroying tribes as sovereign entities, this time by terminating reservations and absorbing Indians into the great American melting pot. In reaction, the Indian Civil Rights Movement of the 1960s and beyond included a strong element of traditional heritage—a desire to return to, and reclaim the legitimacy of—tribal roots. Two decades later, this was to bring tribes into the cultural resource management picture as major players. With shallower roots in North America, African-Americans and other minority groups didn't have the same kinds of connections with the physical environment that Native Americans did, and so have not as a group been as integrally involved in such activities as historic preservation (though there are notable exceptions: see Lee 1987). During the '60s, however, virtually all minority groups began to insist, with increasing intensity, on respect for their cultural traditions. The resulting perception of diversity as a positive thing, though still rather controversial today, has had profound impacts on cultural resource management.

Into the 1970s

Back in historic preservation, NPS reorganized its existing archeological and historic preservation programs into a new "Office of Archeology and Historic Preservation" (OAHP) to coordinate NHPA implementation. The National Register and the ACHP were made parts of OAHP, with Earnest A. Connally of the University of Illinois School of Architecture at its head. Robert R. Garvey, Jr. and William J. Murtagh of the National Trust were wooed away by NPS to head the ACHP and National Register respectively. Both were important additions from the standpoint of making preservation relate to the broader cultural environment. Garvey was a grass-roots preservationist without academic credentials, who very much saw preservation as something for people where they lived, and Murtagh had (and has) a keen sense of the need for historic properties to be living parts of the contemporary environment.

While NPS was organizing OAHP, the environmental movement was gaining increasing congressional attention. With the publication and widespread popularity of Rachel Carson's *Silent Spring* (Carson 1962), the need for federal government action to protect the environment came to be widely recognized. One expression of this new recognition was enactment of the National Environmental Policy Act (NEPA) in 1969. NEPA articulated national policy favoring environmental protection, created the Council on Environmental Quality (CEQ), and required agencies to consider the effects of their actions on the environment.

The new law was especially important for CRM because it caused all federal agencies to begin to look at their environmental impacts, and to create the infrastructure to do so. Thus each agency—more or less—began to develop some kind of environmental staff, and procedures to ensure—more or less—that its actions were viewed through environmentalist eyes. Because NEPA explicitly focused on the "human environment," and called for interdisciplinary analyses involving the social sciences, social impact assessment (SIA) soon became an important part of the NEPA mix, and began to develop an identity of its own (cf. Freudenburg 1986). SIA addressed both the relationships between human sociocultural systems and the natural environment, but also the impacts of proposed actions on aspects of the environment that are purely social—such as lifeways and value systems.

The relationship of historic preservation to the consideration of environmental impacts was not yet very well developed—although one of the very first Section 106 cases, involving a proposed nuclear power plant across the river from Saratoga Battlefield, involved such core environmental issues as indirect and visual impacts. The reason that historic preservation stayed out of the mainstream was that Section 106, as enacted, required agencies to concern themselves only with impacts on places *included* in the National Register. These, of course, were few in number since the Register had just been created, and all an agency had to do to avoid dealing with impacts on historic properties was to keep them from being nominated. This problem was alleviated in 1972 when President Nixon issued Executive Order 11593. In effect, this executive order directed agencies to treat eligible properties as though they were listed in the Register, and ordered NPS to establish procedures for determining eligibility. The executive order, and a number of court cases and other rough-and-tumble historic preservation tussles in the early 1970s, got the agencies' attention, and they began to incorporate preservation expertise and procedures into their environmental programs.

The Three Executeers and the Rise of Archeology

This process was greatly hastened, and pointed in a particular direction, when NPS dispatched three "Executive Order Consultants" to the field to proselytize the agencies. Larry Aten, Jon Young, and Roy Reeves were very effective in their roles as knights errant, and jawboned a number of agencies into hiring preservation specialists and creating programs for executive order compliance. All three EO Consultants were archeologists, and the agencies they targeted for greatest attention were those with the greatest impacts on archeological sites—construction agencies like the Corps of Engineers and land managing agencies like the Forest Service and Bureau of Land Management. Partly as a result, these agencies came more or less to equate historic preservation with archeology, and to hire archeologists to run their preservation programs. The perception of historic preservation as something that is done by and for archeologists, using archeological sites, remains common in the construction and land management agencies to this day.

Another contribution to this perception was the fact that the archeological community under the leadership of the University of Arkansas' Robert McGimsey, undertook in the late 1960s to expand the scope of the 1960 Reservoir Salvage Act to require all agencies to identify archeological resources threatened by their actions, and to fund recovery of the data they contained. Although this initiative was undertaken quite without reference to the consolidation and growth of programs under NHPA and Executive Order 11593, Aten in particular took pains to build bridges between OAHP and the archeological agitators. McGimsey had meanwhile formed a liaison with Richard Leverty, head of the Corps of Engineers environmental program. As a result, when the desired amendment was enacted as the "Moss-Bennett Act" in 1974 (that is, the Archeological Data Preservation Act), things were in place to ensure that its implementation would be integrated into OAHP's programs, and that the Corps would provide a model for other agencies in how the whole business of archeology and historic preservation could be done.

The Birth of "CRM"

Archeologists, however, were not entirely sanguine about hopping into bed with historic preservation. Some feared that the National Register would become a catalogue of archeological sites for misuse by looters. Some objected to being thought of as "historic preservationists" because their primary interests were in prehistory. Some regarded preservationists as rather effete, parts of an eastern establishment which they, as mostly rough-tough westerners, viewed with some disdain. At the same time, there was interest in relating what was coming to be called "conservation archeology"—that is, the practice of archeology under the environmental and preservation laws—to the rapidly coagulating body of policy and practice called "natural resource management." So it was archeologists, in the southwestern United States in the early 1970s, who coined the term "cultural resource management" for what they did (Lipe and Lindsay 1974).

This had unfortunate results that are with us today. The equation of "CRM" with archeology, at worst, and general historic preservation, at best, while using a term that implies responsibility for all types of "cultural resources," has allowed a considerable range of such resources to be ignored by federal planners and decision-makers—indeed it has encouraged them to do so (cf. King 1998). When archeologists invented cultural resource management to pair up with natural resource management, they didn't bring the full panoply of cultural resources into the mix; they brought archeology. But natural resource managers, project planners, and agency officials didn't know that, so they assumed that when they funded "CRM" they were taking care of cultural resources in general.

Tribes and Folklife

There were other forces at work during the 1970s, however, that would keep the scope of CRM at least somewhat broad. Native American groups were important in this process. With enactment of the Indian Self-Determination and Education Act (25 U.S.C. 450-451n, 455-458e) in 1975, tribes attained a new level of authority in the government's administration of its trust responsibilities. Tribes and intertribal organizations soon began to press for, among other things, more governmental attention to their traditional cultural values. These included protection of ancestral sites that were often of interest to archeologists, but it also included concern for spiritual places that were not archeological sites, subsistence and ceremonial use of natural resources, and the integrity of cultural and religious practices themselves. It also included a deep concern for ancestral bones and artifacts, which would become a major issue in the 1980s. In any event, tribes and their representatives were successful in forcing increased governmental attention to their cultural concerns, and in effecting passage of legislation like the American Indian Religious Freedom Act (AIRFA) in 1978 (42 U.S.C. 1996).

In 1976, responding to a growing popular interest in American traditional culture, Congress enacted the American Folklife Preservation Act (20 U.S.C. 2101), creating the American Folklife Center (AFC) in the Library of Congress. The Center has since undertaken a wide range of folklife documentation and encouragement projects, some of them in cooperation with historic preservationists in NPS, state historic preservation offices, and elsewhere. The same set of interests spawned the Festival of American Folklife in Washington, D.C. as an annual event, and folklife festivals and documentation programs at the state and local levels across the country.

Land Management and ARPA

Meanwhile, land managing agencies that had gotten along poorly for generations with uncertain legal mandates had their missions clarified by Congress in laws like the Federal Land Policy Management Act of 1976 (16 U.S.C. 1701 et seq. [FLPMA]) and the National Forest Management Act of the same year (16 U.S.C. 1600 et seq. [NFMA]). These laws, and particularly the implementing regulations drafted by the agencies to which they related—which by now had embedded CRM programs—often alluded to the management of cultural resources along with those of natural character.

In 1974, in *United States v. Diaz* (449 F.2d 113 [9th Cir. 1974]) the Ninth Circuit Court of Appeals found the Antiquities Act of 1906 to be unconstitutionally vague because it failed to indicate the age an object had to be in order to be an "object of antiquity." This provided an opportunity for archeologists who had long seen the 1906 law as grossly out of date. The result was enactment of the

Archeological Resources Protection Act (16 U.S.C. 470aa-mm: ARPA) in 1979. ARPA greatly clarified requirements for managing the disturbance of archeological sites, features, and objects on federal and Indian tribal lands.

The PANE Decision and CEQ's Regulations

The 1970s were a period of great activity on the litigation front, under NEPA, Section 106, and other authorities. One particularly important Supreme Court decision had a chilling effect on the practice of social impact assessment. The Court in *Metropolitan Edison Co. v. People Against Nuclear Energy* (460 U.S. 766, 103 S.Ct. 1556 [1983]) declared that social and psychological effects were not by themselves sufficient to require preparation of an environmental impact statement. This followed issuance of NEPA regulations by the Council on Environmental Quality that included similar language about social and economic effects. Some agencies as a result concluded that social effects didn't have to be considered at all in NEPA analyses—an incorrect assumption, but one that has been hard to overcome in some cases.

The Rise of SHPOs, Local Governments, and Amendments to NHPA

Another important development in the 1970s was the growth in the power, effectiveness, and organization of the State Historic Preservation Officers (SHPOs). Originally provided for in NHPA as State Liaison Officers to administer NPS historic preservation matching grants, the SHPOs became increasingly consolidated and professionalized during the 1970s, and gradually clarified their relationships with NPS. They formed the National Conference of State Historic Preservation Officers (NCSHPO) to represent their interests in Washington.

The Carter administration was activist in environmental matters. Among other things, President Carter issued a Presidential Memorandum on Environmental Quality and Water Resources Management on July 12, 1978, which included direction for the Advisory Council on Historic Preservation to issue binding regulations on Section 106 implementation. Until that time, the ACHP had issued procedures that were not necessarily binding. As a result of Carter's memorandum, the Council issued its procedures as a true regulation, legally binding on all agencies, for the first time in 1979. One important thing the regulation did was to create a very explicit role for State Historic Preservation Officers. Given that most agencies did not have much historic preservation expertise, while SHPOs increasingly did, the regulation prescribed that agencies should turn to the SHPOs for consultative assistance at every step in the Section 106 review process. This direction remains with us today, with mixed results.

NPS grants to the SHPOs also hit a high point during the Carter years, at almost $60 million divided among the 57 entities that then qualified for such grants. This largesse was not to last.

Local governments had long led the way in some aspects of historic preservation—since the nineteenth century, when they were in the forefront of government involvement in preserving landmark buildings, and since the 1930s, when they pioneered the idea of historic districts as urban planning tools. In the 1970s, the federal historic preservation system began to pay more attention to them. In part, this resulted from the evolution of highly centralized Kennedy-era programs in the Department of Housing and Urban Development (HUD) into more flexible "block grant" programs that emphasized local initiative. The 1974 Community Development Act allowed HUD to delegate its NEPA and Section 106 responsibilities to local government recipients of block grants. Some preservationists viewed this allowance with alarm, fearing it would lead to widespread noncompliance with Section 106. It may have, but it also led many local governments to beef up their environmental and historic preservation staffs and procedures, or to create them *de novo*. This created a ripple effect that had positive impacts on local preservation in general—and created a good many jobs for preservation specialists—while it positioned local governments for participation in the developing national preservation system.

During the 1970s, NHPA itself was amended several times. Importantly, the requirement of Executive Order 11593 to address places eligible for but not yet listed in the National Register was integrated into the law itself, by amending Section 106 to refer both to registered and eligible properties. The Advisory Council, whose staff had been lodged in NPS, was given independent agency status after conflicts of interest with NPS project planning became apparent.

Finally, in 1980, sweeping changes were made in almost every section of the law. In a new Section 110, the 1980 amendments specified responsibilities for federal agencies; in an expanded Section 101 they identified the responsibilities of State Historic Preservation Officers. The amendments recognized local government participation in a number of ways, notably by creating a role for "certified local governments" and by mandating local participation in National Register nominations. They also included a couple of provisions relating to the cultural environment beyond historic properties. One provision directed NPS and the AFC to conduct a study of how to preserve "intangible aspects of our cultural heritage" (16 U.S.C. 470a note). Another established a program of grants to Indian tribes and minority groups to support "the preservation of their cultural heritage" (NHPA Sec. 101[e][3][B]).

The Reagan Revolution

The ink was hardly dry on the 1980 amendments when the Reagan administration took office with a very different take on environmental matters and government activism. The '80s were a time of struggle, retrenchment, cutbacks, and a great deal of head-ducking on the part of the federal environmental and historic preservation establishments. It was also a time when a good deal of initiative devolved to the state and local levels. Although NPS grants to the SHPOs were cut drastically (the administration was unsuccessful in doing away with them altogether), some SHPOs were able to exercise a good deal of initiative and develop their programs in new and positive directions. Many states had established "little NEPAs" (or "SEPAs") during the 1970s, and more did so during the '80s. The Certified Local Government program developed, with many local governments getting their historic preservation programs certified to qualify for NPS grants through the SHPOs and for increased technical assistance. The Reagan administration emphasized encouraging historic preservation through tax benefits, and for awhile, federal income tax credits became a tremendous impetus for the rehabilitation of income-producing buildings and structures. NEPA and CEQ survived by keeping low profiles, and the ACHP survived a major assault on the Section 106 process. The Section 106 regulations were revised, but actually (in my view) came out rather better than their 1979 iteration—despite the best efforts of the Administration.

The Rising of the Tribes

The 1980s also saw a dramatic rise in Indian tribal participation in historic preservation and other cultural resource management activities. A number of tribes created historic preservation programs or built on programs that already existed. Some of the larger tribes, and intertribal organizations like the National Congress of American Indians, the Native American Rights Fund, and American Indians Against Desecration (an offshoot of the American Indian Movement) were active influences on the ACHP in revising its Section 106 regulations. Tribes and intertribal groups became major players in NEPA and Section 106 litigation, and began agitating for the return and reburial of ancestral remains and cultural items. This agitation led to enactment of the Native American Graves Protection and Repatriation Act (NAGPRA) in 1990. The Supreme Court's 1988 decision in *Lyng v. Northwest Indian Cemetery Protective Association* (discussed in Chapter 7) had a chilling effect on tribal efforts to protect spiritual places under the First Amendment, but this tended to make tribes more interested in alternative means of protecting such sites—such as Section 106. In 1989, Congress directed NPS to study tribal historic preservation needs (Senate Report No. 191-85). This study, carried out in consultation with many tribes and intertribal organizations, resulted in a report entitled *Keepers of the Treasures* (NPS 1990a). Keepers reflected the tribe's interests in historic preservation in the context of a broader concern for the management of cultural resources in general. Congress began appropriating, and NPS began granting, funds under NHPA Section 101(e)(3)(B) which recommended a wide range of projects not only in historic preservation per se but in language transmission, lifeway documentation, education, skills retention, and other aspects of cultural resource management.

The 1990s

In 1992 NHPA was amended again, this time notably expanding federal agency responsibilities and establishing a program for support of tribal historic preservation programs. Under these provisions, tribes could take over SHPO responsibilities and substitute their own procedures for the ACHP's in Section 106 review.

Around the same time the Environmental Justice (EJ) movement breathed important new life into social impact assessment by emphasizing the need to involve diverse minority and low income communities in decision-making about environmental impacts. EJ found its federal expression in 1994 in Executive Order 12898 and an accompanying presidential memorandum directing agencies to consider environmental justice matters in their environmental impact work. President Clinton continued on a roll, from a CRM point of view, by issuing Executive Orders 13006 and 13007 in 1996. These executive orders deal respectively with use of historic properties in center cities and with protection of Indian sacred sites.

This thumbnail sketch brings us to the "present" as of the time this book is written (early 1998). I've left a great deal out, and refrained from a great deal of elaboration. I've also emphasized the historic preservation aspects of CRM, because these are the ones I know best and, I believe, those that have the most established body of practice, most thoroughly grounded in law.

Chapter 3

The Players

We've already introduced a number of the institutions that a CRM practitioner needs to know about, but before we plunge into the details of CRM practice, let's summarize:

Advisory Council on Historic Preservation

Created by NHPA, the ACHP has two parts. The "Council itself," sometimes referred to (by me, anyway, and it's gotten at least one of its members into a terrible snit) as "the magnificent twenty," is a twenty-member board made up of a presidentially appointed chair, several presidentially appointed "citizen" and "expert" members, the heads of several federal agencies, presidentially appointed representatives of local governments, state governments, and Native American interests, and two outside organizations specified in the statute—the National Trust for Historic Preservation and the National Conference of Historic Preservation Officers. The agency members include permanent members—the secretaries of the Interior and Agriculture, and the Architect of the Capitol—and other agency members appointed by the president. The magnificent twenty meet only four times a year or so; their work is done by a staff of about forty, divided between two offices, one in Washington, one in suburban Denver. The staff is headed by an executive director, and is responsible for overseeing NHPA Section 106 review, poking into agency programs to see how they're doing with historic properties, doing special studies, conducting education and training, and otherwise serving the members, the Congress, and the president. Most CRM practitioners will come into contact primarily with ACHP "Historic Preservation Specialists," the staff members who handle participation in and oversight of Section 106 casework.

American Folklife Center

The AFC is a small part of the Library of Congress, and is responsible for collecting and maintaining data on folklife resources. The AFC sponsors fieldwork as funds permit, and cooperates with others in the conduct of fieldwork, to document traditional lifeways, arts, crafts, expressive culture, and oral history.

Council on Environmental Quality

Created by NEPA, the Council on Environmental Quality (CEQ) is lodged in the Executive Office of the President. This has certain advantages vis-à-vis the Advisory Council on Historic Preservation, which is an independent agency; CEQ is closer to the president's ear. On the other hand, CEQ is much more vulnerable to presidential whim than is the ACHP—a vulnerability that became acute in the early days of the Clinton administration when some sort of misfire by the president's environmental advisors almost resulted in CEQ's demise. CEQ, like ACHP, consists of a council and a staff, but both are much smaller than their ACHP counterparts. The council in CEQ's case has only three members, but unlike the ACHP's magnificent twenty, most of whom are salaried in their posts only when they meet, CEQ's members are supposed to serve full time for their tenure. The council, like the ACHP, is served by a small staff, based in Washington. CEQ is much less involved than the ACHP in individual cases; it oversees NEPA review in general, provides an annual report to the president and Congress, gets involved in resolving particularly difficult cases with national policy implications, and develops government-side policy on environmental matters. The average cultural resource practitioner never runs into a representative of CEQ, but CEQ is there to oversee NEPA review, and it's an important presence.

Environmental Protection Agency

The Environmental Protection Agency (EPA) is a large independent agency with a wide range of responsibilities both for regulating aspects of environmental protection and for assisting in projects designed to protect or clean up the environment. EPA's primary areas of expertise and authority are in preventing and cleaning up air and water pollution, but it is also responsible for promoting implementation of Executive Order 12898, and in this context it has become significantly involved in CRM matters, notably on behalf of Indian tribes whose cultural environments may be disproportionately adversely affected by federal actions. EPA also receives and reviews all Environmental Impact Statements (EIS) prepared under NEPA, and an adverse EPA comment can stop an agency project cold in its tracks until the deficiency EPA has identified is repaired. So EPA is a powerful agency and it's one with which CRM practitioners may come into contact more frequently than in the past, assuming interest in environmental justice continues at a high level.

Federal Agencies

Of course, the ACHP, CEQ, and EPA are federal agencies, as is NPS (discussed below), but whereas each of these has a quite specific role to play in the review of impacts on some kinds of cultural resources, federal agencies in general have a more general but altogether central role. They are, after all, the ones whose actions are reviewed. There are a couple of things about federal agencies that every CRM practitioner ought to know.

There are several types of federal agencies. Agencies like the Bureau of Land Management (BLM) and the Forest Service manage land. The Federal Highway Administration (FHWA) and Department of Housing and Urban Development (HUD) provide financial assistance. Agencies like the Corps of Engineers and Bureau of Reclamation build things. The Federal Energy Regulatory Commission (FERC) issue permits and licenses. Some agencies do multiple things; the Corps of Engineers, for example, manages land around its reservoirs, constructs flood control facilities, and issues permits to fill waterways and wetlands.

Land Management Agencies

Land management agencies have, perhaps, the most elaborate responsibilities under the cultural resource laws, because they actually control land on which people do cultural things and have left cultural things (artifacts, buildings) lying and standing around. They're often said to have "stewardship" responsibility for such resources, as well as project review responsibilities.

Assistance Agencies

Agencies that provide financial assistance to others tend to work closely with, and often through, those who use their money. The Federal Highway Administration (FHWA), for instance, works in very close concert with state departments of transportation, and the Department of Housing and Urban Development (HUD) delegates many of its environmental review responsibilities to local governments that receive its assistance.

Construction Agencies

Agencies that build things have the cleanest project review responsibilities in some ways, since they simply carry out projects, themselves, that require review. There are fewer and fewer of these simple, one-agency projects these days, however; more and more is done through assistance and partnerships.

Permitting and Licensing Agencies

These agencies—the Federal Energy Regulatory Commission (FERC), for example—typically require those who apply for their permits and licenses to do all the legwork required for environmental impact review, though they hold the ultimate ace of being able to issue the permit or not. Some permitting programs, such as those under the Coastal Zone Management Act and the Clean Air Act, are delegated to state, local, and regional agencies.

Central and Regional Offices

Most agencies are organized into some sort of central office/regional office relationship, but the offices are called different things from agency to agency, and the boundaries of regions don't correspond with one another. There are "standard" federal regions, but not all agencies have regional offices in all regions, so regions are combined and split depending on the agency's needs, and some agencies—like the Corps of Engineers, which is organized with reference to river basins—don't use the standard regions at all. Other agencies, like the Bureau of Land Management, place most authority in state offices. However they're organized, there is always tension between "the field" and "Washington." People from Washington are regarded by the field as autocratic and out of touch; people from the field are regarded by Washington as dangerously loose cannons who don't understand policy.

Federal Preservation Officer

Under NHPA, each agency is supposed to have a designated official responsible for overseeing its compliance with the law. This official is referred to as the "Federal Preservation Officer" or FPO. The statute states that the FPO is to be "qualified," but no one has ever quite established what this means. Most agencies have FPOs, but their locations in the agency's organizational system, their authorities, and their expertise vary widely. The "Federal Preservation Forum" is a group made up of FPOs that tries to promote coordination among its members and give them a unified voice.

National Park Service

NPS as a Land Manager

Most people know NPS as the manager of the nation's national parks, monuments, recreation areas, seashores, and other special places designated for the protection and enjoyment of natural and cultural resources. In this role, NPS is a land and resource manager much like the Forest Service, Bureau of Land Management, or Tennessee Valley Authority. As such it has responsibilities under NEPA, Section 106 of NHPA, the Native American Graves Protection and Repatriation Act, and other authorities just like any other agency. CRM practitioners come into contact with it fairly frequently as it exercises these responsibilities. Having preservation and public interpretation as parts of its mission, NPS also does a good deal of CRM work in and around the various units of the National Park System, and CRM practitioners often interact with it as contractors on things like "historic context studies," historic property surveys, preparation of historic structures reports, historic structure rehabilitation and restoration projects, and Native American coordination projects.

NPS External Programs

NPS also has a number of "external" or "outhouse" functions, in the context of which it interacts with other agencies, states, tribes, local governments, and the public on cultural resource matters having nothing to do with the National Park System. The external programs include:

The National Register, as both a list of properties and as a staff unit that manages the list, processes nominations, and so on.

Archeology and Ethnography programs, which deal with Archeological Resources Protection Act (ARPA) and Native American Graves Protection and Repatriation Act (NAGPRA) issues, provide an annual report to Congress on the "national archeology program," and publish a magazine called *Common Ground* that's loaded with good news about archeological and Native American matters.

The HABS/HAER program—the acronyms stand for "Historic American Buildings Survey" and "Historic American Engineering Record"—which oversees the documentation of historic architecture and engineering works.

Architectural preservation programs that promote the proper treatment and rehabilitation of historic buildings and structures under the tax code, through participation in Section 106 review, and through moral suasion.

Grants programs that provide grants to State Historic Preservation Officers, Indian tribes, local governments, preservation technology researchers and educators, and, occasionally, to others to carry out historic preservation and some other CRM activities. The grants programs for the states and tribes get NPS involved pretty directly in state and tribal historic preservation program development and oversight; NPS routinely audits its grantees and provides pretty directive advice about how they ought to do their businesses.

I hasten to say that the titles I've given the various programs above are not those by which they are currently known, nor are the programs necessarily divided up precisely as I've divided them. NPS, like every other agency, reorganizes with the phases of the moon, and you can never be sure who's going to be whom next week. The external programs are particularly vulnerable to reorganization, renaming, reconfiguration and redirection because they are forever trying to sort out their relationships with the much more powerful, higher-profile internal programs. So sometimes the external programs have distinct separate identities, and other times they flow together with various internal programs. The situation is complicated by NPS's more or less decentralized organization, which features regional offices, various kinds of support offices, centers, parks and park clusters—all in more or less continuous power flux. Generally speaking, though, the five functional areas I've noted above tend to be represented by nodes of people, money, and responsibilities, and it's with these that the average CRM practitioner will most likely come into contact.

National Trust for Historic Preservation

Modeled on the like-named organization in Great Britain, the National Trust was granted a federal charter in 1949 (which means little except that the government officially recognizes and approves of its existence). The Trust was instrumental in promoting enactment of NHPA, and has remained an influential voice in preservation circles. A not-for-profit membership organization, the Trust maintains a number of historic properties, assists others in doing the same, provides advice and assistance to local preservation groups, and performs a range of other good works. Its chairman is a member of the ACHP. One of the most useful things the Trust does these days is litigation; it has an active, if pitifully small and undersupported, legal department that does what it can to promote agency compliance with the historic preservation laws through selective litigation.

State Historic Preservation Officer

There are fifty-nine SHPOs, because, in addition to the fifty honest-to-gosh states, the District of Columbia, Puerto Rico, American Samoa, the Virgin Islands, Guam, the Commonwealth of the Northern Mariana Islands, the Republic of Belau, the Republic of the Marshall Islands, and the Federated States of Micronesia are "states" for the purposes of NHPA. The SHPO's basic function under federal law is to coordinate historic preservation activities supported by federal grant funds in his or her state. Each SHPO receives an annual program grant from NPS—size dependent on appropriation and the allocation formula currently in use. The SHPO uses this grant to carry out a wide range of functions set forth in Section 101(b)(3) of NHPA, such as:

- conducting a statewide inventory of historic properties;
- nominating properties to the National Register;
- maintaining a statewide preservation plan;
- providing assistance to others;
- advising local governments, federal and state agencies, and the public;
- participating in Section 106 and other reviews;
- helping local governments with program development; and
- public education.

SHPO grants must be matched by non-federal contributions. NPS audits the SHPOs periodically, not only to ensure that their grants are being well administered, but that the programs are being run as NPS thinks they should be. In the 1980s, this audit system rather ran away with itself, with some NPS regional offices engaging in some pretty monstrous micromanagement of SHPO programs. Mercifully, NPS audits have become considerably kinder and gentler in recent years.

Many SHPOs carry out functions under state laws as well as under federal law; examples include maintenance of state registers, historic preservation easement programs, participation in state environmental reviews and "State 106 processes," and state-funded grants programs.

The SHPO is designated by the governor. Some states constrain the governor's discretion by stipulating that the SHPO will be, say, the Director of the State Historical Society, answerable to the Society's Board of Directors; others do not. SHPOs tend to be political animals, and some preservation purists decry this fact. In my experience, it's mostly to the good; if a SHPO is going to be effective, she or he needs to know how to play the state's political system. SHPO staff must meet standards promulgated by NPS—that is, the staff must include specialists in history, archeology, architectural history, and other fields who meet NPS professional standards. There also must be a State Review Board with qualified members, whose primary function is to review National Register nominations.

At the national level, SHPOs are represented by the National Conference of SHPOs, a membership organization whose president sits on the Advisory Council. Some SHPOs who haven't joined NCSHPO claim not to be represented by it. Generally speaking, this leaves them simply unrepresented, because as far as agencies like the ACHP and NPS are concerned, when it comes to national issues, NCSHPO speaks for the SHPOs.

SHPO staff are the government officials with whom most CRM practitioners come into contact most often—and indeed lots of CRM practitioners *are* SHPO staff. It's important to remember who the SHPO is and is not. The SHPO is the representative of the state's interests in historic preservation. The SHPO is not the representative of the ACHP, nor of NPS, nor is he or she necessarily an advocate for historic preservation *uber alles*. Perhaps most important of all, the SHPO is not responsible for doing a federal agency's work for it—for identifying historic properties that the agency's actions may affect, telling the agency what the effect will be, or dictating to the agency what to do about the effect. The SHPO consults with the agency, assists the agency, but is not supposed either to dictate to the agency nor to perform functions on the agency's behalf.

Tribal Historic Preservation Officers

The 1992 amendments to NHPA contained a number of provisions designed to increase and improve participation by Indian tribes, Alaska Natives, and

Native Hawaiians in the historic preservation system. One of these provisions was for the substitution of tribal preservation programs for SHPO functions within the external boundaries of reservations. To substitute for the SHPO, a tribe must be approved by NPS. The tribe can also substitute its preservation procedures for those of the Advisory Council under Section 106; to do this it must enter into an agreement with the council.

The first dozen-and-a-half or so Tribal Historic Preservation Officers (THPOs) have been established under agreements with NPS. A lot of contentious issues remain about THPO authorities both within and outside reservation boundaries. Generally, CRM practitioners can expect to see more of THPOs in the future, and I hope that THPOs and their staffs, like other practitioners, will find things of use to them in this book.

Part Two

Law and Practice

Chapter 4

The Umbrella: The National Environmental Policy Act (NEPA)

What Is It?

NEPA is a cultural resource management authority, but of course it is also a natural resource management authority, a pollution prevention authority, a clean water authority—an authority for managing the impacts of federal government actions on all aspects of the human environment. "Human environment" is defined as:

> ...the natural and physical environment and the relationship of people with that environment. (40 CFR 1508.14)

NEPA has two parts. The first, set forth in Section 101, establishes national policy. Section 101(a) declares that:

> ...it is the continuing policy of the Federal Government, in cooperation with state and local governments, and other concerned public and private organizations, to use all practicable means and measures, including financial and technical assistance, in a manner calculated to foster and promote the general welfare, to create and maintain conditions under which man and nature can exist in productive harmony, and fulfill the social, economic, and other requirements of present and future generations of Americans.

To carry out this policy, Section 101(b) goes on to articulate:

> ...the continuing responsibility of the Federal Government to use all practicable means, consistent with other essential considerations of national policy, to improve and coordinate Federal plans, functions, programs and resources to the end that the Nation may—
> 1) fulfill the responsibilities of each generation as trustee of the environment for succeeding generations;
> 2) assure for all Americans safe, healthful, productive, and esthetically and culturally pleasing surroundings;

3) attain the widest range of beneficial uses of the environment without degradation, risk to health or safety, or other undesirable and unintended consequences;

4) preserve important historic, cultural, and natural aspects of our national heritage, and maintain, wherever possible, an environment which supports diversity, and variety of individual choice;

5) achieve a balance between population and resource use which will permit high standards of living and a wide sharing of life's amenities; and

6) enhance the quality of renewable resources and approach the maximum attainable recycling of depletable resources.

The aspect of NEPA that federal agencies deal with on a day-to-day basis is set forth in Section 102. Section 102 begins by directing that to the fullest extent possible:

...the policies, regulations, and public laws of the United States shall be interpreted and administered in accordance with the policies set forth in this Act.

It goes on to detail—again to the fullest extent possible—that:

...all agencies of the Federal Government shall...(u)tilize a systematic, interdisciplinary approach which will insure the integrated use of the natural and social sciences and the environmental design arts in planning and in decisionmaking which may have an impact on man's environment.

It further directs that agencies:

...(i)dentify and develop methods and procedures, in consultation with the Council on Environmental Quality...which will insure that presently unquantified environmental amenities and values may be given appropriate consideration in decisionmaking along with economic and technical considerations.

Finally, it lays out certain procedural requirements, discussed below. Many people think of these as NEPA's *only* requirements. This is unfortunate, because the procedural requirements are vacuous in the absence of policy to guide their implementation.

Regulations issued by the Council on Environmental Quality (CEQ) govern how agencies are to carry out the procedural requirements. The regulations, which are pretty extensive and not (in my opinion, anyhow) terribly logically organized, are found at 40 CFR 1500 et seq. Cantor (1996) provides a good general introduction to NEPA practice, though I think his treatment of the sociocultural environment is weak and rather off point.

MFASAQHE

NEPA is often misunderstood as requiring analysis only of "major federal actions significantly affecting the quality of the human environment," which a training package for the Central Intelligence Agency perhaps expectably reduced to the acronym MFASAQHE (pron. "Mafasakwee"). Actually, MFASAQHE is the threshold for doing an environmental impact statement (EIS)—the most detailed kind of NEPA analysis—but there are other kinds of analysis that effectively extend NEPA's embrace to *all* federal actions. This is as it must be, given the scope of the policy articulated in Section 101.

The fixation with MFASAQHE arises from the last parts of Section 102—the procedural requirements—which, among other things, require that agencies:

> ...(i)nclude in every recommendation or report on proposals for legislation and other major Federal actions significantly affecting the quality of the human environment, a detailed statement by the responsible official on—
> i) The environmental impact of the proposed action;
> ii) Any adverse environmental effects which cannot be avoided should the proposal be implemented;
> iii) Alternatives to the proposed action;
> iv) The relationship between local short-term uses of man's environment and the maintenance and enhancement of long-term productivity; and
> v) Any irreversible and irretrievable commitments of resources which would be involved if the proposed action should it be implemented.

Thus MFASAQHE is the threshold for production of a "detailed statement" of environmental impacts—that is, an EIS. But doing an EIS is only one way of addressing the national policy set forth in Section 101.

In point of fact, one has to do some level of environmental analysis even to determine whether an action *is* a MFASAQHE, and that's what a great deal of NEPA analysis is really about.

The range of federal actions to which NEPA applies is outlined in the CEQ regulations. Actions subject to NEPA review include:

> 1) Adoption of official policy, such as rules, regulations, and interpretations...; treaties and international conventions or agreements; formal documents establishing an agency's policies which will result in or substantially alter agency programs.
> 2) Adoption of formal plans...which guide or prescribe alternative uses of federal resources, upon which future agency actions will be based.
> 3) Adoption of programs, such as a group of concerted actions to implement a specific policy or plan...
> 4) Approval of specific projects, such as construction or management activities located in a defined geographic area. (40 CFR 1508.18)

It's in the context of the last class of action that most people most often come into contact with NEPA review. The regulations go on to clarify that:

Projects include actions approved by permit or other regulatory decision as well as federal and federally assisted activities. (40 CFR 1508.18)

Categorical Exclusions

CEQ's regulations direct federal agencies to develop their own NEPA procedures, consistent with the regulations. One thing these procedures do is to list "categorical exclusions." A categorical exclusion, usually referred to as a "CX," "CATEX," or "CatEx," is:

a category of actions which do not individually or cumulatively have a significant effect on the human environment and which have been found to have no such effect in procedures adopted by a Federal agency in implementation of these regulations. (40 CFR 1508.4)

In other words, agencies decide for themselves (subject to CEQ approval of their procedures) which of their actions do and do not have the potential to be MFASAQHEs, and hence to require analysis. CATEXs are absolutely necessary to government operations; otherwise, one would have to analyze the environmental impacts of every paperclip purchase.

But CATEXs also have a downside—things that really do have the potential for impact may be miscategorized. To deal with this, the regulations go on to say that:

...(a)ny procedures under this section shall provide for extraordinary circumstances in which a normally excluded action may have a significant environmental effect. (40 CFR 1508.4)

What this means in practice, of course, is that if you're following the regulations to the letter you *do* perform some level of environmental review even of a CATEX action, because you've got to determine whether an "extraordinary circumstance" exists.

In 1996, I helped the General Services Administration (GSA) rework its NEPA procedures, and we spent a great deal of time thinking and debating about CATEXs. GSA builds and manages federal buildings, among other things, and these actions have the potential for a wide range of environmental impacts—particularly on the urban sociocultural environment. But the great bulk of its actions are routine administrative matters that are quite legitimate CATEXs. Many others have some remote potential for impact on the environment, but that potential is so slight that it's a waste of the taxpayers' money (which, believe it or not, federal employees *do* worry about) to spend much time in reviewing them.

We concluded that there were really two types of CATEX, and the procedures now reflect this. One type is the "automatic CATEX" (also called the "no-brainer") which requires no environmental review at all. This is the kind of action for which it's virtually unthinkable that an "extraordinary circumstance" could exist; examples are hiring and firing personnel, and routine purchase of office supplies.

The other type of CATEX is the "checklist CATEX" (or "low-brainer"). An action falling into one of these categories requires a quick analysis to ensure that extraordinary circumstances don't exist; this is done using a short checklist (GSA 1997). Examples of "checklist CATEXs" include:

Checklist CATEX (a): Acquisition of land which is not in a floodplain or other environmentally sensitive area and does not result in condemnation.

Checklist CATEX (b): Acquisition of space by Federal construction or lease construction, or expansion or improvement of an existing facility, where all of the following conditions are met:

1) The structure and proposed use are substantially in compliance with local planning and zoning and any applicable State or Federal requirements (referenced in appendix);
2) The proposed use will not substantially increase the number of motor vehicles at the facility;
3) The site and the scale of construction are consistent with those of existing adjacent or nearby buildings; and
4) There is no evidence of community controversy or other environmental issues.

Checklist CATEX (j): Disposal of properties where the size, area, topography, and zoning are similar to existing surrounding properties and/or where current and reasonable anticipated uses are or would be similar to current surrounding uses (e.g., commercial store in a commercial strip, warehouse in an urban complex, office building in downtown area, row house or vacant lot in an urban area).

The "quick analysis" of a project that appears to be a Checklist CATEX naturally involves completing a checklist, which is shown in Figure 3.

You can see what I mean, I hope, when I say that NEPA analysis actually extends to all levels and kinds of federal action. Even automatic CATEXs require a sort of categorical analysis; in preparation of the agency's NEPA procedures one has to think through whether, as a category, hiring or firing people or buying office supplies could affect the environment. Checklist CATEXs require a fair bit more analysis on a case-by-case basis.

GSA: CATX Checklist

Action Name:
Action Location:
Action Description:
Category:

	YES	NO	Need Data
Is the action likely to be inconsistant with any applicable Federal, State, Indian Tribal, or local law, regulation or standard designed to protect any aspect of the environment?			
Is the action likely to have results that are inconsistent with locally-desired social, economic, or other environmental conditions?			
Is the action likely to result in the use, storage, release, and/or disposal of toxic, hazardous, or radioactive materials, or in the exposure of people to such materials?			
Is the action likely to adversely affect a significant aspect of the natural environment?			
Is the action likely to adversely affect a significant part of the sociocultural environment?			
Is the action likely to generate controversy on environmental effects?			
Is there a high level of uncertainty about the action's environmental effects?			
Is the action likely to do something especially risky to the human environment?			
Is the action part of an ongoing pattern of actions (whether under the control of GSA or others) that are cumulatively likely to have adverse effects on the human environment?			
Is the action likely to set a precedent for, or represent a decision in principal about future GSA actions that could have significant effects on the human environment?			
Is the action likely to have some other adverse effect on public health and safety or on any other environmental media or resources that are not specifically identified above?			

Conclusions:

1. The action is a CATEX and requires no further environmental review.
2. The action is a CATEX but requires further review under one or more other environmental authorities (list).
3. The action requires an EA.
4. The action requires an EIS.

_____   _____
Program Staff   Date   NCE Representative   Date

Figure 3. General Services Administration CATEX Checklist.

You can also see how sociocultural issues need to be considered in deciding whether an action should be regarded as categorically excluded. Satisfying the conditions of Checklist CATEX (b), for example, is going to require consultation with the local community to ensure compliance with local planning and zoning, a review to make sure other applicable federal and state laws are complied with, and enough contact with the people of the community to judge whether there is evidence of controversy. And for any Checklist CATEX, someone is going to have to consider whether the project may be "inconsistent with locally desired social...conditions," or "affect a significant aspect of the sociocultural environment."

An obvious question here is: "What if the checklist's filled out by somebody who doesn't know anything, or who lies?" That's a problem, and one that can never be wholly solved. If people really want to get out of looking at an environmental impact, there's usually a way to do it. In trying to plug the holes in any environmental review system, one has to balance costs and benefits: how thoroughly can we protect ourselves from errors and omissions before we create a system that's too complex, or too expensive, to sustain? In the case of GSA NEPA procedures, each CATEX Checklist is supposed be signed off by a trained environmental staffer, and everybody involved is supposed to get some level of training, so the forms shouldn't be filled out unknowledgeably. There are guidelines for responding to each checklist question. The guidelines for Checklist CATEX E, for example, state:

Think about whether your action is likely to cause changes in the ways members of the surrounding community, neighborhood, or rural area live, work, play, relate to one another, organize to meet their needs, or otherwise function as members of society, or in their social, cultural, or religious values and beliefs. Is your action likely to:

- *Cause the displacement or relocation of businesses, residences, or farm operations;*

- *Affect the economy of the community in ways that result in impacts to its character, or to the physical environment;*

- *Affect sensitive receptors of visual, auditory, traffic, or other impacts, such as schools, cultural institutions, churches, and residences; or*

- *Affect any practice of religion (e.g., by impeding access to a place of worship)?*

Give special attention to whether the action is likely to have environmental impacts on a minority or low income group that are out of proportion with its impacts on other groups. Consider, for example, whether the action is likely to:

- *Result in the storage or discharge of pollutants in the environment of such a group;*

- *Have adverse economic impacts on such a group;*

- *Alter the sociocultural character of such a group's community or neighborhood, or its religious practices; or*

- *Alter such a group's use of land or other resources.*

Also consider possible impacts on historic, cultural, and scientific resources. Think about whether the action is likely to have physical, visual, or other effects on:

- *Districts, sites, buildings, structures, and objects that are included in the National Register of Historic Places, or a State or local register of historic places;*

- *A building or other structure that is over 45 years old;*

- *A neighborhood or commercial area that may be important in the history or culture of the community;*

- *A neighborhood, industrial, or rural area that might be eligible for the National Register as a district;*

- *A known or probable cemetery, through physical alteration or by altering its visual, social, or other characteristics;*

- *A rural landscape that may have cultural or esthetic value;*

- *A well-established rural community, or rural land use;*

- *A place of traditional cultural value in the eyes of a Native American group or other community;*

- *A known archeological site, or land identified by archeologists consulted by GSA as having high potential to contain archeological resources; or*

- *An area identified by archeologists or a Native American group consulted by GSA as having high potential to contain Native American cultural items.*

Particularly in rural areas, give special consideration to possible impacts on Native American cultural places and religious practices. For example, consider whether the action is likely to alter a place regarded as having spiritual significance by an Indian tribe or Native Hawaiian group, impede access to such a place by traditional religious practitioners, or cause a change in the use of, or public access to, such a place.

Is anybody really going to do all this kind of thinking and questioning? We hope so, and people are supposed to be trained to do so, using GSA's NEPA guidelines. For the great majority of GSA actions, there isn't going to be that much thinking and questioning to do. Checklist CATEX (i), for example, is:

Disposal of...personal property, demountable structures, transmission lines, utility poles, railroad ties, and track.

It's not going to take long for somebody to run through the guidelines and decide that the average CATEX (i) action has no earthly potential for significant effects on the sociocultural environment. On the other hand, a CATEX (j) action, involving land disposal, will require more attention, more questioning—a modicum of research.

Each agency has its own list of CATEXs, and its own way of screening CATEX actions to make sure they won't have significant impacts. Many use checklists of one kind or another. How carefully and professionally they're used varies from agency to agency and person to person. Making any CATEX decision properly, though, requires at least some thinking about potential impacts on the environment, including the sociocultural environment.

Let's suppose, now, that you have an action that's *not* a CATEX, but it also isn't obviously a MFASAQHE. What do you do?

The Environmental Assessment (EA)

Obviously if you don't know whether something is a MFASAQHE you have to do some analysis to figure out the answer. This analysis is referred to as an Environmental Assessment (EA).

According to the regulations, an EA is:

...a concise public document for which a Federal agency is responsible that serves to:

1) Briefly provide sufficient evidence and analysis for determining whether to prepare an environmental impact statement or a finding of no significant impact;
2) Aid an agency's compliance with the Act when no environmental impact statement is necessary;
3) Facilitate preparation of a statement when one is necessary. (40 CFR 1508.9)

CEQ estimates that some fifty thousand EAs are done each year across the federal establishment, as compared to about a tenth that many EISs. It can be fairly said that EAs are the bread and butter of NEPA review.

The regulations aren't very fulsome about what an EA should contain. They only require that the resulting document:

> ...include brief discussions of the need for the proposal, of alternatives..., of the environmental impacts of the proposed action and alternatives, and a listing of agencies and persons consulted. (40 CFR 1508.9)

What an EA is supposed to do, though, is to help you determine whether an action is a MFASAQHE, and therefore needs an EIS. The critical part of the acronym is the "SA" part; the critical thing an EA must do is to determine whether an action "significantly affects" the quality of the human environment. The regulations go into considerable detail about what the word "significantly" means, and much of the definitional language is redolent relevant to the sociocultural environment:

> Significantly as used in NEPA requires considerations of both context and intensity:
>
> a) Context. This means that the significance of an action must be analyzed in several contexts such as society as a whole (human, national), the affected region, the affected interests, and the locality. Significance varies with the setting of the proposed action. For instance, in the case of a site-specific action, significance would usually depend upon the effects in the locale rather than in the world as a whole.
>
> b) Intensity. This refers to the severity of impact. ...The following should be considered in evaluating intensity:
>
> > 1) Impacts that may be both beneficial and adverse...
> > 2) The degree to which the proposed action affects public health or safety.
> > 3) Unique characteristics...such as proximity to historic or cultural resources, park lands, prime farmlands...
> > 4) The degree to which the effects on the quality of the human environment are likely to be highly controversial.
> > 5) The degree to which the possible effects...are highly uncertain...
> > 6) The degree to which the action may establish a precedent...
> > 7) Whether the action is related to other actions with individually insignificant but cumulatively significant impacts...
> > 8) The degree to which the action may adversely affect districts, sites, highways, structures, or objects listed in or eligible for listing

in the National Register of Historic Places, or may cause loss or destruction of significant scientific, cultural, or historical resources... (40 CFR 1508.27)

So the core of the EA, its analytical part, holds the action's potential effects up against the regulatory definition of "significantly," and asks: "Given the context of the action's effects, and applying the measures of intensity, will the action significantly affect the quality of the human environment?"

You first need to ask: "In what context(s) may effects occur?" Suppose we're planning a timber sale on the Kindling National Forest. In terms of geography, there clearly will be effects in a local context—the context of the forest and its environs, or of the ecosystem in which the sale will take place. Perhaps there will be regional impacts—on the economy of the region, let's say, or on the regional wildlife habitat. In terms of society, there may be economic, visual, and auditory impacts, among others, on a local community—the nearby town of Matchless, say—but you'd also need to think about other contexts. Perhaps there's an Indian tribe that used to occupy the area, but that was long ago relocated to Oklahoma. This tribe might have concerns about the area, and they might even have legally binding treaty rights to resources there. The bottom line is that you've got to do some thinking, some research, to establish the context(s) in which analysis of effects should be done. And don't make the mistake of thinking that the sequence given in the regulations—"society as a whole (human, national), the affected region, the affected interests, and the locality"—represents a hierarchical ordering. Impacts on society as a whole are not necessarily bigger and more important than impacts on a locality, or on affected interests. The regulations are just trying to say that you don't ignore the local negative effects, or the negative effects on affected groups, because the effects on society as a whole will be positive.

Having established our contexts—let's say they comprise the National Forest and its neighborhood, and the concerns of the Motomak Tribe—we then turn to intensity, and look at each measure of intensity given in the regulations. So, for example:

1) Impacts that may be both beneficial and adverse...

We're going to stimulate the local economy and give people jobs (beneficial). We may muck up the ecosystem (adverse). We may disturb places of cultural significance to the Motomak (adverse).

2) The degree to which the proposed action affects public health or safety.

Cutting on slopes greater than 30% could cause erosion that would increase downstream flooding, possibly drowning people or polluting the Matchless water system.

3) Unique characteristics...such as proximity to historic or cultural resources, park lands, prime farmlands...

We'll need to do studies of some sort to identify historic and cultural resources—consult with the Motomak and others who may have cultural links to the area, look for archeological sites, check for historic buildings, and so forth. This is often taken as a rationale for doing archeological surveys, but it can require both less and more than that. If we're planning to do helicopter logging, or logging over snow, there may not be much need for archeological surveys because we won't mess up the ground. Even if this is the case, though, if the sale will result in a swath of clear-cut visible from a nearby peak, we'd better talk to the Motomak and others to make sure the peak isn't a spiritual place where people go to gain enlightenment in ways that require a natural view.

4) The degree to which the effects on the quality of the human environment are likely to be highly controversial.

There's only one way to find out about this: we've got to talk with people—both local people and people at a distance who may be concerned, like the Motomak.

5) The degree to which the possible effects...are highly uncertain...

Suppose we're planning to log over snow, but we don't really know how effective that's going to be for the protection of sensitive plants and surface archeological sites. Or suppose we don't know whether that peak is a place where Motomak people go to seek visions. These sorts of uncertainty need to be addressed, and if possible eliminated, in the EA.

6) The degree to which the action may establish a precedent...

Maybe if this project is "successful" in controlling environmental impacts, the Forest Service is going to make logging over snow standard practice. If this is likely, we'd better be sure we've really thought through all its impacts, and we'd probably better go back and re-think the contexts in which we're doing our analysis. Now maybe we'd better look at a nationwide context, and think about different regions. If we do logging over snow where the buffalo roam, for example, is it going to create trails that bison will follow from the high country down onto the cattle range, raising the fear of spreading brucellosis? Not a problem on the Kindling, where the biggest animal is the jackalope, but if the project is a precedent for logging on the Big Blue Bison National Forest, it could be another matter.

7) Whether the action is related to other actions with individually insignificant but cumulatively significant impacts...

How much logging has already gone on in the area? Are we creeping up toward a point at which we could go over some critical threshold and lose a resource? Is the speckled mugwump's habitat so mucked up by logging, roadbuilding, and mushroom gathering on the Kindling that one more timber sale will push it into extinction? Or in a cultural context, is there now just enough old growth timber on the forest, or in the Stony Owl drainage, or on the east slope of Mt. Moron, to allow the Motomak to continue carrying out their Universe Salvation ritual, but will this timber sale reduce the old growth below critical levels? Or will the sale reduce the number of mine sites left from the 1876 quartz rush to a point where we'll never be able to answer important research questions about this fascinating part of Washafornia's history?

8) The degree to which the action may adversely affect districts, sites, highways, structures, or objects listed in or eligible for listing in the National Register of Historic Places, or may cause loss or destruction of significant scientific, cultural, or historical resources...

Here again we need to get out and look—not only within the boundaries of the sale itself, but in other areas where visual, auditory, land-use, or other effects might occur. This look should be carefully coordinated with work under Section 106 of the National Historic Preservation Act (see Chapter 5), but note that this measure of intensity isn't limited to *historic properties*. The clause about "significant scientific, cultural, or historical resources" must mean something other than historic properties, or it wouldn't be there as a separate clause.

We need to think about *scientific resources* like paleontological sites, and pack rat middens that can provide information on past climates.

We need to think about *cultural resources* like the religious practices of the Motomak, the use of Stony Owl Creek for baptismal purposes by the local Pentecostal Church, the gathering of mushrooms on the slopes of Mt. Moron by the residents of Matchless for the annual Mushroom Festival, and the use of the area by landscape painting classes from Southeastern Washafornia State University.

We need to think about *historical resources* like the records of the Mt. Moron Mine, locked in a safe in the old mine headquarters, like the oral history of medicinal plant use in the area, and like the history of local logging itself.

Some of these resources may relate to historic properties, but others don't. They are resources that can be affected by the action, whether they're subjects of concern under laws like the National Historic Preservation Act or not, and impacts on them need to be considered in the EA. And, importantly, finding out about a lot of them requires talking with people, consulting with them, getting their opinions. Although the CEQ regulations don't say much about public participation in EA preparation, it's an absolute necessity with respect to cultural effects, because it's in people's collective consciousness that such effects take place.

So preparing the EA is an analytical activity that should be organized around the regulatory definition of the word "significantly." It must lead to a report, which should be as succinct as possible, and which must (in theory) be considered as the action moves along toward a decision.

The EA leads to one of two results. Either you decide to do an EIS, because the action is a MFASAQHE, or that you don't need to do an EIS because it's not. In the latter case, your agency issues a "Finding of No Significant Impact" (FONSI or FNSI) before proceeding. Many times, the FONSI will include a list of actions that the agency has decided to do—or agreed with others to do—to reduce impacts below a significant level. Some courts have found this to be inconsistent with NEPA, holding that if there are going to be significant impacts, you have to do an EIS, not fiddle around to try to make them insignificant. Generally, however, "mitigated FONSIs" are regarded as reasonable, cost-effective ways to handle impacts without going through costly and unnecessary review. The important point to remember, though, is that in order to have a legitimate mitigated FONSI, the agency must be able to show that it has mitigated or will mitigate the impacts down to a level of non-significance.

The "Socioeconomic Exclusion"

Section 1508.14 of the NEPA regulations says that:

...economic or social effects are not intended by themselves to require preparation of an environmental impact statement. When an environmental impact statement is prepared and economic or social and natural or physical environmental effects are interrelated, then the environmental impact statement will discuss all of these effects on the human environment. (40 CFR 1508.14)

The Supreme Court, in *Metropolitan Edison Co. v. People Against Nuclear Energy* (460 U.S. 766, 103 S.Ct. 1556 [1983], commonly called the PANE decision), similarly concluded that social and psychological impacts were not sufficient by themselves to require preparation of an EIS.

Some agencies have interpreted this exclusionary language to indicate that impacts on social, economic, and cultural resources don't have to be considered under NEPA (cf. Thompson and Williams 1992). However, neither the regulations nor the Court in PANE said this. What the regulations and PANE say, taken together, is that if an action will have effects on social, economic, or psychological factors only, then the proponent agency *doesn't have to do an EIS*. That's a lot different than saying the agency doesn't have to consider these factors under NEPA. In fact, an agency *does* have to consider them in its EA, along with all other possible environmental impacts. If it turns out that there are *only* social, economic, or psychological effects, then the project does not rise to the level of a MFASAQHE, and environmental impact analysis ends with a FONSI. If there are social, economic, or psychological effects that are linked somehow to effects on the physical (natural or built) environment, and the latter effects are significant, then an EIS has to be done.

Suppose that Mr. Jones really, really, really likes the view from his front window out across the valley of Stony Owl Creek. Suppose that Megazap Corp. plans to build a 750 kV power line through the valley, crossing Mr. Jones' view. If Mr. Jones can't find anything wrong with Megazap's proposal except that it's really going to upset him, cause his social standing to decline, or decrease his property value, he's not going to be able to force the Forest Service, or the Federal Energy Regulatory Commission, or whoever's regulating Megazap, to do an EIS. But his concerns will have to be considered in any EA that's prepared on the project, and if he can show that there are impacts that go beyond his psychological, social, or economic well-being, then perhaps he *can* force preparation of an EIS.

What might Mr. Jones find as an impact that goes beyond the social, economic, and psychological? Well, obviously he might find that construction will cause erosion, or that endangered owls will alight on the lines and be fried, but rather, closer to his own concerns, he might argue that the project will have serious cultural effects.

Note that the "exclusion" provided by the regulations and PANE extends to social, economic, and psychological effects; nothing is said about culture. So if Mr. Jones can argue that the Stony Owl Creek valley may be a historic property, a place of high cultural attachment for the people of Matchless, a spiritual place in the eyes of the Motomac Tribe (or the Zen Buddhists, or the Baha'i), or a popular local picnic place, then he may be able to give Megazap a run for its money. How much of a run he can give them will depend on how good a case he has.

Note, though, that there's very little in the CEQ regulations to force Megazap or its regulator ever to talk with Mr. Jones or anybody else, as long as all they're doing is an EA. The regulations go on at some length about public participation in EIS preparation and review, but don't say much about such participation in EAs. It's possible for an agency never to reveal its EAs to the public except in response to a Freedom of Information Act request—this was, in fact, recommended to us at GSA by a consultant whose opinion was politely listened to and dismissed. Logically, one can't very well figure out the intensity of an impact in the context of affected interests without trying to figure out what those interests are and talking it over with them, but there's nothing in the regulations that comes right out and says: "talk with people." That's a weakness in the regulations, I think, and one that cultural resource managers need to watch with some vigilance.

The Environmental Impact Statement (EIS)

The EIS is the "detailed statement" that is required on any action that's a MFASAQHE. The CEQ regulations go into pretty loving detail about what goes into an EIS, and how it's prepared and reviewed.

You begin by deciding what the "purpose and need" for the project are. This seems like a pretty self-evident thing—you obviously ought to know why somebody needs the project before you start analyzing its impacts. There are good reasons for thinking seriously about purpose and need, however, because the way you define them limits the range of alternatives you'll consider. If you define the purpose of your project as meeting the need to alleviate traffic congestion in East Armpit, you can consider a wide range of alternatives—rapid transit, bicycle subsidies, euthanasia—but if you say the purpose is to move traffic more efficiently from downtown East Armpit to the suburbs, you're pointed pretty clearly in the direction of highway improvements.

Having decided why you need to do the project, and having already determined that an EIS is in order, you publish a Notice of Intent (NOI) in the Federal Register. The Federal Register (not the National Register, which is another thing entirely) is a daily publication of federal agency announcements, draft and final regulations, guidelines, standards—just about everything but a "Personals" section. Few real people ever read the Federal Register, of course, so if an agency seriously wants people to know that it plans to do an EIS, it will publish notice elsewhere as well.

Then comes "scoping"—one of the most widely abused elements of the NEPA process. Scoping is a terribly sensible thing to do—the term means figuring out what the scope of the EIS should be. You don't want to hire water quality specialists to work on your EIS if the scope of effects doesn't include doing anything to the water. According to the regulations, scoping includes:

- Inviting interested parties to participate in the EIS work;

- Identifying significant issues for analysis;

- Eliminating nonsignificant issues;

- Allocating assignments for the work that's to be done;

- Identifying other studies being done that relate to the subject of the EIS, so work can be coordinated;

- Identifying environmental review requirements other than NEPA that need to be addressed; and

- Establishing the relationship between preparation of the EIS and the project planning schedule.

The regulations go on to say that as part of scoping, the agency can set page limits on the EIS, set time limits on preparation, combine scoping with EA preparation, and hold a public scoping meeting. Unfortunately, a lot of agencies and consultants read that last clause and seem to ignore everything else, reducing scoping to the conduct of a public meeting. More on this later. What scoping is *supposed* to be is an analytic activity—you take an analytic look at the project and the area, and try to get an idea of what you're going to need to do to analyze impacts. Getting public input is an important part of this analysis, but it's only one part, and it doesn't have to involve a mind-numbing public hearing. It can involve interviews, workshops, focus groups, facilitated working sessions—whatever makes sense under the circumstances. And again, it shouldn't be the only thing you do in scoping; you also ought to apply your own brain, and those of your interdisciplinary colleagues, and those of others you may consult, to the questions: "what impacts *might* this action have, and what kinds of environmental factors *may* need to be considered," as a basis for designing the scope of work for the actual EIS. Your conclusions are going to be provisional, of course; you may discover unexpected impacts as you go along, or find that some anticipated impacts really aren't going to occur.

Although the regulations talk about scoping only in the context of EIS preparation, it's really necessary in planning how to do an EA, too, and even in screening a CATEX. Whether you *call* it scoping or not, you've got to figure out what you're going to do, and you ought to do that systematically, based on analysis and consultation with knowledgeable and interested parties.

Having established the scope of the EIS, the next step is to *do* the analysis—whatever that may entail. Naturally, this is a flexible process; you do such analysis as is needed to identify and make sense of the project's impacts. Of course, if you haven't done a very good job of scoping, you may wind up analyzing the wrong things.

The regulations spell out what the format of an EIS should be; in outline, it goes like this:

- Cover sheet.

- Summary.

- Statement of purpose and need for the proposed action.

- Description of alternatives, including the "no action" alternative (not taking the action at all). All reasonable alternatives are to be "rigorously explored," and the agency's preferred alternative is to be identified, if there is one. Mitigation measures can also be described.

- Description of the environment affected by each alternative.

- Discussion of the environmental consequences of each alternative, including direct, indirect, and cumulative impacts.

- List of preparers.

- Appendices as needed.

So, the core of the EIS answers the following questions:

- What are our options (alternatives) for meeting the purpose and need?

- What is the environment that would be affected by each option?

- What impacts will each option have on the environment?

The analysis leads to a Draft EIS (DEIS), which must then be circulated for comment to agencies with jurisdiction or expertise, to local governments, Indian tribes, and other groups, and made available for public review. Once the comment period is up, comments are considered and—unless the project has been blown out of the water by public opposition or canned for some other reason—a Final EIS (FEIS) is prepared. The FEIS must respond to all comments received, and presumably adjusts the analysis to address deficiencies identified by commenters.

The FEIS is then considered by whoever makes the decision about whether and how to proceed with the project. Once the decision is made, a Record of Decision (ROD) must be published, informing the world of what the decision is. The ROD may (and should) include a description of whatever the agency has decided or agreed to do to mitigate environmental impacts.

NEPA and Cultural Resources

Now that we have something of a handle on the basic NEPA process, let's look at how the cultural environment can—and, I suggest, should—be addressed. Then we'll look at how it usually *is* addressed in the real world.

Remember that NEPA requires agencies to consider *all* environmental impacts, on *all* aspects of the environment. Thus it's NEPA that gives agencies their broadest authority, and direction, to address the sociocultural environment writ large, as well as its interactions with the biophysical environment. NEPA is often referred to metaphorically as an umbrella, that extends over all the other resource-specific laws, but it also extends beyond them, to cover aspects of the human environment that are not the subject of other more specific laws and executive orders.

Let's start with scoping—and by scoping I mean formal scoping for an EIS, the less formal scoping one must do to plan an EA, and the even more informal scoping one may have to do to figure out whether extraordinary circumstances exist that prevent an action from being regarded as a CATEX.

During scoping, an agency should try to figure out what sorts of sociocultural issues may need to be addressed—what sociocultural aspects of the environment may be affected. This is not necessarily going to be apparent as the result of a public meeting or two, though interactions with the public during scoping are important. Scoping should involve whatever kinds of consultation are necessary with authorities and stakeholders, as well as background research. Where traditional communities are concerned—for example, many Native American communities—it's often important to consult with them *before* any sort of public discussion of the action, because they may have cultural concerns (e.g., about spiritually important places) that can't be revealed in public. Consultation with federally recognized tribes must be carried out on a "government-to-government" basis that respects tribal sovereignty.

Scoping may reveal a host of potential issues—impacts on traditional land uses, lifeways, hunting or gathering or agricultural practices, social interactions, religious practices, historic places—which have to be considered in designing the study team that will perform the NEPA analysis, and in designing the analysis itself.

Moving on to the analysis itself—the *Guidelines and Principles for Social Impact Assessment* (Interorganizational Committee 1993; NOAA 1994) set forth nine basic principles that should be followed in analyzing social impacts. These principles can be applied to the study of all types of sociocultural impacts.

1. Involve the diverse public. Figure out who the affected "publics" are, and involve them in ways that are sensitive to the cultural, economic, linguistic, educational, and other variations among them. The NEPA analysis needs to be carried out in consultation with the people who may be affected. Consultation should mean more than just having meetings or sending letters; it ought to involve real, face-to-face exchanges of information and ideas. Special efforts may have to be made to make it meaningful—for example, use of an indigenous language and attention to local social norms that may be foreign to the analyst.

2. Analyze impact equity. Determine if you can who's going to win and who's going to lose if this, that, or the other alternative is pursued. As we'll discuss later, Executive Order 12898 provides specific direction about this aspect of the analysis.

3. Focus the assessment. As the *Guidelines and Principles* say, the analyst should "deal with issues and public concerns that really count, not those that are just easy to count." What's of interest to the analyst, or what the analyst finds easy to deal with, is not necessarily what's important to the people. On the other hand, of course, what people don't know *can* hurt them, or the environment. One shouldn't be slavish to the concerns of the affected public; you need to look both at what specialists think is important *and* what the locals are concerned about.

4. Identify methods and assumptions and define significance. This is basic methodology. To the extent possible, your research should be replicable, or at least the steps you went through to reach your conclusions should be understandable. And the bottom line of any impact analysis is to determine how significant the impacts may be. In a NEPA context, this means analyzing impacts with reference to the definition of significance in the regulations—analyzing the intensity of the impacts in their relevant contexts.

5. Provide feedback to project planners. The analysis should be dynamic; a continual flow should exist back and forth between analysts and planners.

6. Use qualified practitioners. NEPA calls for interdisciplinary research. It's important to distinguish between *inter*disciplinary and *multi*disciplinary research. Multidisciplinary research simply means a bunch of disciplinary specialists working on the same project; interdisciplinary research means interaction among the specialists—and hopefully a fruitful symbiosis. The specialists needed for the sociocultural side of a NEPA analysis will probably be social scientists—anthropologists, sociologists, cultural geographers, archeologists—practitioners of such fields in the humanities as history and architectural history, and people in hybrid disciplines like landscape history. It's important to have them work *with* the other scientists involved in the assessment effort, as an interdisciplinary team. The people doing the water quality studies, for example, will have much to say to the people studying the indigenous community's use of fish or shellfish or wild rice.

7. Establish monitoring and mitigation programs. This, of course, should be one of the end results of the analysis, assuming the proposed action goes forward in some manner.

8. Identify data sources. This is another basic methodological point. It can present some problems, however, where sensitive sociocultural information is involved. It may just not be possible for a traditional religious practitioner to reveal much about a spiritual place, and if he or she does, it may be inappropriate for *you* to put much about it in print, or say where you got the information. I'll have more to say about the "problem of confidentiality" later.

9. Plan for gaps in data. Nobody ever has complete data, and it's unlikely that you'll get all the information you'd like to have for your impact analysis. The important thing is to recognize the missing information *as* missing, and decide explicitly how important it is. Then you can decide—or your sponsor can—whether it's worth extending the study to get it.

In a MFASAQHE, the analysis results in a DEIS, which then gets circulated for review. This shouldn't be the only time the analysts interact with the interested public, but it's one important opportunity. Ideally, review of the DEIS should be seen as an opportunity for creative communication, for the identification of gaps and flaws, for filling the former and correcting the latter, for challenging assumptions and defending or adjusting them. It should also be an opportunity to make sure that the affected public knows what the hell the analysis is about, and understands what impacts the various alternatives may have on their lives and cultural values. In short, it should involve a carefully constructed program of public review and participation.

The public review period is also a key time for consultation with regulatory/advisory agencies like the State Historic Preservation Officer (SHPO). The analysis leading to the DEIS should have at least generally defined the affected resources and the character of the effects, so it's at this point that it's appropriate to consult about how to manage the former and resolve or mitigate the latter. This consultation needs to be carefully coordinated with the public review, so that each can inform and be informed by the other.

In an EA/FONSI case, the regulations don't require public review, but the wise agency will provide for it to the extent the issues seem to demand it. The same principles apply to this sort of informal review as apply to more formal review in an EIS context.

The results of public review and consultation with oversight bodies should be organized, responded to, and reflected in the final EIS or EA. Then they should be considered in making the agency's final decision about whether and how to proceed, and any needed mitigation measures should be developed and implemented—again in consultation with the affected parties.

That's the way it ought to be done. Now, in the real world...

It is common to hear EIS consultants talk blithely about "the scoping meeting" as though that's all scoping is. And in fact, that's the way they often behave. Scoping is often thought of as a pro forma exercise in public relations. CEQ staff grumble about agencies exhibiting "the rent-a-gym syndrome"—set up a meeting in some local public facility, explain the project in great detail to the public, stonily absorb such comments as the (by now stunned and somnolent) attendees can launch, and then say goodnight. Since such meetings often have little evident influence on the actual analysis, this is also referred to as the "Triple-I" approach: "Inform, seek Input, and Ignore."

Having thus engaged the public, the analysts go on to perform a study that matches their—the analysts'—template of a proper EIS. This may have more to do with the disciplines represented on the preparer's staff than with actual impacts of the action.

Where the NEPA analysis is an EA, and there is no formal requirement for public participation, there often isn't any. The entire analysis is performed in the blackest possible box, with as little public input as possible, in order to minimize costs and expenditures of time.

The affected sociocultural environment typically is divided into two parts. There is usually a section on "cultural resources" and another on "social (or socioeconomic) impacts." In most cases neither term is defined. When they are, however—and by implication when they aren't—"cultural resources" are equated with "historic properties" (i.e., places included in or eligible for the National Register of Historic Places) or sometimes with archeological sites, or occasionally with historic properties and Native American cultural objects (see NAGPRA in Chapter 7). "Socioeconomics," meanwhile, is typically reduced to variables that, in the pungent words of the *Guidelines and Principles*, are "easy to count" (Interorganizational Committee 1993; NOAA 1994:20): demographics, use of services, numbers of kids in school, purchasing power, tax base, employment. Everything else of a sociocultural nature falls through the cracks between these two narrowly defined foci of interest, and isn't discussed at all (King 1998; King and Rafuse 1994).

So the DEIS, or EA, ends up addressing historic properties at one end of the spectrum, and easy-to-count socioeconomic phenomena at the other, and then it may go out for public review. Members of the public may well be frustrated by the fact that things of cultural importance to them aren't addressed, and they may comment on this when they review the DEIS, but they are in a slippery position. Suppose you don't feel that a DEIS has properly considered the effect of a reservoir on the places where your community has fished for the last couple of hundred years. What do you call these places? Are they historic properties? Well, you can try to call them that, but the response is likely to be that the analyst's archeologist looked over the place and determined there was nothing there because, after all, the sand bars from which you fish move around all the time. Hence there are no intact archeological deposits and so, you're told, there's nothing eligible for the National Register of Historic Places, and hence no historic property.

Or you can complain about the EIS's failure to consider the importance of subsistence fishing to maintaining your community's traditional lifeways. This complaint will get bounced to the socioeconomist to answer, and he or she will spew out a bunch of statistics about fish yield and per-pound market value.

This sort of obscurantism doesn't necessarily mean that anybody is *trying* to ignore your fishing place; it merely means that nobody knows how to deal with it, because they're all looking at impacts through narrow, disciplinary lenses.

You *can* get past all this, if you know how, but most people don't. You can argue that the sandbars comprise a National Register eligible traditional cultural property. You can point out that NEPA is about more than National Register properties anyway. You can talk about the special sociocultural importance of fishing in your community, and about how taking away the fish may be a disproportionate adverse impact on your low-income or minority group, thus raising the red flag of Executive Order 12898 (see Chapter 7). But you've got to know to do this sort of thing, to speak this way, to say the right things at the right time to the right people. And most people don't know all those obscure words and concepts.

So the chances are excellent that the project will go forward with impacts on the most important parts of the sociocultural environment—at least those that are most important to you—virtually undisclosed, and entirely unconsidered by the agency in making its decision.

So what do you do? If you can afford to, you hire somebody like me to help you frame your argument, get yourself a lawyer, and sue the bastards. And if you're lucky, you may force them to back up and do more analysis—perhaps even an analysis that's relevant to the impacts you're concerned about.

Return to the African Burial Ground

The African Burial Ground, in New York City—discussed in Chapter 1 to show how the unrecognized complexity of the cultural resource universe can cause an agency great trouble—is also an example of NEPA gone bad. The NEPA analysis was an EA, leading to a FONSI, despite the fact that the EA revealed the mapped location of a "Negro burial ground" on the site. It was assumed, first, that NEPA analysis was a sort of meaningless hoop through which the project's proponents merely had to jump. Second, it was assumed that the project would have no significant effects—after all, this was downtown Manhattan. So it was assumed that if anything remained of the burial ground, it would be something the contract archeologists could take care of, reducing the impact of the project below significance. So, there was no EIS, and hence no formal scoping, no organized context in which the concerns of the African-American community might have surfaced. The project went forward, and of course *did* have significant impacts, for which the General Services Administration (GSA) paid dearly.

The African Burial Ground also illustrates the need for interdisciplinary coordination in NEPA analyses. The archeologists reasonably enough assumed that most of the burial ground would have been destroyed by the basements of the buildings that had been built on the site during the 19th century. Better coordination with geomorphologists involved in site characterization might have revealed that the burials had taken place in a low swale between sand dunes, and that the 19th-century basements had gone mostly into the fill that had later been dumped into this low spot to level it—thus preserving the burial ground under the basements but right in the path of GSA's construction.

Conclusion

It's in the context of NEPA that cultural resources as a whole have the best chance of being considered early enough in planning a project that changes can be made to protect them. But there are plenty of things to keep a NEPA analysis from being successful from a cultural point of view. The project may be misassigned to a CATEX category. It may be the subject of an ill-planned EA that's done without adequate input from people outside the agency, or even from internal agency experts. Scoping may be so poorly done that significant issues aren't identified, or aren't identified until too late. Or the issues may be identified, and fully discussed, but ignored in decision-making. All these things *can* happen, but they don't need to. If you're working inside the agency, or as a consultant to the agency, it should be your business to keep them from happening. If you're an affected citizen, you need to know enough about the NEPA process—and I hope you've just learned it—to stand up and fight to make sure the resources you're concerned about get properly considered.

Always remember, though, that in the final analysis there's nothing in NEPA that says an agency can't nuke the environment. The agency has to *consider* the environmental impacts of its project, but it doesn't have to refrain from having them. It's got to have a reasonable rationale for deciding to do something damaging, however, and it ought to consider reasonable mitigation measures. If it doesn't adopt such measures, and it's doing an EIS, then it needs to document in the ROD *why* it hasn't adopted them. If it's doing an EA and fails to ratchet its impacts down to a level of insignificance, then of course it's not supposed to do a FONSI; a significant impact will occur, and it's going to need to go through the extra time and expense of doing an EA.

Here's a word to the wise. I can't document it, but I'll bet it's true that agencies often negotiate mitigation measures for cultural resources—for example under Section 106 of the National Historic Preservation Act with regard to historic properties—that nobody outside the agency really thinks are adequate, but that people buy into because the agency refuses to do anything better, and then the agency issues a FONSI and proceeds. If you're a project opponent, or a regulator like a SHPO, you may have a bargaining chip in being able to say: "OK, we'll agree to this mitigation measure because you're such S.O.B's that you won't accept anything else, but we do *not* think it reduces your impacts below significance, and we'll object if you issue a FONSI based on adoption of this kind of mitigation." Agencies don't like to do EISs; they take time and money and are exposed to a lot of scrutiny. If you can threaten the validity of the agency's FONSI, you may find the agency getting a whole lot more reasonable.

Chapter 5

Impacts on Historic Properties: Section 106 of the National Historic Preservation Act (NHPA)

What It Is and How It Works

If NEPA is the broadest of the cultural resource authorities, Section 106 of NHPA is one of the most specific, at least as it has been interpreted by its rulemaker, the Advisory Council on Historic Preservation (ACHP).

The Basic Requirements

Section 106 (Figure 4) is deceptively simple. It says that federal agencies must do two things:

"Take into account" the effects of their actions on historic properties; and

"Afford the Advisory Council...a reasonable opportunity to comment" on their actions.

> *The head of any Federal agency having direct or indirect jurisdiction over a proposed Federal or federally assisted undertaking in any State and the head of any Federal department of independent agency having authority to license any undertaking shall, prior to the approval of the expenditure of any Federal funds on the undertaking or prior to the issuance of any license, as the case may be, take into account the effect of the undertaking on any district, site, building, structure or object that is included in or eligible for inclusion in the National Register. The head of any such Federal agency shall afford the Advisory Council on Historic Preservation...a reasonable opportunity to comment with regard to such undertaking. (16 U.S.C. 470f)*

Figure 4. Section 106 of NHPA

The Section 106 Process in Historical Perspective

When NHPA was enacted, one of its major authors, the late Robert R. Garvey, Jr., became the first Executive Secretary (later Executive Director) of the fledgling ACHP, and was promptly faced with the need to decide what Section 106 meant. How were agencies supposed to "take effects into account?" And what did it mean to give the Council a "reasonable" opportunity to comment?

At the time, another obvious question was easily answered. The only thing agencies had to give the Council an opportunity to comment *on*, or to take into account, were effects on places already included in the National Register. Since the Register was about as new as the Council, there weren't a great many places on it, so Section 106 business was pretty slow for awhile. However, a National Register was assembled pretty promptly by NPS using its existing list of National Historic Landmarks (NHLs) and its inventory of properties documented by the Historic American Buildings Survey (HABS). Agencies began finding that they *did* have Section 106 to deal with from time to time. But what did this mean?

Based on what seemed to work in the first few cases the ACHP took part in, Garvey and his colleagues, then embedded in NPS, decided that what "taking into account" meant was figuring out what effects one's action was likely to have, and considering what might be done to reduce, or mitigate, any effects that were adverse. Moreover, since agencies at the time almost universally didn't know a thing about historic preservation, this consideration of effects and mitigation ought to be done in consultation with people who *did* know something about it—that is, the ACHP's small Park Service staff, and the newly created State Liaison Officers (later State Historic Preservation Officers or SHPOs). Finally, because the rationale for even having a Section 106 was that preservation was construed to be in the public interest, the consultation process should be a public one.

The rest is history. The ACHP first put out non-binding procedures for Section 106 review, which were promptly the basis for litigation that gave them additional authority. Executive Order 11593 added clarity to the ACHP's role, and brought eligible but unlisted historic properties under the Section 106 umbrella. President Jimmy Carter gave the ACHP rulemaking authority, through the backdoor mechanism of a Presidential Memorandum on water resource management, of all things. Congress eventually made this authority, and the inclusion of eligible properties, official. It also separated the ACHP from NPS, giving it independent status. The Section 106 procedures were issued as formal regulations in 1979. They're codified at 36 CFR 800—that is, Title 36, Part 800 of the Code of Federal Regulations.

36 CFR 800 Today

36 CFR 800 was significantly revised in 1986—after a firefight in the Reagan administration that I hope someday to write about, when a few more of the

participants are dead or retired. The 1986 version has guided Section 106 process for a bit over ten years as I write, but today the regulation is being changed again—not for the better, in my opinion, but more on that later. This places your author in something of a quandary. Do I explain the now-existing 1986 regulation, with the expectation that it will be irrelevant by the time this book is published, or do I try to explain the revised regulation, understanding the possibility that it will not be issued, or will be substantially changed, by the time this book is in your hands?

Happily for me as author, though it disappoints me as a practitioner, the revised regulation doesn't change the core Section 106 review process much. In the name of simplification it complicates the process; in the name of clarity it obscures it; in the name of enhanced public participation it limits public participation, and in the name of reduced paperwork it's longer than the existing regulation, but it isn't really all that different in *structure*. So we're probably safe in addressing the basic steps in the Section 106 process, using the revised regulation where we need to deal with specifics, but I'll try to avoid getting wrapped up in regulatory language. There will be plenty of opportunity for hair-splitting once the revised regulation is in effect.

Strategies and Terminology

"Step-by-Step" Approach

I mentioned that we'd look at the steps in the process. One of the unfortunate things about Section 106 is that people look at it as prescribing a rigid, step-by-step process. The ACHP actually encourages this kind of thinking, through the structure of its publications and training. I have come to think that this has very unfortunate consequences, but it does make things clearer, easier to understand—if unduly inflexible. As we go along, I'll try to point out places where the process can usefully be flexed, but there is a sort of logic to a stepwise approach, so we'll use a step-by-step explanation to structure this chapter.

I'll illustrate each step with a real-world (if somewhat dated) example of a case—the "G-O Road" in Northern California, and with other cases where they help clarify the process and its pitfalls.

Terminology

Wherever I refer to "the regulation" I mean either the 1986 regulation or the version that presumably will be issued in 1998—either because both say approximately the same thing or because the context makes it clear which version I'm referring to. When I need to be specific, I'll refer either to "the 1986 regulation" or "the revised regulation."

The revised regulation routinely refers to the "SHPO/THPO," recognizing that the State Historic Preservation Officer and the Tribal Historic Preservation

Officer fulfill the same roles within their respective jurisdictions. Because in the vast majority of cases agencies deal with SHPOs, not THPOs, I'll refer routinely only to SHPOs. I don't mean thus to denigrate the roles of THPOs; I just think the reader is smart enough to understand that when I refer to the SHPO I mean to include the THPO where one exists.

The revised regulation also regularly provides for various forms of consultation with the SHPO/THPO and any Indian tribe whose lands are affected by the action under review. Where it's too cumbersome to include this full recitation of parties, I'll refer to them all as "the usual core parties."

Undertaking: The CATEX Filter of Section 106

Just as NEPA filters out projects that have little potential for significant effect through the mechanism of the CATEX, the Section 106 process filters out such projects through its definition of the term "undertaking."

Under NHPA itself (Section 301[7]), an "undertaking" is any:

> ...*project, activity, or program funded in whole or in part under the direct or indirect jurisdiction of a Federal agency, including*—
> (A) *those carried out by or on behalf of the agency;*
> (B) *those carried out with Federal financial assistance;*
> (C) *those requiring a Federal permit, license, or approval; and*
> (D) *those subject to State or local regulation administered pursuant to a delegation or approval by a Federal agency.* (16 U.S.C. 470w[7])

So the first key question, in terms of the statute, is: "is there some kind of federal involvement in the action?" Or, as it's often put, "is there a federal handle?"

This is an important point that people sometimes miss. *Section 106 (like NEPA) applies only to actions with federal involvement!* If the Mount Vernon Ladies' Association, which owns George Washington's old home, wants to cover its facades with vinyl siding and add a twenty-story tower complete with battlements, it is perfectly free to do so as far as federal law is concerned, provided it doesn't use federal funds or require a permit from a federal agency or a state or local agency operating under federal delegation or oversight. And no, the fact that Mount Vernon is a real important historic place does *not* mean that the Ladies' Association needs a permit to muck about with it. Why not? Because Congress hasn't made it so.

However, Congress *has* dictated that permits are required before one can discharge fill into a wetland—Section 404 of the Clean Water Act requires that. Approval is required from the Federal Deposit Insurance Corporation before a bank can install an automatic teller machine. Permits are required from state coastal zone management authorities before a variety of things (sometimes, depending on the state, including single-family house construction) can be done in the vicinity of a coast, and issuance of this permit occurs (if it occurs) under a federal program overseen by the National Oceanic and Atmospheric Administration. All these actions have federal handles, so they *are* subject to Section 106 review.

In other words, the arm of the federal government can be pretty long, and hence the statutory definition of "undertaking" can embrace a host of actions carried out by, for, with the assistance of, or under the direct or indirect regulatory authority of a federal agency.

But just as in the case of NEPA, if Section 106 review had to be done on every conceivable action the federal government is involved in, either the wheels of government would grind mighty slow, or we would have to develop a *very* attenuated Section 106 process. So just as CEQ invented categorical exclusions (CATEXs) to avoid review of things that couldn't possibly be major federal actions significantly affecting the quality of the human environment (MFASAQHEs), in the Section 106 regulations, the ACHP included a way to filter out actions that don't need to be reviewed. It's important to note, however, that many actions that are not MFASAQHEs under NEPA require review under Section 106. The fact that something is a NEPA CATEX does not mean it doesn't require Section 106 review. Conversely, however, in some agency NEPA regulations, if an action requires review under Section 106 it can't be a CATEX.

The Section 106 regulation provides that to be reviewable, an action must be the kind of thing that has the potential to affect historic properties. Thus firing your mail room attendant is not an undertaking that requires Section 106 review; nor is purchasing office supplies. If you build a new mail room, however, or convert the old one, or if you build a road to carry the office supplies from one place to another, that *is* an undertaking that requires review, because it has the potential to change buildings or land, hence affecting any historic properties that may be standing or lying around in the neighborhood.

Note that an action is an undertaking if it's the *kind of thing* that can affect historic properties—if it *has the potential* to affect them. Knowing that something has the potential to affect something doesn't mean that you have to know that something is there to be affected. Checking to see if something is indeed there is what you do *after*, and *because*, you recognize the potential for effect.

If I have a live hand grenade and want to pull the pin and toss it out the window, I know I run the risk of doing injury to someone walking by. I don't need to know that somebody's out there to know that this *potential* exists. Knowing that the possibility of hurting someone exists—and assuming I don't want to hurt whoever happens to be out there—I need to take a look before I throw, or leave the pin in the grenade. In the same way, I know that knocking down a building, or digging up the ground, or painting a facade, or changing traffic patterns through a neighborhood, has the *potential* to affect historic properties. Recognizing this, I need to check to find out if anything really is out there to be affected, and that's the next step in the Section 106 process.

The G-O Road as Undertaking

In the mid-1970s, the Forest Service proposed to construct a logging haul road across the Six Rivers National Forest in northern California, from the town of Gasquet to the town of Orleans (hence, called the G-O Road). The purpose was to open up virgin timber reserves on the interior, eastern side of the north coast ranges and make them accessible to financially strapped sawmills on the coast. No historic properties of any kind were known to exist in the vicinity of the proposed right-of-way.

Discussion Question: Was construction of the G-O Road an undertaking subject to Section 106 review?

The Hairy APE

Before I start actually finding out what an undertaking may affect, I need to decide where I'm going to look. This is called is defining the "area of potential effects," or APE.

Going back to our grenade analogy—one thing I need to know, in order to be sure I won't blow anybody up, is the blast radius of the grenade. It's within that radius that I need to make sure there's no one strolling around. I'll have to take several things into account in determining the radius. How powerful is the grenade? Will the wall containing the window through which I'll toss the thing deflect the blast away from itself? Are there other walls, rocks, cliffs, groves of trees, or whatever, that will shape the blast's effects? Are there secondary sources of explosive power? Cars with gas in their tanks, an ammunition dump, a fireworks stand? What kind of grenade is it? Will it spew shrapnel? Is it highly incendiary? Will it discharge tear gas or mustard gas or botulism? Will it blind people?

In the same way, I need to figure out the size and shape of the area within which my proposed undertaking may affect historic properties. This is the APE, which the regulations define as the geographic area or areas within which the action may affect historic properties, if any such properties are there.

One of the most common mistakes agencies make is to equate the APE with the actual "footprint" of the undertaking—for example, the construction site. This is like considering the APE of a grenade to be only the location where it may bonk somebody on the head.

As with my grenade's blast radius, a lot of things can affect the size and shape of the APE. Obviously the place where the undertaking will have direct physical effects (if there is such a place) is part of the APE, but it's *only* part—analogous to the precise location where the grenade lands. Just as the grenade's effects may be felt in different locations and different ways depending on the character of the area, the grenade itself, the wind direction, atmospheric conditions, and so forth, so the effects of an undertaking are shaped by the character of the undertaking, the local environment, and other factors. Typically, in defining the APE you'll need to consider not only direct physical effects but at least the potential for:

- Visual effects (Consider the areas within which the undertaking's effects will be visible);

- Auditory effects (Consider the areas within which the undertaking's noise, if any, will be audible);

- Sociocultural effects (Consider the areas within which the undertaking may cause changes in economic activity, land use, tax rates, traffic, quality of life);

- Effects on culturally significant natural resources such as plants or animals used in subsistence or for religious purposes; and

- Indirect or secondary effects like induced erosion or public use.

Defining the APE based on multiple variables will usually result in several differently bounded areas—an APE for physical effects, an APE for visual effects, and so on. This is all right. In fact, a troup of APEs is perfectly expectable. In some cases it may not be possible even to define APE boundaries. This is all right, too, as long as you're explicit about it. In the case of Crandon Mine, a surface copper-zinc mine in Wisconsin urgently opposed by the Mole Lake Band of Sokaogon Chippewa on cultural grounds (among others), the Corps of Engineers (which had Section 106 responsibilities because it had regulatory authority under Section 404 of the Clean Water Act) decided that the APE for archeology was the mine site and its appurtenant access roads, power lines, and the like, but that the APE for "traditional cultural properties"—in this case, places of cultural importance to the Chippewa—had no boundaries at all. As a Corps representative quipped, if someone wanted to complain about impacts on a traditional cultural property in Los Angeles, this would be perfectly OK, because the Corps wouldn't have to waste much time on considering such an implausible impact.

The Bureau of Indian Affairs (BIA) and Rural Electrification Administration (REA) got themselves in trouble in New Mexico by defining the footprint of a proposed power substation as its APE. The substation, designed to supply power to San Ildefonso Pueblo, was next door to a graded parking lot used by the adjacent hispanic community of El Rancho. BIA and REA had the project site surveyed for archeological sites (without talking with the El Ranchitos), and, having found nothing, proceeded with construction. The El Ranchitos then took BIA and REA to court for violating Section 106. The parking lot, it developed, was where the hispanic community carried out its "Matachines Dance," a culturally important tradition that made the place eligible for the National Register of Historic Places. The power station, it was argued, would be so intrusive that it would make it hard to continue the dance, thus adversely affecting the integrity of the site. At this writing, the case is still in court and the station is idle pending an outcome. Had BIA and REA considered visual and auditory impacts in defining the project's APE, and talked to the community about the potential for such effects, they probably would have sited the station elsewhere and the whole problem would have been avoided.

The G-O Road's APE

The Forest Service recognized that the G-O Road was an undertaking. It was obviously under the direct jurisdiction of a federal agency, and it was the kind of action that had the potential to affect historic properties. So the Forest Service proceeded with Section 106 review, and needed to define the APE.

Discussion Question: What factors should the Forest Service have considered in establishing the G-O Road's APE?

Finding Historic Places: Some Myths

Once we've defined our APE, we're ready to try to identify historic properties within it—in other words, historic properties that may be subject to effect by the proposed action.

There's a widespread belief that Section 106, or the regulation, require agencies to do some kind of survey to identify historic properties. This is a myth. A related myth is that the regulations require agencies to identify all historic properties in the APE. In order to accomplish this complete identification, it's often assumed that some specified kind of "complete" survey is required—usually referred to cryptically as a "Class One" or "Phase One" survey. This too is myth, all myth.

In fact, the regulation doesn't require any particular kind of identification program. It simply requires that the agency make a "reasonable and good faith effort" to identify historic properties. And that's "historic properties," not "*all* historic properties." The regulation doesn't require identification of all historic properties for two reasons. First, it's an impossibility; you can never be sure you've identified everything. Second, it's unnecessary. The rule of thumb is that you should do enough identification to provide a basis for reasonable decisions about effects and what to do about them. How much and what kind of identification thus requires depends on the nature of the likely effects, the nature of the area, and the nature of the likely historic properties, among other things.

One of the big problems with the "Class One" or "Phase One" myth is that it encourages rote thinking. It's assumed that a "Class One" survey will identify all historic properties. But what does such a survey entail? Standards for such surveys are set forth in various state, regional, and agency guidelines; they vary widely from place to place, but one thing tends to be pretty universal: they emphasize archeological field survey. Survey standards typically go into loving detail about how closely spaced (sic) archeologists should be over the landscape, and at what intervals they should dig holes, in order to find "all the sites." But some historic properties aren't "sites," and some aren't best found or evaluated based on looking at or digging in the ground. Historic buildings, districts, landscapes, and traditional cultural properties require different kinds of survey strategies, ranging from aerial remote sensing to talking with local residents to background historical research to geomorphology. Whenever we assume that a particular "class" of survey will automatically be sufficient—and that it is automatically required—we fail to think through what kinds of identification strategy is really needed. This can lead you to miss truly important stuff, however closely you pack your archeologists and holes.

Bottom line: There's no specific kind of survey you've got to do to satisfy Section 106; the kind of survey you do depends on the character of the project and its likely effects, and on the character of the properties likely to be present—which can only be determined through background research. You don't necessarily have to identify every single historic property subject to effect, but you do need to consider all *kinds* of historic properties, not just those you happen to be trained to identify and appreciate. The basic rule is: make a reasonable and good faith effort.

Finding Historic Places: Some Reality

First Step: Scoping

Since the kind of fieldwork you do is so dependent on what you think might be out there to find, it follows that the first step in identification is to figure out what might be out there. And where it might be, and how one might recognize it. This requires knowledge of various kinds of background data. So the first step in identification is background research to, in the words of the regulations, "scope" the identification (1998 draft regulation) or "assess information needs" (1986 regulation). The regulations ask us—by implication, not in so many words—to posit what might be out there and what it might look like, and then to construct an identification strategy based on what we've posited.

What does scoping entail? As usual, "it depends." In general, you need to find out what's already known about the APE. What surveys have already been done, what historic properties have already been identified? What areas have been studied and found to be devoid of historic properties, or of this, that, or the other *kind* of historic property?

At a somewhat higher level of abstraction, what do we know about the area that suggests anything about the kinds of historic properties that *might* be there, or about where they might be? What does the area's history, traditions, sociology, geography, geomorphology tell us about what may have been left there by people in the past?

And what do people *think* might be there, and why? What can be said by extrapolation from other areas, or based on sociological, anthropological, or other theory?

This is, I know, beginning to add up to look like a lot of research, but again, it depends. For a small area, where it's relatively easy to see what's standing or lying around on the ground, you're not going to have to do much background research. For a bigger, more complex area, more such research will be needed.

In almost no case, though, is it enough just to send an archeologist (or anybody else) out to look around, whether they're just looking aimlessly or looking in a highly organized manner, on five-meter transects digging holes every four meters. There's a famous case in Indiana in which the archeologists surveying a highway borrow source missed the big Hopewell mound into which the borrow pit would be dug, because it was *so* big that it dwarfed the survey area. That's a pretty unusual situation in archeology, but it's easy to have a historic landscape or an urban historic district that stretches far, far beyond the project site, or even beyond the boundaries of the APE. You've got to back up and look at the big picture in order to see it. Some kinds of properties don't look like anything at all—or rather, they just look like hills, or streams, or rock outcrops, or groves of trees, or meadows, or commercial streets. To understand their importance you've got to talk to the people who value them, find out from them what it is they think is important. To know that you may need to talk to people, and to figure out who to talk with, you need to back up and look at what's known and believed about the area. That's what the assessment of information needs is all about. Incidentally, this sort of assessment—or overview, as it's sometimes called—is another piece of work that's sometimes referred to as a "Class One" or "Phase One" survey, to the endless confusion of those who use the same term to mean a basic field inspection.

The "Reasonable and Good Faith Effort" Standard

So, you've scoped your identification effort and discovered, let's say, that:

- The APE includes the Hoitytoit Historic District, a group of high-style classical revival mansions along Hoitytoit Road, a locally designated historic district that's included in the National Register.

- The Motomak Indian Tribe, now resident on a reservation 50 miles away, used to occupy the area.

- Part of the APE is a floodplain covered with sediments deposited in the last 5,000 years.

- Much of the floodplain is farmed by Amish families.

- The Town of Crossroads, near the east end of the APE, has been occupied by African-American families since the end of the Civil War.

- The Crooked Bend Unpleasantness, in which local militiamen massacred the fleeing Motomaks, occurred somewhere along a bend in Messy Creek, which flows through the APE.

- The overworked, understaffed SHPO's office has given you a form letter recommending a "Class II.A cultural resource survey."

- Prof. R.T. Toulle of Giant State University's Geographic Research Center advises that the area may produce information important in the study of climatic change over the last 10,000 years; this information may be present both in archeological sites and in natural floodplain deposits.

So, what do you do now? The regulations require that—based on the assessment of information needs—you make a "reasonable and good faith effort" to identify historic properties. In this case, given the above data, what does this mean?

One of the commonest and least useful responses is to do what the SHPO tells you to do. This is not meant to insult SHPOs; it's just that in this case, as often happens, the SHPO's staff person has been busy with other things, and has given you an off-the-cuff recommendation that isn't very useful.

What does the SHPO mean by a "Class II.A cultural resource survey?" Like a "Class One" or "Phase One" survey (which naturally leads to a Class Two or Phase Two), it's probably a standard kind of fieldwork promoted up by the state's archeological community. It's probably defined in terms of personnel qualifications, spacing on the ground, and test pit intervals. Or it may be product-oriented: "a sufficiently detailed study to serve as the basis for determining eligibility for the National Register." When you ask what this means, you usually wind up being told something about test excavations.

The problem, of course, is that a survey that assumes the need for test excavations to determine eligibility may not identify anything but archeological sites. And a standard-form archeological survey that doesn't consider local conditions may not even identify archeological sites if they're deeply buried in those floodplain sediments. You may spend much time and money traipsing archeologists over the floodplain, digging holes every few meters and never getting down to the level where there are actually archeological sites. And of course, while you're spending your time and money thus, you're probably *not* identifying any of the non-archeological kinds of historic properties that are out there.

So what should you do? Use your background data, and your head.

- The Hoitytoit Historic District is already known, recorded, and listed in the Register, but don't trust the Register data to be comprehensive. It may well be that Hortense Hoitytoit nominated the district back in '72 on the basis of a very narrow range of significance criteria. Perhaps she discussed only the district's association with Harry Hoitytoit, her grandfather, who brought the railroad to the area, so the documentation doesn't tell you that the district is characterized by elegant homes that look eastward over the broad expanse of the adjacent valley, and are subject to visual impacts by, say, a highway that passes up the valley as much as five miles away. It may not tell you about the mature oak trees in the district, that are subject to damage by air pollution. Hortense may have drawn the boundaries of the district more or less arbitrarily, and left properties out that are significant in their own right. There may be buildings outside the district that are identical with those inside, or maybe a little bit younger or less high-style but still significant. There may be a group of commercial buildings a block away, important in the history of the community's economic development. Hortense probably ignored the prehistoric archeological site that lies under 725 Hoitytoit Road. None of this indicates that Hortense was ill-intentioned or stupid; she just nominated what was important to her, and the Register accepted it as such. The point is, the fact that something is included in the Register doesn't mean it's the only eligible thing around, or that its eligibility has been comprehensively considered. You're going to want to take another look at the District with specific reference to the potential impacts of your project, and you're going to need to consider its boundaries and character seriously, too. All this is probably a job for a historian and/or an architectural historian. In addition, you're going to need to look for other kinds of historic properties.

- The fact that the Motomak Tribe previously occupied the area tips you off that there may be places around that are culturally important to the tribe. These may be archeological sites, and/or traditional cultural properties, which may in turn comprise whole landscapes. To find them, you may need to do some kind of archeological survey, but perhaps most important, you need to get out and talk with the Motomak. This may be a job for a cultural anthropologist, sociologist, or folklife specialist, and for an agency line officer if the Motomak are a federally recognized tribe entitled to a government-to-government relationship with the U.S. government. You may need to do some kind of archeological survey—which may or may not fall into the "Class II.A" category.

- Speaking of archeological sites, the fact that the APE includes a floodplain covered with 5,000 year-old sediments suggests a couple of things. First, there may be deeply buried archeological sites in those sediments, that could be quite old and, perhaps, quite significant for research and public interpretation. Second, as mentioned above, it suggests that surveying the surface of the floodplain may be a pretty fruitless endeavor—though this of course depends on how fast the floodplain has built up, and how young the sediments are on the surface.

With deeply buried archeological sites, you also need to think about whether your project can affect them. If the project will disturb only the top meter of the floodplain, and the sites are likely to be twelve meters down, there's probably not much point in disturbing the floodplain sediments to find them; you'll probably do more damage than the project's construction will.

- Since the floodplain is farmed by Amish families, you need to think about whether as a working landscape it's got historical value for its association with the Amish and their traditional lifeways. And you'll need to talk with the Amish, too—again, work for a cultural anthropologist, sociologist, or folklife specialist, or perhaps for a landscape historian.

- Similarly, you're going to need to talk with the people of Crossroads, and look into the community's history, to see whether it constitutes a historically or culturally significant resource or whether there are places in the area that its residents value—the pool in the creek where baptisms are carried out, perhaps, or the fishing bridge. More work for the anthropologist or other cultural specialist.

- Archival research into the Crooked Bend Unpleasantness, perhaps coupled with aerial photography or other forms of remote sensing, may help you identify the massacre site, which may well be eligible for the National Register. Interviewing willing Motomaks is likely to be important, too; there may be traditions about the place and the event that can help pinpoint the location and elucidate its significance.

- Finally, in considering the possible significance of archeological sites in the floodplain, you'll need to keep Professor Toulle's concerns about climatic change in mind. These research interests aren't the only basis for possibly regarding archeological sites (or other sites) as eligible for the National Register, but they're certainly *one* basis, and they shouldn't be ignored.

So, it looks like you need to deploy an army of historians, architectural historians, archeologists, landscape historians, and cultural anthropologists to figure out what's in your project's APE. In some cases this is true, particularly if your project is a big one with lots of far-reaching, complex, potential effects. But in most cases it doesn't have to be true; you need to look at what kinds of impacts your project is actually likely to have, and adjust your identification accordingly. If you're planning a 500 kV power line on giant towers marching through the countryside, you're going to have to worry a lot about visual effects on things like historic buildings, districts, and landscapes, and a lot less about impacts on archeological sites. If you're planning a fiber-optic cable in the ground through the same landscape, archeology's going to be a problem but visual effects probably won't be. The nature of the likely effect determines the kinds of properties that are likely to be affected, and how they're likely to be affected, and hence the kind of work you need to do to identify them and the kinds of specialists you need to do the identifying.

In some cases—particularly where the project is a relatively small one, with a limited range of probable impacts—all the requisite expertise may reside in a single head. Because they've tended to be the ones who've wound up running "Section 106 shops" in the agencies, SHPO offices, and consulting firms, there are quite a few archeologists who have perforce become more or less familiar with the identification and evaluation of things other than archeological sites—buildings, structures, landscapes, traditional cultural places. Some historians, too, have become jacks and jills of all historic preservation trades, and rather more rarely you'll find an architectural historian who's developed multi-disciplinary, multi-resource expertise. People who've come through "historic preservation" or "cultural resource management" (CRM) graduate programs or graduate certificate programs may have developed this kind of expertise, too, but don't count on it; lots of "historic preservation" programs basically train people in applied architectural history and historical architecture, while many CRM programs teach little more than applied archeology.

Hint for students: if you want to be really employable in CRM, get training in more than one preservation-related discipline. It will make you a hot commodity.

One last point. It's during identification—notably during the first step, assessing information needs—that you can most effectively identify not only historic properties but also *people* who may be concerned about the project's effects. The regulation requires you to consult with people who may have knowledge of or concerns about historic properties in the area. You should treat this as an opportunity, not an onerous requirement. Far better to identify concerned people, ascertain their concerns, and begin to consult with them at this early stage, than to wait for them to pop up in court when you're ready to go into construction.

Identification on the G-O Road

The Forest Service never explicitly defined an APE for the G-O Road, but implicitly, it acted as though the construction corridor—the right-of-way itself and a rather ambiguously defined buffer on each side of it—was the APE. It proceeded to identification.

Discussion Question: What should the Forest Service have done to identify historic properties within the APE?

Evaluation

OK, so let's suppose you've completed an identification effort—whatever this may have entailed—and you've found something that *might* be eligible for the National Register, but you don't *know* whether it is. What do you do in order to decide?

First let's think a little about the phrase we've just used: "something that might be eligible for the National Register." In deciding that this thing might be eligible, and this other thing surely is not, we're making some value judgements that we want to be pretty careful about. It's generally good practice to err on the side of caution, and assume something might be eligible unless it clearly, demonstrably isn't. Why? Maybe because you really, really don't want to mess up something that might be important. If you're not that altruistic, there's this: finding that something you thought was insignificant really *is* significant, late in the game, can be really embarrassing, and really costly. Suddenly your agency's or client's project is stopped, the bulldozers are idling and eating up money, the contractor is charging quintuple fees for being forced to sit around twiddling his thumbs, your boss or your sponsor or your congressperson is screaming at you about being obstructionist, and the local citizenry, or the archeological community, or Indian tribe, or the SHPO, or somebody is screaming at your agency or client about violating the nation's cultural patrimony.

But of course, there has to be a rule of reason. The scatter of beer cans along the roadside is not something that qualifies as a "might be eligible." Unless, of course, the road is pretty old, and the people who drank out of the cans were pretty important, and—

Well, where *do* you draw the line?

As usual, it depends. Age is part of the issue. Last night's beer can's don't usually make up a site that might be eligible for the Register, but a scatter of cans from 75 years ago just might. Association is another issue. Your cans or mine don't make an eligible site, but cans left by the first Vulcan expedition to Earth might be another matter. But how do you know whether the cans—or the old foundation, or the nondescript building, are associated with someone or something important?

You don't. You have to guess. When push comes right to shove, we have to exercise more or less unsubstantiated judgement, or we'd never get anything done. We look at the scatter of cans, or the corrugated tin garage, or the fence line with adjacent cow trail, or the concrete foundation slab, or the local gas station, and say "no, it's not worth even thinking about." And having made that statement, feeling pretty comfortable that nobody will argue with us about it, we then ignore the place and don't think about it any more.

Of course, an educated guess is a lot better than an uneducated one. This is one reason local expertise and background research are important. Having knowledge of the local area and its history because I've studied it, I know that this isolated concrete slab may be all that remains of the abortive real estate development that serendipitously led to the discovery of gold in the area, so I know we'd better pay some attention to it. You haven't studied the area, so you don't know that the old slab may be important, and this may get you or your client in trouble.

In an attempt to level the playing field, and objectify the threshold of "might-be significant," people sometimes establish more or less arbitrary criteria for historic property-ness. This tends to be something archeologists do—if there are fifteen flakes of chert per square meter, it's a potentially significant site; if there are only fourteen, it's not. This sort of thing is fraught with problems, of course—problems of variation among observers, variation with season, with vegetation cover, with the number of cows that have walked over the site, and so on, and problems of the relationship between what's on the surface and what's present at depth—to say nothing of the fact that it is, at base, an arbitrary measure whose relationship to the actual significance of a place is tenuous at best.

I belabor all this because some people get preoccupied with it, and it can be a source of great, and sometimes expensive, frustration. One SHPO of my acquaintance used to be terribly worried about causing people to spend money unnecessarily taking care of insignificant archeological sites. To avoid this fearsome result, he insisted that the significance of any site be proved through intensive subsurface testing. Testing, of course, costs money and takes time, so project proponents sometimes found themselves spending far more of both than they probably would have if they'd just accepted sites as significant and gotten on with managing them.

Bottom line: there aren't any simple answers. We make judgement calls about what might and what might not be significant, and sometimes we're wrong—just as we're sometimes wrong about the decisions we make about marriage, child rearing, and which way to turn on an unfamiliar road. That's life.

So we come out of an effort to identify historic properties in an APE with a list of places that *might* be eligible for the National Register, as well as, perhaps, a probably shorter list of places that we know are eligible, perhaps because they've already been nominated and accepted for placement. How do we decide whether something that hasn't been formally evaluated is eligible?

Naturally, we apply the "Criteria of Eligibility," which are found in NPS's National Register regulations at 36 CFR 60.4 (Figure 5).

The quality of significance in American history, architecture, archeology, engineering, and culture is present in districts, sites, buildings, structures and objects that possess integrity of location, design, setting, materials, workmanship, feeling, and association.

(a) That are associated with events that have made a significant contribution to the broad patterns of our history; or
(b) That are associated with the lives of persons significant in our past; or
(c) That embody the distinctive characteristics of a type, period, or method of construction, or that represent the work of a master, or that possess high artistic values, or that represent a significant and distinguishable entity whose components may lack individual distinction; or
(d) That have yielded, or may be likely to yield, information important in prehistory or history. (36 CFR 60.4)

Figure 5. The National Register Criteria for Evaluation.

The National Register Criteria

There are four National Register Criteria, labelled "A" through "D." Lee Keatinge, architect and attorney at the ACHP, has coined a simple way to keep track of them. "A" is for "association," "B" for "big people," "C" for "cute buildings," and "D," of course, boringly, for "data." Or perhaps "dig." National Register Bulletin 15 (National Register 1991) provides details about their application, as do other bulletins with respect to particular property types and situations.

A is for "Association"

Here we ask ourselves: is the property associated with some important event, or set of events, or pattern of events, that's important in our past? Note that "our" can refer to us local folks, us members of a community, us members of an Indian tribe, us residents of a state or region, us Americans, or us residents of the world. Historic properties are to be judged in whatever spatial and social contexts are relevant to them.

A property can be eligible under Criterion A if it's associated with a specific event, such as a battle, an invention, the first occurrence of this or the last occurrence of that. Or it can be associated with a pattern of events—westward movement, the development of complex political organization in the prehistoric midwest, the growth of the poultry industry in Sonoma County. The events can be traditional events in, say, the oral history of an Indian tribe—Earth Maker's battles with the monsters; the emergence of the ancestors from the lower world.

B is for "Big People"

Again, the people here can be "big" in a variety of contexts. George Washington is a Big Person, but so is Marin de Likatuit, the Coast Miwok chief who launched a revolt against the Spanish in northern California in the early 19th century. So is Montgomery Blair, whose plantation became Silver Spring, Maryland. The "person" also doesn't have to be a demonstrable member of the human race. Tahquitz Canyon in southern California is included in the Register in part for its association with the spirit Tahquitz, who in the traditions of the Cahuilla tribe emerges from the canyon in the form of a blue comet, to devour people's souls.

C is for "Cute Buildings"

Criterion C could also be called "catch-all," though, to be nice some people, just call it the "characteristics" criterion. A property that displays the characteristics of a class, a style, a school of architecture, a period of construction—all these can be eligible under Criterion C. Generally speaking, this is the architectural historian's favorite criterion—a dog-trot house, a Classical Revival courthouse, a parkway designed by the Olmsted Brothers; all these can be eligible simply for being what they are. So can an example of engineering like, say, a rocket launch tower or a nuclear reactor, a sewer system or an automobile assembly line. Or a piece of artwork like a WPA mural or a prehistoric rock art panel.

A place can display characteristics if it's typical of its class—a good example of a shotgun house. On the other hand, it can be eligible if it's the best or only example—the last tobacco barn in Emphysema County—or if it's an *atypical* example, like the biggest or smallest tobacco barn.

Finally, there's that marvelous last clause: a property can be eligible if it represents "distinctive entity, the individual components of which may lack distinction." Say what? This is what "districts" are all about, and it reflects the notion that the whole can be greater than the sum of the parts. A historic mining area may have shafts, adits, chunks of rail line, spoil heaps, collapsed buildings, garbage piles—any one of which, by itself, might be of little or no historical value, but when you put them all together, the whole complex is pretty neat. Such a "distinctive entity" can be eligible as a district, even though its individual components "lack distinction."

D is for "Data"

The archeologists' fave, Criterion D, makes a place eligible if it contains—or may contain—information significant in history or prehistory. Some archeologists think D is the *only* National Register Criterion, and argue that a place can't be eligible *unless* it contains significant data. This, of course, is not true; there are three other, quite independent, criteria, and a property need meet only one of them to be eligible.

Arguably, though, to be eligible under Criterion D a place must also be eligible under Criterion A. How can a place have important information about the past if it's not associated with some sort of important pattern of events? A rhetorical question; it really doesn't matter.

Note that it's not necessary to know for sure that a place contains significant data; it's enough to think it probable. This is helpful because it means you don't have to dig the bejeebers out of an archeological site to determine whether it's important, and hence eligible. You can give it the benefit of the doubt, based on informed judgement.

Archeological sites of all ages and types can be eligible under Criterion D, and so can any other kind of property. A building that can be studied to learn about 18th-century carpentry, a landscape that can be studied to learn about Shaker agricultural practices, a highway that can tell us about early twentieth century engineering—all these can be eligible under Criterion D, as well as, probably, other criteria.

Integrity

There's another thing a place must exhibit in order to be eligible for the National Register: "integrity." The regulations refer to "integrity of location, design, setting, materials, workmanship, feeling, and association." One can go into loving detail about what this means (cf. National Register 1991:44-48), but the bottom line is that the place can't be so screwed up that it no longer has whatever made it significant in the first place. The National Register's first Keeper, Dr. William Murtagh, used to use the example of the location in St. Louis, Missouri where the various immigrant trails to the west began. Clearly a tremendously important historic site, but now it's downtown St. Louis, and there's simply nothing left there to convey its association, or the feeling of the place's history.

Of course, things like feelings can be pretty tricky to define. Who does one have to impress in order to demonstrate integrity? Can we guess what the answer is, class?

Logically, this time it ought to depend on two major factors:

1. What's it significant for? If you think the place is important for its potential contribution to historical or prehistorical research, then it has integrity if the information in it is intact enough to be studied; it doesn't matter a bit what sort of "feeling" it has, or what it looks like. If you think it's important because of the feelings of inspiration, enlarged vision, or historical perspective it can engender, then integrity of feeling—generally requiring a visually intact property and environment—is necessary. Of course, this answer begs another question: what do we mean by visually intact? The Gettysburg Battlefield can inspire, enlarge one's vision, give one historical perspective, and it's not "intact" in having gunsmoke in the air and gore underfoot. Yet if it were covered with tract housing, surely it would not

inspire. But it's OK, apparently, that it's covered with monuments. Where do we draw the line? There's no obvious answer, but a partial answer may be found in the other factor on which integrity depends.

2. Who thinks it's significant? If the people of Bayonne, New Jersey regard a place in Bayonne as significant to them, then surely it should be up to them to decide how much and what kind of integrity it needs to have. National Register Bulletin 38 is most explicit about this with regard to "traditional cultural properties," (TCPs) when it says that:

(T)he integrity of a traditional cultural property must be considered with reference to the views of traditional practitioners; if its integrity has not been lost in their eyes, it probably has sufficient integrity to justify further evaluation. (National Register 1990:10)

But the same principle surely applies to all kinds of historic properties. Archeologists think that sites with interesting data in them are significant, and are the best judges of how messed up those data can be before a site loses integrity. Architectural historians like buildings that are good examples of particular styles, or that represent deviations from standard forms, and are the best judges of how much change a building can handle and still retain its significant elements. The people of Bayonne value the places that represent—to them—the character of their community, and are the best judges of whether they retain their integrity.

We sometimes get confused about this basic principle, particularly when "we" are employees of the National Register, or SHPO staff who deal routinely with registration. We begin to think that *we* ought to be the arbiters of integrity, treating the National Register as though it were designed for *us* rather than for the American people.

Consider, for example, the case of Mount Shasta, an extinct volcano in northern California, and a place of great spiritual significance to several Indian tribes (among other people). To make a very long and complex story short, the Forest Service, which administers most of the mountain, determined that its upper slopes were eligible for the Register in connection with Section 106 review of a proposed ski facility. The tribes claimed that the whole mountain was significant, and hence eligible for the Register. The matter was referred to the Keeper of the National Register (hereinafter, "Keeper"), who, after much deliberation, agreed with the tribes. Local property owners were outraged, because California law provides special protections for Register-eligible properties, which they felt would impinge upon their property rights. They and their representative in Congress put political pressure on the Keeper, who felt it and became inclined to undo his decision. But how to do it? Integrity showed the way. The Keeper toured the mountain (without talking with the tribes) and observed, to his consternation, that the lower slopes had long ago been transformed from forest primeval to timber plantations. Obviously, the Keeper then opined, the lower slopes had lost integrity and the Forest Service had been right all along. The Keeper revised the eligible property's boundary accordingly.

The problem here, of course, is that it wasn't the Keeper to whom the mountain was significant; it was the tribes. Hence it should have been for the tribes to decide what did and did not compromise its integrity. Had the Keeper done his job honestly, he would have talked to the tribes, asked them whether the long-ago conversion of the woodland from natural to managed forest made it lose integrity in their eyes, documented the results and opined accordingly. By substituting his own taste in forests for theirs, the Keeper acted as though the Register were his own plaything, rather than a tool to be used in the service of people who value their heritage.

So integrity is very much in the eye of the beholder, and it is possible to get into some pretty esoteric arguments about whether a place has it or doesn't. The best advice I can offer is, go with the opinions of those who value the place. If their opinions seem strange to you, it's perfectly appropriate to get them to explain them, but I do not believe that it is your business or mine to impose our values on places of importance to other people.

One last word about integrity. In discussions of the subject, much is often made of whether the property retains the ability to "convey" its significance. This notion that the property must somehow speak to the viewer arises largely from the origins of the National Register in the traditions of architectural history—where the appearance of a building is key and in the National Park Service, where interpretation for the public is a central concern. Surely the property must convey something to someone, but you want to be careful not to slide into thinking of integrity entirely in terms of what the property might convey to a visitor seeking enlightenment about the property's life and times. An archeological site may convey its significance only to an archeologist armed with appropriate tools; a Native American spiritual place may convey its significance only to someone initiated in the traditions of the tribe that values it. Again, we need to consider integrity through the eyes of those who value the property. If those people are interested in public interpretation, fine, but it's not only the public in general to whom historic properties may convey something.

This brings us to a simple rule of thumb that the National Register sometimes uses in considering integrity; it asks: "would a person from the property's period of significance recognize it?" If the answer is "yes," it has integrity; if "no," it doesn't.

Like most simple rules, this one has to allow for a lot of exceptions. A resurrected Clovis mastodon hunter probably wouldn't today recognize the place where he or she sat down 12,000 years ago to flute a spear point, but that place may well retain its integrity as an archeological site. Even where feeling and association are key variables, recognition by a person associated with the place may not be the major thing to consider. A place that has been radically transformed may—even as a result of its transformation—convey something important about the past to a viewer. A resurrected Samurai incinerated at Ground Zero in Hiroshima or Nagasaki would be unlikely to recognize the place today, but the very transformation of the cities, both by atomic bombs at the end of World War II and by post-war recovery, conveys history-based feelings to any visitor with an iota of sensitivity.

The "recognizability to those associated" rule of thumb is ONE rule to apply, but you always need to remember that history, and culture, are dynamic, and the significance of a property may lie less in how well it represents the character of its times than in the role it plays in today's culture.

The Criteria Considerations

It's not enough for a place to meet one of the National Register Criteria and have integrity. It also must *not* reflect one of a series of "criteria considerations" shown in Figure 6—except that often a property *can* exhibit such a "consideration" and still be eligible.

Ordinarily cemeteries, birthplaces, or graves of historical figures, properties owned by religious institutions or used for religious purposes, structures that have been moved from their original locations, reconstructed historic buildings, properties commemorative in nature, and properties that have achieved significance within the past 50 years shall not be considered eligible for the National Register. However, such properties will qualify if they are integral parts of districts that do meet the criteria or if they fall within the following categories:

a. a religious property deriving primary significance from architectural or artistic distinction or historical importance; or
b. a building or structure removed from its original location but which is significant primarily for architectural value, or which is the surviving structure most importantly associated with a historic person or event; or
c. a birthplace or grave of a historical figure of outstanding importance if there is no other appropriate site or building directly associated with his productive life; or
d. a cemetery that derives its primary significance from graves of persons of transcendent importance, from age, from distinctive design features, or from association with historic events; or
e. a reconstructed building when accurately executed in a suitable environment and presented in a dignified manner as part of a restoration master plan, and when no other building or structure with the same association has survived; or
f. a property primarily commemorative in intent if design, age, tradition, or symbolic value has invested it with its own historical significance; or
g. a property achieving significance within the past 50 years if it is of exceptional significance. (36 CFR 60.4)

Figure 6. The National Register Criteria Considerations.

Say what? It's probably clearest to explain the Considerations one at a time,[1] and discuss why a place that reflects each one normally isn't eligible but sometimes is.

CEMETERIES

The Criteria Considerations say that cemeteries are not ordinarily eligible, but that one *can* be eligible if it derives its "primary significance" from graves of people who were of "transcendent importance," or from age, or from distinctive design features, or from association with historic events.

With all those exceptions, it's not too hard to find that a cemetery is eligible. Ancient or just older cemeteries are determined eligible all the time because of their age, and their association with historic events like, say, the development of mortuary ritual in a prehistoric society. Somebody who looks pretty commonplace from one person's perspective may be of transcendent importance from another's. And so on. If you want a cemetery to be regarded as eligible, you have to be pretty slow to be unable to find a way to make it so.

BIRTHPLACES AND GRAVES

Birthplaces are a little more clear-cut. If all that ever happened someplace is that someone important got born there, the property is not therefore eligible for the Register. Yes, Christians, it's a good thing the National Register isn't how significance is judged in Israel.

Similarly, if the only thing a person of importance ever did on a particular plot of ground was to get buried there, that plot is not eligible for its association with the stiff. If this seems slightly at odds with the fact that a cemetery can be eligible if it contains dead bodies of people regarded as transcendently important, it is, but let's not be slaves to consistency.

A birthplace or grave *can* be eligible, though, if it's associated with the productive life of the person who was born or buried there. Martin Luther King's home in Atlanta, Georgia is on the Register not because he was born there but because he lived there as he was beginning his ministry. And if there's no place remaining that reflects the person's productive life, then that person's birthplace or grave can be eligible. Of course, this means that in order to determine a birthplace or grave eligible you have to demonstrate that there's no place around that reflects the person's productive life—a pretty daunting task.

RELIGIOUS PROPERTIES

"Properties owned by religious institutions or used for religious purposes" are not supposed to be eligible, but may be eligible if they derive "primary

---

1 The order of Criteria Considerations given here is the order in which they are initially listed in 36 CFR 60.4. In National Register guidance (e.g., NATIONAL REGISTER Bulletin 15), the Considerations are re-ordered by the way they appear in the EXCEPTIONS to the Considerations, also given in 36 CFR 60.4; thus the "religious property" Consideration becomes "Consideration A," the "moved property" Consideration becomes "B," and so on.

significance from architectural or artistic distinction or historical importance." The bugaboo word here is "primary." "Primary" to whom? In what social or historical or artistic context? At what point in time?

The "religious exception" was included among the Criteria Considerations in order to avoid running afoul of the Establishment Clause of the First Amendment to the U.S. Constitution (Figure 7), which says that "Congress shall make no law…respecting the establishment of religion." The fear was that recognition of a religious property as eligible for the Register *because of its significance in religious doctrine* would be taken as governmental endorsement of the religion, and hence establishment. The "primary significance" exception-to-the-exception was then tacked on to accommodate the fact that religious places may have lots of kinds of non-doctrinal, supra-doctrinal, or extra-doctrinal aspects of significance.

> *Congress shall make no law....*
> *respecting an establishment of religion*
> *or prohibiting the free exercise thereof.*

Figure 7. The Establishment and Free Exercise Clauses, First Amendment to the U.S. Constitution.

It's easy to see that a church can be eligible if it's a fine example of, say, Romanesque architecture. It's also easy enough to see that a synagogue could be eligible if it was the site where proto-fascists tarred and feathered a leader of the local Jewish community before World War II (this happened in my home town). It's not hard to understand that a mosque might be eligible as the community center for Moslem immigrants to a community.

Things get a little trickier when we get to Native American spiritual places, which are given considerable attention in National Register Bulletin 38 as traditional cultural properties. The problem is that those who value such properties, through whose eyes we are supposed to consider their significance, often express their significance in spiritual—i.e., religious—terms. So if we recognize a place as eligible for the National Register because those who value it regard it as spiritually significant, are we not placing the government's imprimatur on those people's religious doctrine? Are we not establishing religion?

Hold that question for a moment and look at the First Amendment's other religious clause—the "Free Exercise" clause. Congress, the First Amendment says, not only will make no law respecting the establishment of religion; it will also make no law "prohibiting the free exercise thereof." Just as an agency cannot constitutionally interpret the law in such a way as to "establish" religion, so it cannot administer the law such that it prohibits someone from the free exercise of her or his religion.

Both the Establishment and Free Exercise Clauses have been the basis for voluminous litigation, and case law provides extensive if sometimes confusing guidance about how both are to be interpreted. Suffice to say that agencies must operate in a sort of "window" between the Clauses, carrying out their affairs in such a way as to avoid prohibiting anyone from carrying out their religions while not going so far as to support—i.e., "establish" the beliefs or practices of a particular religion. Grimm (1997) has provided an excellent summary discussion of all this with reference to the management of Native American spiritual places.

It's pretty obvious that destroying someone's place of worship may prohibit that person from practicing his or her religion—though of course this depends on how integrally associated the practice is with the place. In Native American traditional religions there tends to be a pretty close association between place and practice, so it's a fair general statement that an agency should try not to destroy Native American spiritual places lest it run afoul of the Free Exercise Clause. On the other hand, it's equally obvious that if the government sets a place aside for use only by Native Americans in carrying out religious rituals, and prohibits others from using the place, it may be supporting traditional religion in a way that is probably at variance with the Establishment Clause. Between these extremes there's a host of situations and possibilities to be sorted out, some of which have been addressed by the courts, some of which have not. We'll return to some of these possibilities in Chapter 6.

What does all this have to do with the National Register and the religious properties Criteria Consideration? First, we have to ask: does recognizing a property as eligible for the National Register "establish" religion? The answer, as usual, is "it depends."

Consider the example of the "Sacred Wood" in upstate New York. According to the traditions of the various churches of Jesus Christ of Latter Day Saints (LDS—including but not limited to the "Mormon" Church), it was here that the founder, Joseph Smith, received a vision from God telling him where to find the Book of Mormon, a collection of golden tablets upon whose revelations the religions are based. If we were nominating the Sacred Wood to the National Register and said "The Sacred Wood is significant because it was here that God told Joseph Smith where to find the golden tablets that contained God's revealed word about the Levites, Nephites, and Jesus Christ in the New World," the Register would do very well to look at our nomination askance, because we'd be asking the U.S. Government to validate the doctrine of the LDS churches. If instead we said that "The Sacred Wood is significant because in the traditions of the LDS churches it was here that God told Joseph Smith where to find the tablets containing the Book of Mormon, which led to the creation of the LDS churches, which are of great cultural importance to those who subscribe to their beliefs," the Register could be much more comfortable about accepting our nomination. We would not be asking the government to support anybody's religion; we would simply be asking the government to recognize the importance of a set of beliefs in the cultural life of a community, and the association of that set of beliefs with a place.

Consider, then, the other side of the coin. If we built a highway through the Sacred Wood, would we prohibit the free exercise of LDS religion? Once again, of course, it depends—in this case on how tight the association is between the Sacred Wood and the integrity of LDS religious practice. We don't know whether bulldozing the woods will destroy LDS religion, and we certainly won't find out if we don't consider the significance of the Sacred Wood to LDS practitioners. Viewing the Sacred Wood as eligible for the National Register, and hence ensuring the consideration required by Section 106, is one way of ensuring that its significance will be considered.

And if we *don't* consider the Sacred Wood eligible for the Register, are we not potentially running afoul of another amendment to the Constitution—the Fourteenth? Are we not discriminating against LDS practitioners on the basis of their religion, saying that because they happen to ascribe religious importance to the Wood, it cannot be considered in agency decision-making, while the old building down the road can and will be considered? This particularly becomes an issue where Native American spiritual places are concerned, because Indian tribes and other indigenous groups tend not to make clear separations between the secular and the sacred. If we decline to consider impacts on properties simply because an Indian tribe talks about them in terms of spirits and supernatural power, we may be discriminating against consideration of the tribe's cultural values, on the basis of the tribe's ethnicity and religion.

The bottom line is that religious places can be, and routinely are, determined eligible for the National Register, but in doing so—and in managing impacts on them—one has to be careful not to appear in any way to be giving the government's blessing to the values ascribed to a property in the religious doctrine of the group that values it. We regard a spiritual place as eligible because of the important roles that beliefs about it have in the cultural life of a community, *not* because the government endorses those beliefs.

MOVED PROPERTIES

If a property has been moved from its original significant location, it is generally taken not to be eligible for the Register. The Register does not want to encourage the creation of architectural petting zoos, in which historic buildings are relocated into what amount to outdoor museum settings. Historic properties are supposed to remain in their cultural and environmental contexts.

Of course, a property that is inherently mobile—an airplane, or a ship—can be moved with impunity and retain its eligibility. You have to be careful about the context in which it's moved, though. A railroad car that's moved along a rail line is one thing; one that's moved to the middle of a shopping mall is something else again. Though, even this depends on, say, the character of the mall; if it's the Railyard Mall, built around and incorporating an old roundhouse, moving the car there might be just fine.

A moved property can also become significant on its new site. Fort John Wayne is dismantled and reconstructed fifty miles away as Fort Clint Eastwood, where it gains significance in the Madison County Bridge Wars.

Districts that contain some moved buildings, or buildings that include a moved-in wing or two, don't automatically become ineligible, nor does a building that's moved up or down on its foundation—but as always, it depends. It's a matter of degree; if your proposed district contains one old building in place and sixteen that are moved in, it's not going to be eligible as a district (the single *in situ* building may be eligible), but if it's sixteen buildings in place and one moved in, it probably will be eligible. If you raise the building six inches on its foundation it's probably no problem; if you raise it twenty feet it's probably another matter.

RECONSTRUCTED BUILDING

If you reconstruct a vanished building, it will probably not be eligible for the Register, because it lacks integrity—it's not the real McCoy. This doesn't mean that you can't remodel a *real* historic building and have it retain its eligibility, though of course if you remodel it too much, or with too little sensitivity to its original character, it *will* lose integrity and will become ineligible. How much remodeling is too much? Check the *Secretary of the Interior's Standards and Guidelines for the Treatment of Historic Properties* (NPS 1992; see Chapter 6) and related NPS publications for guidance.

The "Reconstruction" Criteria Consideration is meant to keep what amount to speculative reconstructions off the Register. You've got the foundations of Fort Clint Eastwood, and you make up what the walls and innards of the place looked like based on your impressions from old movies; the Fort is not going to be eligible.

As always, though, there are exceptions. If you do a *really good job* of reconstruction, accurately reconstructing the place based on good historical, archeological, and other information, and if it's in an appropriate environment (usually its original environment), then it may be eligible. Any reconstruction is going to be viewed by the Register with something of a jaundiced eye, though, so if you want to have such a property considered eligible, be prepared for some tough questions.

COMMEMORATIVE PROPERTIES

A statue or other marker of some historical (or other) event is not itself eligible for the National Register, though of course the site of the event it commemorates may well be eligible. Gettysburg Battlefield is eligible; the monuments that litter it are not themselves eligible—though by now, they have become such parts of the scene that they might be regarded as contributing to the integrity of the Battlefield.

A commemorative property can be eligible for its design—as an indicator of the designs associated with a particular period, or because it's the work of a master. Or if it's really something special—the Statue of Liberty—it may be eligible. Actual direct association with (as opposed to commemoration of) an important event may also make a commemorative property eligible. There's a statue on the island of Guam representing the indigenous leader who misguidedly welcomed Spanish missionaries to the island; it's not eligible for the Register for its association with indigenous culture or Spanish missionaries. A few years ago, however, an important local political figure chained himself to the statue and committed suicide; it may be that history will show this to be an important event, association with which will make the statue eligible.

PROPERTIES WITH SIGNIFICANCE EXTENDING
LESS THAN 50 YEARS INTO THE PAST

Finally, there's what's widely referred to as "the Fifty Year Rule." This Criteria Consideration is often misstated as "a property isn't eligible if it's less than fifty years old." Actually a property can be *more* than fifty years old and still not be eligible if it didn't become *significant* until less than fifty years ago. The Dallas Book Depository is well over fifty years old, but nobody thought it significant until Lee Harvey Oswald used one of its windows to shoot John F. Kennedy. Had Oswald been a less proficient shot, the Book Depository might not be regarded as eligible today. But it is, which illustrates the exception to the rule. A property whose significance lies less than fifty years in the past *may* be eligible if it is of "exceptional significance." The assassination of President Kennedy is regarded as an exceptionally significant event, so the Dallas Book Depository is eligible. The U.S. Space Program is regarded as exceptionally significant, so Cape Canaveral and Houston Mission Control are eligible.

Of course, this begs one to ask: "exceptionally significant to whom?" This question has become a hot one in recent years in the context of properties associated with the Cold War. In 1991, Congress directed the Department of Defense to:

> ...*inventory, protect and conserve the physical and literary property and relics of the Department of Defense, in the United States and overseas, connected with the origins and development of the Cold War.* (DoD Appropriations Act of 1991, Section 8120)

With more enthusiasm than good sense, some DoD officials decided that this meant that Cold War properties were by definition exceptionally significant and therefore might be eligible for the National Register, even though such properties were almost universally less than fifty years old. Upon realizing that it had backed itself into viewing virtually all its domestic real estate holdings as historic properties, DoD tried to recover by holding that really, a Cold War property was eligible only if it was "nationally significant"—i.e., a National Historic Landmark. The Alaska SHPO, among others, rightly objected to this contention, pointing out that the Register deals with properties of national, state, and local significance. Surely, she argued, a Cold War property can be "exceptionally significant" in a state context—for example, in terms of its impact on the socioeconomic development of Alaska. Although the Register appears to agree with this position, and although it is manifestly logical, DoD does not as yet seem to have bought into it.

In any event, properties that have been regarded as significant for less than fifty years usually aren't eligible for the Register. The reason for this rule is obvious; we need some historical perspective in order to judge something's historical significance. Fifty years is the rule of thumb the Register uses, though it is very careful to point out that it's a sliding rule, that shouldn't be applied rigidly. When the significance of a property—or for that matter, the property itself—has hung around for forty years or so, one ought to start thinking about whether it might be eligible; on the other hand, the mere fact that a property has turned fifty doesn't automatically make it eligible. If you want to assert the eligibility of something whose significance lies less than fifty years in the past, be prepared for some argument.

Significance, Eligibility, and What You Want to Do With the Place

Remember that when you're evaluating a property to determine its historical significance, that's *all* you're doing. You're not determining what will be or should be done with the property. To put it another way, you're not letting management considerations affect your evaluation. Evaluation is supposed to be done *only* on the basis of historical, cultural, and other aspects of significance. You're not supposed to consider what you, or your client, or anybody else wants to do with or to the place. You may be working for somebody who really wants to knock the old building down, and you may entirely support this intent—maybe it's a matter of national defense, or maybe the building is full of toxic wastes that are poisoning the community—but that's no reason to say the building isn't historically or architecturally significant if it really is. It's perfectly all right to say: "It's historically significant *and* we want to knock it down;" what's *not* all right to say is, "We want to knock it down, and therefore it's not historically significant."

By way of analogy, imagine that you're examining a wetland. You're up to your knees in muck, alligators nibbling at your tush. Your client wants to fill the wetland to build a hospital for abandoned urchins. You don't say that the wetland is dry just because you want to see the project go forward, or even because you're tired of the 'gators. You acknowledge that it's a wetland, and go on to consult with the Corps of Engineers and others about whether to fill it. It's the same thing with a historic property. It may well be that nobody wants to preserve the thing; that doesn't matter. If it's historically significant, you determine it to be, and *then* think about whether to preserve it and, if not, what else you can do with it—for example, document it and let it go.

For this reason, it's important not to get too righteous about the importance of preserving historic properties. If you decide the world ought to preserve everything that's historic, then you can't possibly determine that something *is* historic but *doesn't* need to be preserved; it follows that if it doesn't need to be preserved, it must not be historic. In fact, the world is full of stuff that's got historic value but can't realistically be preserved—maybe shouldn't be preserved even in the most perfect of worlds—but should be documented before it's destroyed, or commemorated in some way, or compensated for. If you let physical preservation and significance get equated, you're inevitably going to wind up recognizing only a very narrow range of properties as significant.

As an example, consider a steel launch tower at Vandenberg Air Force Base in California, used during the Cold War to launch intercontinental ballistic missiles on test-firings into the Pacific. Steel, rusting on an active military base; no potential for public interpretation. Should we invest scarce tax money in preserving such a tower? Probably not. Should we document it before we demolish it? Probably so. But if we say that historical significance means a place must be preserved, we cannot recognize the historical significance of the launch tower without committing ourselves to preserving it. Frugal responsibility for the taxpayer's dollar will accordingly drive us to consider the tower to be non-historic, and therefore not even record it.

The bottom line is that you don't consider management factors when evaluating whether a property meets the Register Criteria. That's not to say that you don't consider such factors when you decide *how much* analysis you need to do to determine eligibility, or how far you have to go to "prove it." Agencies regularly decide to agree that something's eligible and get on with figuring out how to manage it, rather than going through the trouble of exhaustively analyzing its significance. On the other hand, project sponsors who feel they're being jerked around by being pressured to preserve sub-marginal properties may want to invest the time and treasure needed to nail down or disprove eligibility. Yep; it depends.

"Potential Eligibility" and Still Another Definition of "Cultural Resource"

So, let's say you've found something you think *might* be eligible for the National Register, but it hasn't been formally evaluated yet. Perhaps you're a consultant, and you've applied the National Register Criteria and decided the thing is eligible, but the sponsor agency and SHPO haven't done so officially. Or perhaps even *you* haven't applied the Criteria yet; maybe you don't think you have enough data. What do you call this thing?

Sometimes such properties are referred to as "potentially eligible." This practice seems sensible enough, but there is some danger in using it. Remember that Section 106 requires agencies to consider impacts on places that are included in or *eligible* for the National Register, not *potentially eligible*. In theory—and in fact this has happened in practice, particularly in the regulatory program of the Corps of Engineers—an agency can say "well, we need to consider properties that have been *determined* eligible, but we don't have to consider properties that are only *potentially* eligible until somebody else—other than us—determines them eligible." This effectively puts us right back where we were before Executive Order 11593, when Section 106 applied only to properties actually included in the Register. The agency can ignore its impacts on a property until the SHPO, or the Keeper, or God determines it eligible.

The eligibility determination process, and the notion of agency responsibility for formally unevaluated properties, turn on the notion of "inherent eligibility." Under this doctrine, a property either inherently does or inherently doesn't meet the Register Criteria. A property that nobody's ever even seen can be lying out there in the woods, throbbing with eligibility; another can be weeping softly for its failure to possess this happy quality.

Of course, this notion is epistemologically absurd. Eligibility is a human mental construct, not a fundamental characteristic of a place like "yellowness," or "acidity," or "Pony Trussness," or "Dogtrotness." And what's not eligible today may be eligible tomorrow, or vice versa. But if you carry this thinking very far, the whole National Register concept becomes pretty silly. A point worth considering, but for the moment let's just note that unless we assume the inherence of eligibility, we have no logical basis for saying that agencies have the responsibility to concern themselves with—and hence even identify—places that *may be* eligible; they are responsible only for those that are *known to be* eligible.

Going back to our wetland analogy: when we go out to see if there's a wetland on a development site, and we sink into the muck up to our knees, we don't say: "This is a potential wetland." We say "This looks and feels and smells a helluva lot like a wetland; let's check it against the definition in the Corps of Engineers' Section 404 regulations." Wetlandness is an inherent quality of the property; our task is to recognize it. Just so with historic properties.

But if we don't call it "potentially eligible" until we determine it to be or not to be, what *do* we call it?

Some people, unfortunately, call it a "cultural resource." There's some logic in this; since "cultural resource" embraces a wider range of phenomena than "historic property," it's reasonable to say that something is a cultural resource but may or may not be a historic property. However, this doesn't really solve the problem of ensuring agency responsibility for considering the place—or at best, it complicates it. You're basically saying that the agency is responsible for considering the place as a cultural resource under NEPA and other authorities, but has such responsibilities under Section 106 only once somebody determines it to be eligible for the National Register by applying the Register Criteria. Worse, it leads to the impression that "cultural resource" means "ineligible property" or "property whose eligibility is undetermined," as opposed to all the other, broader things that the term logically embraces.

So, what to call a place until its eligibility has been determined, either formally by the Keeper or informally by agency/SHPO consensus? I'd call it a "property that may be eligible," or a "property whose eligibility still has to be determined," or "property that appears to be eligible" (or ineligible—or something like that—something that makes clear its uncertain status without implying that it falls definitively into some category other than eligible or ineligible). This may seem like a pretty unartful way to express uncertainty about eligibility, and pretty hard to differentiate from a simpler bit of terminology like "potentially eligible," and if everybody knows what you're talking about when you say "potentially eligible," maybe that's fine terminology to use. You've always got to remember, though, that your reports may wind up being interpreted in a court of law, by people who *don't* know what you're talking about and who may have reasons to give your words their own particular twists. You need to be careful not to give the court a basis for concluding that a property is *not* eligible (by virtue of being only "potentially" so) until somebody officially pronounces on its status.

Determining Eligibility

All right, then. You've found something that *may* be eligible, but you don't know whether it *is* eligible. What now?

The Section 106 regulations are pretty flexible on this point. They provide that the SHPO and responsible agency can agree to "regard" a property as eligible for the Register. When they do, then they treat the property as eligible for purposes of Section 106. Technically, this is not a formal "determination" of eligibility; only the Keeper makes formal determinations. But it's often referred to as a "consensus determination of eligibility."

The regulations don't spell out any particular documentation requirements for a consensus determination; it can be made based on whatever documentation the agency and SHPO agree on. The National Register naturally prefers to see people use National Register forms as the basis for their documentation, and encourages SHPOs toward the same preference. SHPOs often buy into this, or they may have their own forms or other documentary standards that they insist on. There's nothing in the law or regulations that requires agencies to accede to such demands, but they usually do, because it would take more time and trouble to argue with the SHPO than just to do it. However, this step in the process is one at which a good deal of delay and unnecessary costs are generated by "requirements" not only for completing particular forms but for collecting the information necessary to do so—for example, through intensive archeological testing and other activities of sometimes marginal relevance.

The SHPO and agency can also agree to "regard" a property as *not* eligible, in which case (with the exception discussed below) it is so treated for purposes of Section 106. In other words, as far as Section 106 is concerned, it can be blown away without further consideration. This is not to say that it doesn't need to be considered under NEPA and other authorities, but in practice it generally means that it's not going to get very much consideration under any statute, unless somebody really makes a fuss about it.

If the SHPO and agency *don't* agree, then the agency has to seek a formal determination of eligibility from the Keeper. Before we look at how that's done, let's consider another circumstance in which a formal determination must be sought. It may be clearest to give some historical background.

In the early 1980s, the Forest Service was considering an application for a special use permit to allow expansion of a ski facility on the San Francisco Peaks in Arizona. The San Francisco Peaks (a single mountain, really, with multiple summits) comprise a very important sacred place for both the Navajo and Hopi, as well as for other tribes. In Navajo cosmology they make up one corner of the world; to the Hopi they're home to the Kachina, very important spirit beings. The Navajo and Hopi both alerted the Forest Service to the cultural importance of the Peaks, and suggested that they were eligible for the Register.

The Forest Service had an archeological survey done, which revealed nothing. Accordingly, the Forest Service determined that the project would affect no eligible properties. The SHPO, allegedly under pressure from the governor, concurred. The tribes disagreed, pointing out that the very significance of the Peaks discouraged people from going there and creating archeological sites, and that Kachinas leave no middens. The Forest Service and SHPO stuck to their guns.

Under the regulations then governing eligibility determinations (36 CFR 63), an agency had to seek a determination from the Keeper under either of two circumstances:

1. When the agency and SHPO agreed that a property was eligible; in this case, the Keeper in effect had to concur in their determination.

2. When a "question" existed about eligibility. Under the regulations, a question existed when the responsible agency determined it did.

You can doubtless see the problem; all an agency had to do was decide the property was not eligible, get the SHPO to concur, and determine that there was no "question" about ineligibility, in order to proceed with its undertaking without considering impacts on the property.

Parenthetically, I worked on the creation of 36 CFR 63 in the early 1970s, and expressed concern about letting the agency decide whether a question existed. I was rather grandly advised by the solicitor who was calling the legal shots that no agency would ever be so crass as to decide a question did not exist when one in fact did. The solicitor and I are both a good deal older and, I hope, wiser now.

Because, of course, the Forest Service displayed precisely such crassness in the case of the San Francisco Peaks. The tribes had gone to court insisting that the Forest Service comply with Section 106, claiming that the Peaks were eligible. The Keeper and the ACHP had both written the Forest Service recommending that it seek a formal determination of eligibility. In the face of this, the Forest

Service determined that since the SHPO concurred in its opinion about eligibility, no question existed. Taking 36 CFR 63 at face value, the court agreed, and the project proceeded without further Section 106 review.

This case obviously illuminated a very large loophole in the Section 106 process, which we sought to seal up in the 1985 version of 36 CFR 800. At the same time, we tried to do away with the manifestly ridiculous requirement to have the agency seek the Keeper's blessing when the agency and SHPO agreed that a property *was* eligible.

So, under the Section 106 regulations, an agency must seek a determination from the Keeper if:

a) the agency and SHPO don't agree; or

b) the Council or Keeper so request.

The second provision is designed to take care of situations like the San Francisco Peaks, without opening the door to mandatory Keeper review every time anybody objects to an agency/SHPO determination for however frivolous a reason. The Keeper and Council serve as a screen, but if either so requests, the agency must seek a determination from the Keeper.

Incidentally, 36 CFR 63 is still on the books, as a source of confusion in the eligibility determination process. When the ACHP changed the Section 106 regulations in 1985-86, NPS assured us that it would do away with 36 CFR 63 and replace it with regulatory language paralleling what we said in 36 CFR 800. However, NPS then got cold feet about opening *any* regulation up for review during the Reagan administration, and shelved the project. By the time a more sympathetic administration took over, there was a higher degree of tolerance for confusion at both NPS and the ACHP, and nothing has been done about the inconsistency between the regulations. 36 CFR 63 is generally honored in the breach today, but it does still exist. You can use it if you'd like to make some mischief and clog up the system by insisting that agencies comply with contradictory requirements.

So let's assume the agency and SHPO don't agree, or that the Keeper or Council requests that the agency seek a determination from the Keeper. What is the agency to do?

Obviously, the agency needs to bundle up all the pertinent documentation and send it off to the Keeper with a request for a determination. Equally obviously, it's in the agency's best interests to organize the documentation so it's clear and complete, and gives the Keeper a rational and easy-to-use basis for making a decision. Other parties can of course supply the Keeper with their own documentation, and make their own arguments.

The Keeper then reviews the documentation, talks with people as necessary, and makes a decision. The determination of the Keeper is theoretically final, though as we saw in the case of Mt. Shasta, discussed above, the Keeper can be forced by political pressure to re-think a determination.

Eligibility and Nomination

The fact that you, the agency, the SHPO or the Keeper decide that something is eligible for the National Register does *not* mean that you have to, or even should, nominate it for inclusion in the Register. Eligibility determination and nomination are *completely different things.*

Since you determine eligibility as part of the Section 106 process, it often would make no sense whatsoever to nominate the property to become a permanent part of the National Register, since the action you're subjecting to Section 106 review may very well destroy it. In other cases, there's just no particular point in nominating the property; preparing a nomination may not be where you want to put your limited financial and personnel resources.

This kind of thinking tends to upset people at the National Register, and people who make a living doing nominations. Here are some of the arguments they make in favor of nomination, with some responses:

1. *Nomination is required by law.* Nope, it's not. It used to be, in that Section 110(a)(2) of NHPA used to require agencies to nominate "all" historic properties under their jurisdiction and control. This provision was removed in the 1992 amendments; what's required now is simply to have a program that includes nomination. The provision was removed because Congress (that is, the drafters of the amendments) recognized that agencies can often take perfectly good care of historic properties without ever nominating them. So why require them to go to the trouble and expense of doing so?

Executive Order 11593 *does* require agencies to nominate all properties under their jurisdiction, but they were supposed to complete this identification and nomination process by July, 1973. Needless to say, nobody succeeded. So is the requirement still effective? Some people and programs that make money off nomination work would like to think so, but I suggest that they're on pretty shaky ground. Congress has had repeated opportunities to incorporate the Executive Order's provision into law, and has not been inclined to do so. Or rather, they at first did include it, at Section 110(a)(2), and then explicitly removed it.

2. *It protects the property.* Well, maybe. It depends. Actually, the condition under which nomination is encouraged by the statute—when a property's in federal ownership—is precisely the condition under which nomination is the least useful as a preservation device. Federal agencies, remember, are required to manage historic properties under their jurisdiction or control, and historic properties are defined as properties included in *or eligible* for the National Register. So if the property's

eligible, the agency's responsible for managing it whether it's on the Register or not.

Of course, there are those in the federal establishment who are impressed with registration, so it's sometimes helpful to have a property on the Register if, say, we're going to seek funding to rebuild its roof, and our budget people are more likely to approve a new roof for a property on the Register than for one that's merely eligible. But do we want to encourage this kind of thin understanding of what NHPA's all about, if we can help it?

3. It's a good thing to do. Says who? Nomination involves the preparation of paperwork; it doesn't change the property in any way. It *may* help preserve it, as noted above, but in many contexts it's entirely irrelevant to preservation. I think it's fair to say that there is no moral content whatever to the nomination of properties to the Register.

4. It helps keep track of the property. Well, yes, as does any registration device, but the same argument cuts against the Register. If there's another way to keep track of the property, that's no more expensive and no less effective, what's the benefit of the Register? If a land management agency keeps records of its resources in a geographic information system (GIS), for example, it's probably going to be much cheaper, more flexible, and more certain to influence the agency's planning to maintain historic property data in the GIS than to nominate things to the Register, so why not invest scarce dollars in the GIS rather than in nomination?

5. It's an aid to research. This is one of the Register staff's ultimate fall-back positions; they honestly seem to think that the Register can be a great research tool. This strikes me as utter balderdash. Considering that the Register now represents—and surely always will represent—a non-random selection of properties that have happened to be nominated and accepted based on quite uncontrolled and uncontrollable variables, what kind of legitimate research does the Register think anyone's going to use it for? Besides, most research in most of the preservation disciplines is done on a regional basis, where regional records would be at least as useful as a national database. Finally, is the possibility of future research by preservation specialists a legitimate justification for investing tax dollars?

6. It's an educational tool. The Register staff these days really likes this one, too, and it's true, to an extent. Educators do use the Register. But educators would, could, and do use alternatives to the Register, too—like local inventories, state inventories, the databases of land management agencies, Indian tribal data—and these just might have greater pedagogical value than the Register.

7. It honors the property. Yep; sure does. That's what the Register is really good for, and if you feel the need to honor a property, you ought to nominate it. If you simply want to manage it, you might find another tool more useful. And you want to be careful about bestowing the Register's honors too far and wide; the owner of the fine antebellum plantation house may feel that his property's Register status is somewhat cheapened when he finds that it's shared with a tin can scatter in southeast Wyoming.

In a rational world, the Register would be an honorific tool and we'd use other, simpler, cheaper, more flexible tools for planning purposes. We don't live in a rational world, so we struggle along trying to use the Register, and its eligibility criteria, for both honorific and planning purposes. But that doesn't make it sensible, or necessary, to mix up the planning functions of eligibility determination and the honorific function of registration. The fact that the Criteria indicate a property is worth considering in planning does not mean that the property needs to be accorded the honor of placement on the Register.

A Word About Documentation

The Section 106 regulation doesn't require any particular kind of documentation as the basis for an agency-SHPO decision to treat a property as eligible. It does say that agencies are supposed to be guided by the *Secretary of the Interior's Standards for Identification* (included in NPS 1983), but these are pretty flexible. In point of fact you can agree to treat something as eligible based on a one-page description, a polaroid photo, or no documentation at all. This kind of flexibility can be *very* useful.

Consider, for example, the case where an Indian tribe wants to be sure that a spiritual place is considered in planning, but doesn't want to reveal what makes the place spiritual—because to do so, in its belief, would dissipate its power, or cause that power to turn to evil, do harm to people, or whatever. It may be very helpful, efficient, cost-effective, and productive of harmony in such a case to be able to say: "OK, we'll treat this mountaintop as eligible without pursuing why it is. Now, what can we do to manage impacts on it?" At least one National Forest has a "cultural" element in its GIS that identifies areas within which consultation with specified local tribes is necessary before taking action there, without specifying why each such area is culturally important.

Or consider the case where you have seven hundred old houses scattered through an area that may be affected by a redevelopment program. It may save a lot of time and money to say: "We'll treat every building over 45 years old as eligible, and apply the Secretary of the Interior's *Standards for Rehabilitation* to each one." Hundreds of local governments have agreements with their SHPOs and the ACHP under which they do this, without project-by-project Section 106 review.

Or consider a project involving five alternative sites, some of which can't be physically inspected in full at the time analysis needs to be performed under NEPA. If you can make judgements about the relative likelihood of eligible properties in each alternative's APE, you can consider and resolve adverse effects on such properties early in planning. If you have to wait until you can get on the land, dig holes in it, measure its buildings, or whatever, you may not get to looking at historic preservation issues until most of the decisions about the project have been made. It is for precisely this reason that Section 106 review tends to occur late in planning, and to generate last-minute conflicts.

The National Register doesn't have to worry about stuff like this, however, and its people naturally believe in the legitimacy of the documentation requirements it imposes on nominations. It's an article of faith at the Register that an eligibility decision should be based on the same level and quality of information as a nomination. Therefore, if you go to the Keeper for a formal determination of eligibility, you're going to be asked for something equivalent to a nomination package. This will involve a detailed description of the property, with maps, plans, photos, and the like, together with a detailed analysis of its significance.

For the same reason, it's been NPS's practice during its triennial SHPO program reviews to pressure SHPOs to insist that agencies develop equivalent documentation as the basis for "consensus determinations"—that is, for regarding something as eligible. Since NPS holds the SHPOs' federal purse strings, SHPOs tend to be responsive to such pressure. Although this sort of pressure has ebbed in recent years, you still may find a SHPO insisting on a substantial level of documentation as the basis for a consensus determination, simply because NPS has made him or her do it.

And of course, some SHPOs may want substantial documentation for their own reasons—which may be good ones (e.g., not wanting to give undue protection to insignificant resources) or not so good ones (e.g., consistency with some standard operating procedure).

The thing to remember is that the Section 106 regulations themselves don't establish a particular documentation requirement, so what *is* required *should* be negotiable, and should—if you'll excuse it—depend on the circumstances.

Boundaries

The Keeper of the National Register frets greatly about boundaries of historic properties—where they should be drawn, how they should be justified, and so forth. This is necessary in the case of a property that's nominated for inclusion in the Register, because by accepting it onto the Register the Keeper is identifying it for long-term consideration in planning as well as for honorific purposes, and one really does have to know where the thing starts and stops. Boundaries are far, far less important in the world of eligibility determinations. In an eligibility determination we are not saying that the property is going to be listed in perpetuity—we may in fact destroy it—so there's no long-term recordkeeping rationale for detailed boundary definition. And boundaries are often irrelevant for project planning purposes, since many of the effects we may be worried about— visual, auditory, and atmospheric effects, for example—may result from actions that take place far outside the property's boundaries. In fact, defining boundaries may mislead people into thinking that if they can just physically stay outside the boundaries, they've avoided adverse effect, and this is obviously not necessarily true. On the other hand, sometimes it *is* true. If we can physically avoid an archeological site that's valuable only for research, we probably have avoided affecting it. So once again, it depends. In consulting about whether to regard something as eligible, you should think about the extent to which you really need to define boundaries, and don't get wrapped up in trying to do so if it's not important in the context of the project under review. But if you have to refer the matter to the Keeper, expect to have to go into excruciating detail about boundaries, and to draw them someplace even if doing so is entirely irrelevant to your project.

Eligibility and the G-O Road

The Forest Service conducted an archeological survey along the G-O Road right-of-way, and identified a few prehistoric and historic sites, including some cairns of rock in the high country at the crest of the coast range. It didn't undertake any special consultation with interested parties, but several local tribes began to make their concerns known. They claimed that there was a very important spiritual place in the high country, probably close to the road right-of-way. Here, they said, there was a hole in the sky through which knowledgeable religious practitioners could gain access to other worlds of knowledge. It was also an important place for medicine gathering, and those rock cairns were prayer seats, constructed by people seeking visions. They were very concerned about potential impacts to this important location.

After some hemming and hawing, the Forest Service contracted with a cultural anthropologist for an ethnographic study of possible Indian spiritual places along the right-of-way. Based on extensive interviews and work in the field with her tribal consultants, the ethnographer was able to show that people did use the high country for spiritual purposes, and that a particular area, smack dab on the G-O Road right of way at the crest of the coast range, was viewed as a particularly important place for vision questing, medicine making, and communication with the supernatural.

Discussion Question: Don't worry about the archeological sites; they were taken care of. Aside from these sites, do you think there's an eligible property here? Apply the National Register Criteria and the Criteria Considerations. If you think there is an eligible property, what do you think it is? How should it be documented? How should its boundaries be established?

Aside: Traditional Cultural Places and the Identification Process

I've repeatedly mentioned traditional cultural places, or properties (TCPs). Since these are among the more controversial types of real-property cultural resources, and, because a recent court case (as of 1998) that bears on them, gives us some guidance as to what constitutes a reasonable and good faith identification effort, I should say a little more about them.

I first became involved with TCPs in the early 1970s, when I helped the Agua Caliente Band of Cahuilla Indians protect its traditional origin place, Tahquitz Canyon in Palm Springs, California, from a Corps of Engineers flood control project. In this and other cases, it seemed to me that, in dealing with TCPs, we were dealing with the kinds of places that NHPA was really, centrally, about: places that are historically rooted and figure importantly in the lives of communities. In the early 1980s, though, this kind of property was getting shorter and shorter shrift in Section 106 review because National Register eligibility determinations were focusing more and more on the relevance of properties to the professional interests of archeologists and architectural historians. By a long and convoluted path, this led Patricia Parker and me to write, and the National Register to publish, National Register Bulletin 38— *Guidelines for Evaluating and Documenting Traditional Cultural Properties* (National Register 1990). Agencies resisted following the bulletin's guidance, so when Congress amended NHPA in 1992, it added Section 101(d)(6)(A), reminding them that one major (and controversial) kind of TCP could be eligible for the Register:

> *Properties of traditional religious and cultural importance to an Indian tribe or Native Hawaiian organization may be determined to be eligible for inclusion in the National Register.* (NHPA Section 101[d][6][A])

Some people think that Bulletin 38 or the 1992 amendments created a new class of eligible properties, or amended the National Register Criteria. Not true. TCPs have been found eligible for, and included in, the Register since its inception. It was just that in the 1980s agencies, SHPOs, and practitioners began to drift toward thinking that a property couldn't be eligible unless only a professional could love it. First the Register and then Congress sought to correct that impression.

TCPs tend to be controversial for several reasons—some of them good, some of them not so good. One of the not-so-good reasons is that they're hard for a standard-issue professional in preservation to recognize, and impossible for him or her to evaluate. They may look like nothing but rocks, or hilltops, or springs, or run-of-the-mill urban neighborhoods, or agricultural valleys. To learn their significance you've got to talk with the people who value them, and lots of practitioners don't much like to do that.

A better reason, a legitimate one, for controversy over TCPs is that because their significance is in people's heads, it's subject to manipulation. People can lie about them. Indian tribes and others can, in theory, manipulate the significance of places to serve political and economic ends. This is a rational basis for being careful about TCPs—for applying some kind of standard of proof—but it's no reason to ignore them. Nor is it a reason for transferring the burden of proof about the existence or character of a TCP to the community that values it, as some agencies would like to do. No reason for ignoring this kind of property unless the community knocks at your door and hands you a description of the place and its significance.

In 1995 the Tenth Circuit Court of Appeals ruled in the case of *Pueblo of Sandia v. United States*, (50 F.3d 856 [10th Cir. 1995]). This decision speaks both to the identification of TCPs and, more broadly, to what constitutes the "reasonable and good faith effort" to identify historic properties called for by 36 CFR 800.

The case involved a proposed management plan for Las Huertas Canyon on the Cibola National Forest, near Albuquerque, New Mexico, to accommodate increased visitor use. The Forest Service's preferred alternative involved various changes to the road up the canyon, and to visitor use facilities. During review under NEPA and Section 106, the Forest Service determined that there were no TCPs in the canyon, and that the undertaking would have no effect on historic properties. The SHPO concurred.

The Pueblo of Sandia filed suit charging violation of Section 106, alleging that there were important spiritual sites in the canyon and, in effect, that the canyon as a whole was a TCP. The District Court granted summary judgement for the Forest Service, largely on the basis of the SHPO's concurrence. The Pueblo appealed.

Meanwhile the SHPO received additional information that strongly supported the Pueblo's contention about the canyon's cultural importance: an affidavit by a cultural anthropologist associated with the Pueblo and a resolution by the Pueblo's council. It turned out that the Forest Service had this information at the time it made its no historic properties determination, and had withheld it from the SHPO. The SHPO withdrew his concurrence.

The Court of Appeals reversed the District Court's decision, and remanded the case for further proceedings. The ruling largely speaks for itself:

The Forest Service mailed letters to local Indian tribes.... The letters requested detailed information...

Rather astonishingly, the Forest Service wrote tribes in the area and asked them for written descriptions of any TCPs in the canyon, together with a description of their significance and a 7.5 minute U.S. Geological Survey quadrangle with the sites and their boundaries marked.

None of the tribes or individuals provided...the type of information requested...

Hardly a surprise. The Forest Service was asking the tribes to do its work for it, and potentially to reveal highly sensitive cultural information.

We conclude, however, that the information the tribes did communicate to the agency was sufficient to require the Forest Service to engage in further investigations, especially in light of regulations warning that tribes might be hesitant to divulge the type of information sought.

By "regulations" the Court seems actually to mean Bulletin 38. The Court cited Bulletin 38 repeatedly as a methodological guide and as an explanation that the Forest Service should have understood as to why the tribes might not have been willing to speak up about TCPs:

National Register Bulletin 38 warns that knowledge of traditional cultural values may not be shared readily with outsiders, "as such information is regarded as powerful, even dangerous, in some societies."

The Court's basic point was that the Forest Service had the obligation to make its own reasoned decision about whether and what kind of identification effort was needed; it could not do nothing just because the tribes hadn't provided precisely the kind of information it requested.

Going on to discuss what the Forest Service should have done to have made a "reasonable" effort to identify TCPs, the Court said:

Determining what constitutes a reasonable effort..."depends in part on the likelihood that such properties may be present." National (Register) Bulletin 38...The information communicated to the Forest Service as well as the reasons articulated for the lack of more specific information clearly suggest that there is a sufficient likelihood that the canyon contains traditional cultural properties to warrant further investigation.

So the Forest Service should have used the data from the tribes—together with other information as available, one might add—to determine what kinds of identification effort were needed. The indication by the tribes that there were important cultural qualities to the canyon should have been enough to tip off the Forest Service to the need for detailed study.

Turning to what constitutes a "good faith" effort, the Court focused on the Forest Service's misleading interaction with the SHPO:

Affording the SHPO an opportunity to offer input on potential historic properties would be meaningless unless the SHPO has access to available, relevant information. Thus, consultation with the SHPO mandates an informed consultation.

The Forest Service did not provide the SHPO copies of the (relevant information) until after the consultation was complete and the SHPO had concurred...In fact, the Forest Service informed the SHPO during consultation that "(c)onsultation with Pueblo officials and elders, and other users of the Las Huertas Canyon area, disclosed no evidence that the...area contains traditional cultural properties."

(T)he withdrawal of (the SHPO's) concurrence upon discovery of the withheld information suggests that the Forest Service did not put forth a good faith effort to identify historic properties...

By withholding relevant information from the SHPO during the consultation process...the Forest Service further undermined any argument that it had engaged in a good faith effort.

The decision in this case tells us that courts are going to take seriously the obligation that federal agencies have to identify and consider TCPs under Section 106. More broadly, it gives us some tests to apply in determining what constitutes a "reasonable and good faith effort" to identify not only TCPs but historic properties of all kinds:

- Writing letters to others asking them about historic properties is all right as part of background research, but it's not enough. The agency has to apply its own mental processes to the information it collects, and reach a defensible decision.

- Cultural factors that may affect a group's willingness to communicate about historic properties have to be thoughtfully considered.

- National Register bulletins provide standards against which the adequacy of identification efforts can be measured.

- Consultation with the SHPO, and presumably with others, must be informed consultation; an agency isn't acting in good faith if it withholds important data.

Determining Effect

I've belabored the identification and eligibility determination process because it's where a lot of myths accumulate, and a lot of people get hung up—and because it's where a lot of professional practice takes place. It's only one step in the process, however. It's important to remember, and to remind others who may not understand the process as well as you do, that the fact that a property is eligible for the Register does not mean you can't blow it away or muck it up. It merely means that ways of managing it and mitigating effects on it must be considered.

To figure out how to mitigate effects, you naturally need to have some idea what those effects are. For this reason, the regulations prescribe that once you've identified something as eligible, you next seek to determine what kind of effect, or adverse effect, the proposed action may have on it.

The 1986 version of the regulation provides for two—or in a way three—sequential steps in determining effect. The 1998 redraft kind of collapses these steps into one—or two, depending on how you look at it.

Under the 1986 regulation, you first determine whether any historic properties are present at all. If not, then (rather implicitly, as the regulation is written) you determine that there are "no historic properties," and send this determination off to the SHPO and other interested parties. Nobody has to comment on this determination, and there are no set review periods.

If there *are* historic properties, then you apply "Criteria of Effect" to determine whether your action may affect them—positively, negatively, or (if an effect can be so) neutrally. If it won't, you can determine "no effect," send this determination around, and if the SHPO doesn't object within 15 days, you can assume you're OK and proceed.

If you find that you *will* have an effect, or if the SHPO objects, then you apply "Criteria of Adverse Effect" to determine—of course—whether the effect of your action on the historic property will be adverse. If it is, then you go into consultation to resolve the adverse effect. If the effect isn't adverse, then you document this fact, send it around to everyone including, in this case, the ACHP, and if neither the ACHP nor the SHPO objects within thirty days, you can proceed.

Perhaps needless to say, most people have mixed up, collapsed, combined, or otherwise mucked about with the sequential steps. People are forever finding that projects have no effect because there are no properties, or determining no effect when they really mean no adverse effect, or determining effect and adverse effect in one step rather than two. The distinctions were really too precious. The 1998 draft regulation tries (without much success, I think) to correct this problem. The draft provides for determinations of:

- No historic properties affected—which can mean either that there are no historic properties there or that one way or another you're going to avoid affecting them;

- No adverse effect—meaning that there are historic properties and they will be affected, but the effects will be nice, or at least not too bad; and

- Adverse effect.

Determinations of "no historic properties affected" and "no adverse effect" are made with the SHPO, without ACHP involvement unless somebody blows a whistle to the ACHP and it decides to look into the matter. Determinations of "adverse effect" lead to more detailed consultation with the SHPO, other interested parties, and sometimes the ACHP.

You determine whether there will be an adverse effect in consultation with the SHPO or THPO involved, by applying "Criteria of Adverse Effect" set forth in the regulation.

Criteria of Adverse Effect

Consistent with the practice we established at the beginning of this chapter, I'll minimize verbatim quotes from either the 1985 regulation or the 1998 draft. Unless some quite unexpected changes take place, though, under the revised regulation the "Criteria of Adverse Effect" will be a single criterion: you have an adverse effect when your action will (or in some formulations, may) *diminish the integrity of those aspects of the property that make it eligible for the National Register.* The regulation (as revised) goes on at considerable length about how effects can be direct or indirect, and specifies that characteristics not identified in the original evaluation of the property but discovered later have to be considered.

Well now, what do we do with this? Consider what you have to know in order to apply the core criterion here. First you have to know what aspects of the property make it eligible for the Register. This is not necessarily a simple matter. Suppose we have an old building that's been on the Register since 1976, and we want to gut it to create office space. We need to know whether the interior helps make it eligible for the Register, because if it doesn't, then gutting it may not adversely affect it. But whoever nominated the building back in '76 probably wasn't very explicit about what features of the building did and did not contribute to its eligibility; National Register forms don't really elicit that information very well. So we may not know whether the interior contributes or not. This is why the revised regulation says that characteristics identified after the original evaluation have to be considered. But this means, of course, that one more or less has to evaluate every property *de novo*, even those already evaluated through the nomination process.

Even if we're not dealing with some antique nomination or eligibility determination—even if we're looking at the historicity of a property for the first time—reasonable people can disagree, and there's a world of potential for disagreement about what does and doesn't contribute to a property's eligibility.

Assuming we can reach some kind of consensus on what contributes, then we have to decide whether what we're planning to do will diminish its integrity. OK, so gutting the interior will diminish its integrity, but what if we're planning only to paint it? Or remove asbestos? Or bring it up to code? Again, lots of room for argument.

And what if we can do things to reduce the severity of the effect? What if everybody thinks painting it puce would be an adverse effect, but painting it teal would be OK?

Most people, most of the time, avoid dealing with the abstract arguments inherent in the core criterion by using a series of examples that the regulation provides. Examples of adverse effect include:

Destruction. If you're going to knock the building down or bulldoze away the archeological site, that's an adverse effect. No brainer (but see the "research exception" discussed below).

Alteration. A bit trickier. If you're going to alter the property in such a way as to diminish its integrity, that's an adverse effect. There we are, back up against those contentious abstractions. What usually happens, though, is one of two things. Either it's agreed—or somebody like the SHPO forces it down the agency's throat—that *any* alteration is an adverse effect, or it's agreed that there won't be any adverse effect as long as specified conditions are met, such as painting it teal rather than puce. The 1998 draft regulation provides that an alteration is not an adverse effect if it's consistent with the *Secretary of the Interior's Standards for the Treatment of Historic Properties* (36 CFR 68; NPS 1992) and applicable guidelines; it's silent on how one is to demonstrate such consistency.

Removal. If you're going to move a property away from its historic location, under the 1998 draft regulation that's an adverse effect, even if you're moving it for protective reasons. If a property doesn't *have* a historic location—as is arguably the case with a historic ship or aircraft— then presumably removing it *isn't* an adverse effect. But consider the case of the *U.S.S. Missouri,* the battleship on which the Japanese surrendered to end World War II. When it was up for recommissioning to go lob shells at Lebanon during the Reagan administration, it had sat in port at Bremerton, Washington for many years, and had become a popular tourist attraction. Was moving it from Bremerton an adverse effect? The Bremertonians certainly thought so—as they have more recently when the Mighty Mo, once again off-duty, has been scheduled for relocation to Hawaii to serve as a museum ship.

Changing use. Even if you don't touch the property, if you change the way it's used this may have an adverse effect on it. If you drive up tax rates to the point where low-income families may not be able to remain in their old houses, or family farmers are unable to hold onto their land, or if you close off the trail that the Indian tribe uses for access to its sacred site, you're having an adverse effect.

Alterations of setting. Changing the setting of a property can have adverse effects on it—again without touching the property itself. If you build something that's visually incompatible right next to a building whose visual qualities are important, that's an adverse effect. A classic example of setting alteration—and use alteration—as adverse effects is the case of the Matachines Dance site in El Rancho, New Mexico. As you'll recall, in this case the proposed action was constructing a power substation next to the parking lot where the dance was held. The people of El Rancho claimed that this alteration of setting would so compromise the character of the site that they would no longer be able to dance there; this was clearly an adverse effect on the site.

Obviously, though, sometimes an alteration of setting may be irrelevant to the significance of the property. Archeological sites are notoriously insensitive to visual impacts, for example.

The revised draft regulation tries to deal with this disparity by saying that a change in the setting is an adverse effect only if it changes physical features within the setting that contribute to the property's significance. Like the core criterion, this opens the door for some truly wonderful arguments about what does and what doesn't contribute, though some may be closed by the next criterion.

Introduction of intrusive elements. If you erect a cell-phone antenna on the margins of a historic district whose visual integrity is important, this is obviously an adverse effect. The regulation at this point speaks to visual, atmospheric, and audible elements, so it covers things like air pollution and introduction of noise as well as things you can see. The introduction, like a change in setting, must somehow diminish the integrity of the property's significant elements in order to be an adverse effect.

There's a cell phone antenna on the edge of the "Woodhenge" at Cahokia, the ancient urban center east of St. Louis, Missouri. Does this diminish the Woodhenge's, or Cahokia's, significant elements? I'd certainly say so, and probably most people would agree. But does it really? Aren't the significant elements of the Woodhenge the holes into which the poles were stuck to create the structure that's thought to have been an astronomical observatory? What's really affected is the visitor experience at Cahokia, which is very important but is not itself an aspect of the site's historical significance. I can imagine a lot of arguments over things like this—which will distract people from getting on to the real issues of resolving adverse effects.

Consider, for example, the case of a satellite dish that's proposed for construction next to a juniper tree on a western Indian reservation; the tree is regarded as a place where religious practitioners can communicate with the supernatural. Since both the tree and the satellite dish are communication devices, does the dish detract from the tree's significance? At least one traditional tribal religious leader who showed such a site to an NPS official didn't think so (Patricia Parker, personal communication 1996).

Neglect. If you control a historic property, and neglect it so it falls apart, falls down, gets vandalized, or is otherwise adversely affected, the neglect itself constitutes an adverse effect—except, says the 1998 draft regulation, where deterioration is something the property is *supposed* to do according to an Indian tribe or Native Hawaiian organization. This caveat is supposed to handle situations like Indian cemeteries, where the tribe wants the remains of its ancestors to return to the earth.

Neglect is a hard effect to deal with, because agency decision-makers seldom wake up in the morning and say "I'm going to neglect the Joe Smith Plantation House today." But agencies do make decisions all the time that may be neglectful of historic properties—budget decisions, decisions about the priority of projects, and so on. In *National Trust for Historic Preservation v. Blanck* (938 F. Supp. 908 [D.D.C. 1996]) the U.S. District Court for the District of Columbia found that in neglecting historic buildings at the Walter Reed Army Medical Center Annex in Maryland the Army had failed to comply with NHPA, though it also determined (using rather contorted logic) that NHPA did not create a private cause of action to enforce compliance, and did not require agencies to spend substantial amounts of money to maintain historic properties. This decision will certainly be appealed, and is so strange that it would be risky, I think, to put much reliance on it.

Transfer out of federal ownership. Federally controlled properties are subject to the protections not only of Section 106 but of other sections of NHPA and other federal laws. If you transfer a property out of federal ownership—sell it, give it away, exchange it, whatever—it's deprived of these protections, and that's obviously an adverse effect.

Again the 1998 draft regulation contains a caveat. Transfer is all right if you include in the transfer documents adequate and enforceable restrictions to protect the property. What constitutes adequacy or enforceability? That's left for negotiation, as it doubtless should be; what works in one state, or with one kind of property, won't work in another. In the state where I live, for example, there's a very active, pretty well-enforced historic easement program, and that's the system the SHPO wants used to protect transferred property. The recipient is required to grant the SHPO an easement under which the recipient agrees to preserve specified elements of the property that contribute to its significance.

So, those are the examples of adverse effect that illustrate the criterion. They're so widely used and so thoroughly embedded in the determination of effect process that they're referred to as the "criteria of adverse effect," though they're really only examples. There can be other kinds of adverse effect, as long as they meet the core criterion.

Like what? Well, how about if somebody is living on public land, under a special use permit of some kind, and takes it upon himself or herself to keep watch over a nearby cave full of ancient pictographs? The resident keeps track of visitors to the cave, talks to them, encourages them to respect the paintings and not contribute their own spray-can additions. The special use permit expires and the federal agency proposes not to extend it; the resident will have to move. Is the agency destroying the cave? No. Is it altering the cave? No. Is it changing the "character of its use?" Well, one might be able to make an argument for this, but it would be a pretty long bow to draw. Is it altering the setting? No. Is it introducing elements that distinguish its integrity? Probably not. The regulation talks about "visual, atmospheric, or audible elements," and while spray-can vandals presumably could be seen, might smell, and can probably be heard, it would still be hard to squeeze them into this example. Is the agency neglecting the cave? Well, yes, but no more than it's already been neglecting it, and it will probably say that it will, of course, protect it just fine. Is it transferring the cave? No. But is it doing something that, indirectly at least, can alter characteristics that qualify the cave for the National Register? Sure it is.

On the other side of the coin, the draft regulation posits the possibility that an agency can propose that something is not an adverse effect even though the Criterion of Adverse Effect *is not* met. So presumably an agency can propose that, say, burning down Monticello would not be an adverse effect. I don't know what to do with this idea, other than to say "good luck."

What To Do With a Determination

Having applied the "criteria" of adverse effect, you clearly must make one of two determinations. Either the project will have an adverse effect or it won't. If you determine that it *will*, you move on to the next step. If you determine that it *won't*, then under the draft revised regulation you so notify whoever you've been consulting with—at minimum the SHPO or THPO and any Indian tribe whose lands are involved—and provide them with specified documentation. The SHPO, THPO, and tribe have 30 days to object, and if one of them does so you either work with them to persuade them to withdraw the objection, or you treat the effect as adverse. Other consulting parties aren't given the opportunity to object in the same manner, but they can try to influence the SHPO, THPO or tribe to exercise its authority. They can also appeal to the ACHP, as can anyone else, and if the Advisory Council decides to so request—within the 30-day review window—you have to treat the effect as adverse and go on to the next step. Under the 1986 regulation, you must provide the determination documentation to the ACHP, and give the ACHP 30 days to review, object, or propose changes.

Conditional No Adverse Effect Determinations

Often an agency, SHPO or THPO, and others will agree to conditions which, if adhered to, will ensure that there will be no adverse effect. The resulting determination is commonly referred to as a "conditional no adverse effect" or "CNAE" determination. The 1998 draft regulation appears to provide, rather in passing, for CNAEs even where there actually will be adverse effects, while the 1986 regulation provides for them where the Criterion of Adverse Effect applies but certain exceptions are met. Setting aside any disquiet one may feel about this rather large loophole, we can recognize the "CNAE" determination as a useful tool to ensure, within reason, that what's supposed to have no adverse effect will, in fact, have none.

Consider the case where the agency says that constructing a new federal building will have no adverse effect on a nearby historic cemetery because a vegetative buffer will be created between the building site and the cemetery. We might agree in principle that this measure is adequate, but how does the agency translate the principle into on-the-ground reality? What kind of buffer will it be? What kinds of plants will be used? Evergreen or deciduous? Big or small? How big? How close together? This is the kind of thing you want to have nailed down. You want to have a document that reflects an agreement on such matters, and that's signed by the parties involved.

The regulation doesn't prescribe what kind of document it needs to be; often it's done with an exchange of letters. But your rule of thumb should be that the condition as documented should be understandable to the "cold reader"—the person who walks in off the street and is given the document to read. Remember that the project will probably be implemented by people other than those who write the condition; they need to be able to understand what the condition requires them to do. The condition may wind up being interpreted in court, so you need to write with judges and lawyers in mind—which does not mean you've got to lace the document with obscure Latinisms and allusions to parties of the first part; it just means that you've got to make it clear and complete. There are classes in how to do this, and a companion textbook to this one will address it as well.

Aside: The "Research Exception" and Its Brethren

The 1986 regulation includes three "exceptions" to the Criteria of Adverse Effect. These were (and at the moment still are) sometimes referred to as the "Three Rs," standing for research, rehabilitation, and restrictions. I'll refer to them in the past tense, in the hope that by the time this is published they will have gone away.

Rehabilitation: Under the rehabilitation exception, you could treat alteration of a property as not adverse if it amounted to rehabilitation of a building or structure in a manner consistent with the Secretary of the Interior's *Standards for Rehabilitation.* The SHPO had to concur in the agency's application of the *Standards,* and the ACHP had to review the determination.

In the 1998 draft regulation, this exception no longer stands alone; it has been effectively absorbed into the "alteration" example of the Criterion of Adverse Effect.

Restrictions: Under the restrictions exception, you could treat transfer out of federal ownership as a non-adverse effect if your transfer documents contained restrictions adequate to protect the property. The restrictions had to be enforceable under applicable state law, and in theory should run with the property in perpetuity. Their use was subject to SHPO and ACHP concurrence. Like the rehabilitation exception, the restrictions exception has been absorbed into the Criterion of Adverse Effect in the 1998 draft regulation, as a caveat on the "transfer of federal lands" example.

Research: The "research exception" was not absorbed into the 1998 examples, because of strong objections by Indian tribes and others, but it will probably be resurrected as a "standard treatment" (see below), so a little discussion of it may be in order here.

The research exception has its origins in the mid-1970s, when the number of "Section 106" cases (they were really Executive Order 11593 cases) was escalating rapidly as agencies began to implement President Nixon's executive order requiring that eligible properties be given the same consideration in agency planning as registered ones. As discussed in Chapter 2, NPS sent three archeologists out to proselytize the agencies about the executive order; they concentrated on land management agencies, and promoted attention to archeological sites. So the ACHP and SHPOs suddenly found themselves confronted with lots of archeological cases.

The ACHP at the time had no archeologists on staff, and had little experience in dealing with archeological issues. It did have a clever General Counsel, however, Ken Tapman, who came up with a way to minimize the trouble the ACHP would have to put itself to in order to deal with such matters. Tapman reasoned that since archeological sites were important for the data they contained, then if one could remove and preserve those data, one had removed and preserved the importance of the site. Therefore, destroying an archeological site shouldn't be an adverse effect if one first recovered its significant data.

The ACHP floated this idea around the federal family, and got a mixed reaction. Some agencies liked the idea a lot; it could save them some trouble. NPS's Interagency Archeological Services Division, for which I worked at the time, didn't like it at all. We pointed out that one can never recover all the data from an archeological site, so it simply wasn't true that one could eliminate the adverse effects of destruction by conducting data recovery. We objected to the ACHP's assignment of second-class citizenship to archeological sites—you'd never say that demolishing an old building was OK provided it was documented, we sniffed. And (rather as an aside, I'll admit), we pointed out that lots of archeological sites were important to Native American groups for reasons other than research.

The last argument was actually the best, particularly since Tapman had been involved on behalf of the ACHP in the case of *Warm Springs Dam Task Force v. Gribble* (387 F. Supp. 240 [N.d. Cal. 1974]), which had pitted the Dry Creek Band of Pomo Indians and a number of other plaintiffs—myself included—against the Corps of Engineers over the impacts of a dam in California on ancestral Pomo sites. Tapman and I had rather scratched one another's backs; he had given our lawyers and me advice about how to make our case, and we had structured the case to give maximum authority to the ACHP's then-nonbinding Section 106 procedures. We had come to respect each other, and I think Ken had gotten some notion of the extra-research significance of archeological sites.

After a number of quiet meetings with Tapman in what I remember as rather dingy basement bars around Washington, we reached an understanding. The ACHP would issue its exception to the Criteria of Adverse Effect, but say that it could be employed only where an agency showed that the site in question was important *only* for research, and where the agency had an acceptable research design in hand that it was committed to follow. Smug at the sagacity we'd shown in splitting the baby, I went off to Micronesia.

Returning in 1979, I was distressed to find that it had become more or less standard practice to treat all destruction of archeological sites as having no adverse effect on them, provided the sites were found eligible only under National Register Criterion D (for data, remember?) and a data recovery plan would be implemented. NPS still didn't like this much, but was preoccupied with other things; some archeologists griped about it, but most people had accepted it.

Doing away with the exception was not a playable game, so in the 1986 regulation we tried to clarify it, specifying as unambiguously as possible that (a) it could be applied to any kind of property that was "of value" only for research (hence it could be applied to a building, a landscape, or whatever, not just to an archeological site), but that (b) the property could not be of value for anything other than research; (c) the character of the property and its data had to be such that the relevant data could be reliably retrieved; and (d) the agency had to be formally committed to a research design meeting professional standards.

By this time Native American groups were getting more involved in Section 106 review than they had been. Shortly after the regulation was issued, the National Congress of American Indians (NCAI) wrote to the ACHP expressing concern about the exception and saying that in its view, *any* site containing ancestral graves had value that went beyond research. After due cogitation, the ACHP's General Counsel (John Fowler; Tapman had escaped the government) agreed with NCAI, directing the staff not to go along with No Adverse Effect determinations based on data recovery where burials might be found. Fowler's memo made a particularly important point in highlighting the fact that the regulation alluded to properties having *value* only for research, not *significance*. This, he said, made it clear that the historical significance of a site, as measured in a National Register evaluation, did not determine whether the research exception could be applied. The question instead was, did the site have value of some kind, in the eyes of a community, a Native American group, or whoever, that went beyond research.

This distinction and the other caveats on the research exception have been emphasized in ACHP guidance and training, but they continue to be routinely ignored (sometimes, I fear, even by ACHP and National Register staff). The notion that any "Criterion D" site can be salvaged and blown away without adversely affecting it is particularly galling, given that eligibility is supposed to be determined solely on the grounds of historic, cultural, architectural and engineering significance, without reference to how one wants to manage the evaluated property. The "Criterion D = Research Exception" equation violates this fundamental principle.

By the time the ACHP began working on the 1998 draft regulation, Native American interests had become sufficiently powerful, and sufficiently vocal about the discriminatory character of the research exception, that it apparently became untenable for the ACHP to keep it in the regulation. So it no longer appears there, but the regulation does permit agencies and SHPOs to execute quickie agreements to employ "standard treatments" for mitigating effects on historic properties. Such "treatments" are to be issued periodically by the ACHP Can we guess what one of the first standard treatments to be issued will be?

Assuming the research exception is reborn as a standard treatment, with essentially the same caveats as in the 1986 regulation, here are some thoughts about it:

- It should be applicable to all kinds of properties, so if you have an old building that everybody agrees can't be used for anything but as the basis for a document illustrating how it was built or what it was used for, it ought to qualify for the treatment just as much as an archeological site.

- The distinction between "value" and "significance" should be rigorously observed. "Significance" is something to be determined without reference to what one wants to do with the property. As discussed above, a historic property doesn't become non-historic because you want to knock it down, any more than a wetland becomes dry because you want to fill it in. In the same way, a property doesn't lose its association with significant events or significant people, or its status as an exemplar of a type or school, or its artistic importance, or its association with a master, just because you want to demolish it. The moment we let the kind of significance we ascribe to a property drive its treatment, we taint the eligibility determination process. The question asked in determining treatment should not be: "what is the significance of this property in historical, archeological, engineering, or cultural terms," but "what is the value of this property in the contemporary world?" Does anybody want to keep it because it's sacred to them? Does it contain the treasured remains of the ancestors? Does it have potential for adaptive use? Does it have public interpretation potential? Is it important to a community's ongoing cultural life, or its sense of place or identity? If it exhibits any of these characteristics, then there are values that compete with its research value, that require full consideration. If it doesn't have such characteristics, then maybe it's OK to document it or dig it up and destroy it without much detailed review.

- All archeologists know that you can never recover "all the data" from a site, if for no other reason than that we think up new things to ask of sites, and new techniques to employ in asking them, all the time. And the more complicated the site, the less likely it is we can extract all the data. The research exception, under whatever guise, should be used only with properties that are simple enough, or common enough, to give us a reasonable shot at recovering all the data that matter.

- And the agency should have its research design or data recovery plan in hand, together with the money to implement it. It should be able to demonstrate that it has these, and will implement its plan in a manner that's in accord with contemporary professional standards.

I continue to hope, though, that the research exception will simply die a quiet death, and archeological sites will be afforded the same thorough consideration that every other kind of historic property (in theory) receives. Creating it was a mistake, I believe; an understandable mistake, but a mistake nonetheless. I should have poisoned Tapman's hamburger.

Some Advice

Like the eligibility determination process, the process of determining effect is one that can generate a tremendous amount of argument over fine points and procedural issues. My recommendation to clients about such arguments almost invariably is, don't get into them. If someone thinks there's an adverse effect, there's almost always a way to show that there is, given the twists and turns of the criterion and its examples. If you don't think there's an adverse effect, but somebody else does, it's probably not worth arguing with them about it. And if you can find some lawyerly way to split a procedural hair, somebody else can probably find a similar way to splice it back together, or find a hair that's less ratty under some other law. Don't play games; get on with the process.

The Effects of the G-O Road

The Forest Service felt that the spiritual place identified at the crest of the Coast Range was not eligible for the National Register because of the "religious property" criteria consideration. The SHPO, following the lead of the tribes, disagreed. The matter was referred to the Keeper of the Register.

The Keeper determined that the spiritual place was eligible as a district, called the "Helkau Historic District." The Keeper dismissed the religious property criteria consideration argument by noting the intense cultural significance of the property, the role it played in maintaining traditional culture, and its clear association with important local Indian traditions.

The Keeper, as is the Keeper's wont, worried greatly about what the boundaries of the property should be, and eventually established them along the contour line that enclosed all the locations where the ethnographic study indicated that people sought visions and medicine; this enclosed all the prayer seats, but was a pretty small area.

By the time the determination was made—because the Forest Service had not refrained from construction while the process went on—the road was built to the east and west boundaries of the district.

Discussion Question: Assuming the Forest Service wanted to complete the road, what sort of effect determination should it have made? What are its options for avoiding having to make an adverse effect determination?

Resolving Adverse Effect

After effect determination, what's the next step in the process? If you're going to have an adverse effect, naturally the next thing to do is, see if there's a way to keep it from happening, or reduce its severity. Mitigate it, or as the regulations put it, "resolve" the adverse effect.

Unfortunately, I think, the regulation (both the 1986 and the revised version) discuss "resolution of adverse effects" largely in terms of consultation—that is, you consult with other parties about how to resolve the adversity. By saying this is unfortunate, I don't mean to imply that consultation isn't important—far from it. I do think, though, that focusing on consultation tends to divert attention from the fact that the responsible agency *itself* needs to think about how to resolve adverse effects. Take some initiative, do some studies, and perhaps most critically, consider alternatives.

But more on that in a moment. First, what is this thing called consultation?

Why Consult?

In the ACHP's introductory Section 106 class, we used to use a wonderful John Cleese videotape called "Decisions, Decisions," in which at one point Queen Elizabeth I observes that "consultation is a process factual and a process psychological." She then perforce drops out of character to explain that "there are two dead good reasons to consult with people, baby." The reasons are (1) to get information you don't have that might influence your decision, and (2) to make sure people feel like their concerns have been addressed, so they're more likely to accept the decision when it's made.

If everyone attended to Her Majesty's sturdy advice, there'd be a lot fewer silly arguments about who has the "right" to be a consulting party under Section 106. But even in these enlightened times, with a zillion self-help and management principle books around advising folks to talk with one another, there are still a lot of people who think they can best advance their interests by not listening to anybody else, and by keeping others from knowing what they're up to. Such people—and their lawyers—get terribly exercised about who they *have* to consult with under Section 106, what has to be discussed, how long consultation must take, and whether one need only suffer through it or actually *do* something in response to it.

Consultation Under Section 106

ACHP staff sometimes distinguish between "little-c" and "big-C" consultation. Little-c consultation takes place throughout the process. You consult with people about identification, about evaluation, about effect determination, and so on. Big-C consultation occurs once you've determined that there'll be an adverse effect; you then consult with a degree of formality to try to resolve the effect. We've touched on little-c consultation as we've discussed previous steps in the process. Now let's look at big-C consultation.

In principle, it's no different from little-c—it's about reasoning together. Let's sit down and discuss the project's effects and what we can do about them. Let's lay our cards on the table and negotiate. Let's make sure each of us understands the other's concerns, and seek ways we both—all—can gain.

In practice, the notable thing about big-C consultation is that there are some definite standards it's supposed to meet. This may be unfortunate; standards have a way of coming to be regarded as the *most* one needs to do, rather than the minimum.

Consulting Parties

The regulation is most explicit about *who* an agency needs to consult with. Generally, the party you've got to consult in every case is—of course—the SHPO (or THPO). Just as the SHPO must be consulted at each little-c consultation step, so must the SHPO be consulted in seeking to resolve adverse effect.

Other parties who must be consulted under the statute itself and/or under one or the other version of the regulations include:

- Indian tribes whose lands are affected (that is, lands within the boundaries of their reservations, including any historic properties on such lands).

- Indian tribes and Native Hawaiian organizations who may attach religious and cultural significance to affected properties.

- Local governments with jurisdiction over areas affected.

- Applicants for federal assistance (e.g., state highway departments applying for funds from FHWA, or a low-income housing provider seeking HUD assistance).

- Applicants for federal permits, licenses, or other approvals (e.g., the applicant for a FERC certificate or a right-of-way from BLM).

In addition, you can invite other parties to participate as consulting parties. The 1998 draft regulation is a bit ambiguous on this point, in part because it addresses it in several different sections in several different ways, but the bottom line seems to be that:

- An agency may invite anybody it wants to participate;

- Anybody else may ask to participate, but must do so in writing to the agency; and

- If the agency and SHPO or THPO agree that the proposed invitee or requester *should* participate, they participate, and if they agree that they should *not* participate, they don't, but if they don't agree at all, the agency goes to the Council for a final decision.

The agency also has to notify the ACHP when it initiates big-C consultation, and it may invite the ACHP to participate if it wants to (actually, this *does* happen sometimes). It must invite the ACHP to participate if the adverse effect will be to a National Historic Landmark (elitism raises its ugly head), or if the agency wants to do a Programmatic Agreement (more on this later).

In big-C consultation, some parties are more equal than others. To understand why, you have to jump ahead to the end of the consultation process.

The process ideally is concluded with a Memorandum of Agreement (MOA) signed by the consulting parties, which the agency (perhaps with others) then implements. Certain parties must sign the MOA in order to make it official; these are referred to in the regulations as the "signatories." Everyone else may sign, but their signatures aren't necessary to make the MOA go into effect—in other words, if they don't sign, it's no big deal; the MOA can still be finalized and implemented, and Section 106 review as such is over. So signatories (I like to think of them as the "terminators," because they're the ones that can terminate consultation instead of concluding an MOA) pretty much have all the marbles.

Where the ACHP hasn't participated in consultation, the agency and SHPO or THPO are the signatories. Where the ACHP has participated, the agency, SHPO or THPO, and ACHP are the signatories. In rare cases where the SHPO or THPO bows out or terminates consultation, the agency and ACHP may be the signatories by themselves. Where the action will affect tribal land, the tribe must be a signatory. All other consulting parties must be invited to concur in the MOA, but their decision not to concur doesn't keep the MOA from going into effect.

So in the vast majority of cases, it's the agency and SHPO who really have the power in the consultation process. The ACHP and tribes have equal power in certain circumstances, and the ACHP in some cases has power beyond that of the SHPO or THPO. Everybody else is a second-class citizen.

Is this right? Just? Democratic? I don't think so, but it's essentially what both versions of the regulation say, so there you are.

The regulation is also explicit about providing documentation. The agency must provide the consulting parties with documentation necessary for them to participate in the process. And the agency must inform the public of what's going on, provide the public with specified documentation, and consider the public's views.

So, we go into consultation. What do we consult about?

What is Consultation About?

I said above that I thought it unfortunate that the regulation emphasizes consultation so much. I say this in part because when people get too focused on the *process* of consultation—notably on who to consult, who has what rights, who gets to be at the table instead of around the room, and so on—what gets lost is the recognition that consultation has a *purpose*. It's supposed to achieve some kind of results. And however devoted we may be to a good consultation *process*, unless we're willing to consider *substance* we're not going to achieve much. It's the agency responsible for the project that has primary control over substance; it's the one that can either consider alternatives or decline to do so, get more data about something or not, apply expertise to a problem or not, pay attention to someone else's expertise or not. Under NEPA and its regulations, the responsible agency is clearly supposed to do substantive analysis of its impacts and what to do about them. Although pragmatically an agency must do the same kinds of analysis to take into account its effects on historic properties, the Section 106 regulation is very vague about it, while it goes into excruciating detail about consultation. Moreover, the agency's consultation responsibility is overwhelmingly focused on the SHPO, encouraging agencies to transfer their substantive responsibilities to the SHPO as well. Alternatives? What does the SHPO say we should do? Can we avoid an adverse effect? What does the SHPO think?

Bottom line: consultation needs to have substance; it needs to be informed. And it's not a substitute for the agency's own, independent, analysis of impacts and what to do about them.

The regulation says that we consult about ways to avoid, minimize, or mitigate the adverse effect. These three terms are not defined in the regulation, and in the NEPA regulations the first two are subsumed under the third (40 CFR 1508.20). There's a tendency among Section 106 practitioners (encouraged by some of the ACHP's guideline and training material) to think of the three terms in a hierarchical sense. We first seek ways to avoid the impact altogether; if this doesn't work we look for ways to minimize it, and if we can't find these we agree on mitigation measures. "Mitigation" in this formulation tends to be equated with things like archeological data recovery and architectural recordation. We let the property go, but we make a record of it.

Such a simple hierarchy, of course, bears scant resemblance to the real world. Suppose we have a highway that's going to go through an archeological site. Suppose we move the right-of-way a mile from the site's boundaries. Have we avoided adverse effect? Sure—except of course that the new highway may stimulate development in the area which will destroy the site. But suppose the property isn't an archeological site but an historic building, and the highway, while physically distant, is still in its viewshed? Now have we avoided adverse effect, or only minimized it? Suppose we plant trees along the highway; does this minimize the effect further? Or suppose we don't move the highway a mile from the archeological site, but three feet. Suppose that to make sure no bulldozer driver wanders over onto the site, we fence the right of way and guard it with a minefield and machine guns, and provide construction monitoring just in case the site has oozed out beyond what we think its boundaries are. Have we avoided effect, minimized it, or mitigated it? What if we're not talking about a highway but about a footpath? A power line? What if there's a three-foot horizontal separation but a 300-foot vertical drop? What if the site is a Native Hawaiian spiritual site where silence is really important, particularly in the trade wind season, and that's when we have to build? Or not build?

"Avoidance," "minimization," "mitigation" all grade into and among each other, depending on the nature of the action, the nature of the property, the measures proposed, and a range of other factors. We get into a lot of silly arguments when we let ourselves believe that they have absolute definitions. Some Indian tribes, for example, insist that "you can't mitigate adverse effects on a spiritual place." Why? Because they've dealt mostly with archeologists in Section 106 review, and come to think that "mitigation" means archeological excavations. So what they're really saying is "you can't dig up spirituality and put it in a museum." This is doubtless true, but it's *not* true that you can't mitigate impacts on a spiritual place. It depends on the nature of the place, the nature of the impacts, and the nature of the mitigation.

So, what we should have in our consultation is an open, free-wheeling, informed discussion of the proposed project, its effects, and what to do about them. We should consider alternatives, weighing and balancing costs and benefits of all kinds.

Here's another myth. Sometimes people think that we can consult only about "historic preservation matters," by which they usually mean the significance of the property and what might be done with it in terms of archeology, architectural recordation, rehabilitation, and other kinds of historic preservationish activities. Agencies and other project proponents will say this because they don't want the preservation people questioning, say, their traffic volume calculations or their assessment of economic benefits. Preservationists will say it because they don't want to entertain the possibility that something—relieving traffic congestion, promoting economic development—might be more important in some cases than preservation. In fact, of course, if we limit ourselves to "avoidance, minimization, and mitigation measures" that are within the ambit of the historic preservation disciplines, we're going to have a mighty narrow range of measures to consider.

Remember that one purpose of consultation, from the standpoint of the decision-maker, is to reveal and consider information that hasn't already been considered. It's a "process factual," in Elizabeth I's words. The information that needs to be considered may or may not have much to do with historic preservation per se. Building the new shopping mall will create 500 new jobs, but will they be jobs that local residents will be able to get, or will they require skills that must come from outside? If the latter, do the proponent's assertions about local economic development, upon which the local government has relied to justify tearing down a bunch of historic buildings, really make sense? If we swing the proposed airport runway fifteen degrees to avoid overflying the historic district, what does this do to fuel consumption and safety? These kinds of questions have to be addressed, and answered with real data, or consultation has little chance of accomplishing much.

On the other hand, considering such issues not only requires that proponents be willing to gather and share pertinent information; it also requires that preservationists take them seriously. If the jobs at the mall really will go mostly to local people, or if altering the runway alignment will cause aircraft to crash into mountains, scare endangered ducks away from a wetland, or cause a five-dollar per ticket increase in airline fares, these facts can't be ignored as irrelevant to historic preservation.

How is Consultation Done?
Some Process Suggestions

In making much of the need for substance in consultation, I don't mean at all to denigrate the importance of process. A colleague in the Department of the Interior commented to me recently that the older he got, and the longer he spent in the bureaucracy, the more he came to equate "success" with "good process" as opposed to "good outcome." I not only share his view, I think it's an entirely reasonable one—especially in a public servant. As we grow older and more experienced, unless we shut down our thought processes altogether, we all come to recognize a wider and wider range of outcomes that we can regard as "good." Particularly if we work for the public, which almost by definition has multiple, conflicting desires, most of them justified one way or another, we come to be suspicious of simple "good-bad" distinctions. If we believe in serving the public, then we pretty soon come to be satisfied—even happy—with a process that gives everybody a fair crack at making his or her preferences prevail.

Consultation under Section 106—and for that matter under NEPA, AIRFA, and the other statutes—is by definition a process, and what constitutes a "good" outcome, as usual, depends. In this case it depends on your point of view; did the process arrive at what you think is desirable?

But the process itself can be "good" or "bad," depending on how level it makes the playing field, how fairly it allows different opinions to be heard and debated, how open it makes decision-making to varying ideas and alternatives.

There are ways to make consultation work, and ways to make it a sham. Unfortunately, a lot of people know only how to do the latter. Not necessarily because they *want* sham consultation, but because they simply don't know how to do anything else. This is particularly sad since there is a pretty substantial literature on how to make consultations of various kinds work. There's widely available training, and there's a national organization—the Society of Professionals in Dispute Resolution (SPIDR, and yes, it has a web site) that's composed of people for whom processes of consultation are a way of life and a way of making a living.

Consultation-to-agreement under Section 106 is a classic example of what's widely referred to as "alternative dispute resolution" or ADR. It's called "alternative" because it's mostly lawyers who've called it that, and it's seen as an alternative to mainstream dispute resolution—suing your opponent's eyes out.

There are many kinds of ADR—arbitration, mediation, the "mini-trial." Section 106 consultation tends to slip and slide around three types: negotiation, conciliation, and mediation.

Negotiation is where disputants get together without anyone helping them out, to butt heads and work through to a solution. Of course, the extent to which there's major head-butting depends on how far apart the negotiators are, and how serious their beefs are with one another. The great majority of Section 106 cases—perhaps all of them, to some extent—involve negotiation.

In conciliation, you have a third party who helps the disputants communicate with one another. This is a form of what's popularly called "facilitation," but facilitators perform their functions in broader contexts than ADR, helping in processes of decision-making that these days go under such stylish terms as "team building" and "quality management." The conciliator is neutral, and helps the disputants exchange views. Sometimes this can be as basic as persuading them to sit in the same room and talk; often it requires trying to get the disputants not to snipe at each other to such an extent that one drives another out of the room. Sometimes it includes helping them interpret data in something like comparable ways.

Mediation is much like conciliation, but is a bit more structured, and the mediator is a bit more of a person with a mission. But it's an entirely processual mission; the mediator doesn't care what the resolution is, as long as there is a resolution that the disputants are reasonably happy with. The mediator is rather more in control of the process than the conciliator is; she sets the rules and does her best to enforce them. The rules are designed to keep people talking, break down communication barriers, achieve mutual understanding and, where possible, agreement. If agreement is reached, the mediator is equipped to help the parties put the agreement in writing.

In Section 106 review, it is not uncommon for the SHPO or ACHP staff to serve in a conciliator or mediator role between a project proponent and project opponents. When I've served in this role I've often found it to be tremendously rewarding both intellectually and emotionally. Very often I find that the parties are simply talking past each other, or that one side or the other is locked into some kind of absolutist position that's unnecessary or even counterproductive to resolving the issue that one or both sides are concerned about. There's a principal in mediation that one wants to get the disputants away from staking out *positions* and into discussing what their real *interests* are. When you can do that, the results can be almost magical.

There's an extensive literature on ADR; for starters I'll recommend Costantino and Sickles Merchant (1995), Fisher and Brown (1988), Fisher and Ury (1981), Kritek (1994), and Ury (1991). Training is offered at a number of institutions (I'll cheerfully recommend Bowie State University's Center for Alternative Dispute Resolution, where I received my mediation training) and through government and private-sector organizations. Sadly, it's unusual to find a SHPO or ACHP staff person with any training in the subject.

So, how do we consult? Naturally, it depends—on who you represent and what you're trying to do. If you want to clog up the process and bring things to a grinding halt, there are lots of ways to do that. If you want to advance your point of view over everybody else's, there are ways to do that, too—to an extent, but always remember that in the final analysis, somebody can pull the plug and terminate consultation. That's the safety valve in the Section 106 process, that keeps consultation from turning into gridlock. But let's assume that your job is to try to reach a resolution to the dispute over adverse effect that's brought the parties to the table. Let's suppose that you're the honest broker—which you *can be* even if you're working for one of the parties, as long as your role is clearly understood.

Everybody is human. Whoever you're working for, try not to perceive the person on the other side of the table as Hitler or Pol Pot. And if you're in any kind of broker position, try to encourage everyone to think of one another as people with legitimate, if conflicting, needs. Try to separate the people from the problem.

Keep it small. If possible, limit the number of people at the table. This can't always be done, and the process has to be an open one, in which all points of view are represented, but if you can keep the cacophony of voices down, it will help. Sometimes this can be done gradually—you have a great big chaotic meeting at first, and by the second or third meeting everybody's gotten to the point of thinking they should designate spokespeople or form coalitions.

But not too small. On the other hand, be very wary of people who want to exclude other people because they're "disruptive" or "just want to make their points." It's astounding how thin-skinned some people are, even people who routinely deal in conflict. I recently had an attorney tell me that he didn't want a certain citizen activist at a meeting because she was "just preparing for litigation," and would "just use the meeting as a forum for expressing her views." Better, presumably, to exclude her and give her a better case to bring to court.

First, we kill...Speaking of which, be careful about participation by lawyers. You can't keep the devils out of the room, but don't take any guff from them. Despite their self-perceptions, they are not the sole receptacles of all wisdom, and their training and personalities are often precisely at odds with the interests of dispute resolution. That said, I should acknowledge that more and more attorneys are themselves getting trained in ADR, which helps a lot, and there are plenty of lawyers who manage to be human. But don't count on it, and don't be afraid to ask them to explain their obscure legalisms in English.

Seek equity. Try to make the playing field as level as possible. You're likely to have people involved who don't understand the fine points of Section 106 or NEPA very well—who don't know a FONSI from a fuzzy bear, or that it's really legal to knock down a National Register building. You may have participants who don't have English as their first language, or who have cultural barriers to communication. And you may have people with various kinds of disabilities to be accommodated. Make sure you accommodate them not only physically but by trying to keep the discussion sensible to them. Stop and summarize from time to time, try to rephrase things in plain language. Watch their eyes; are they glazing over? Narrowing to suspicious slits? Time to stop and regroup.

Move beyond past hurts. Try to keep people from belaboring the past. Whatever may have irritated them in the past about the person at the other side of the table, it's not likely to get fixed now. Try to stay focused on the future.

Interests, not positions. Try to get people to explain their interests, as opposed to their positions. For example, when somebody says:

"This project will wipe out our community's whole connection with its past..."

Before you let somebody else say:

"It will not, as we've explained a hundred times..."

ask:

"Can you explain how it's going to do that?"

Try to get past sweeping generalizations and down to specifics. How will it wipe out the community's connections with its past? By eliminating the only place where people can park to shop at local stores in rehabilitated historic buildings, thereby driving the stores out of business and thereby causing our downtown to dry up. Well, there's a germ of a solution here, isn't there?

But you want to be careful about suggesting the solution, if you're the honest broker; it's much better to let the parties find it themselves. And often they will.

"You mean that's your problem? What about if we add a parking garage?"

That sounds overly simple, of course, but you'd be surprised how often seemingly intractable conflicts are in fact conflicts between *positions,* rather than really between *interests.* In other cases, addressing the interests that people are willing to talk about may ultimately reveal things that they aren't so willing to discuss but that are really bases for solutions.

Trial solutions. Try to get people to put trial solutions on the table. What would you like to see done? Of course, when you're starting out with one side just wanting the other to go away, and the other wanting its opponent to shut up, this may not be feasible. But you can try to explore hypothetical options, anyhow.

Lots of options. Explore as wide a range of options as possible. Particularly if there are lots of people involved, a technique like brainstorming—where everybody tosses up ideas and nobody shoots them down until they've all been articulated—can be useful.

Look for possibilities for mutual gain. There may be something that party A wants badly enough to put up with impact Z if it gets it. Even if party A is in favor of preservation and against the project, that something may not be strictly a preservation kind of something. There was a case recently in which an Indian tribe was willing to accept certain impacts to a traditional cultural property in return for financial assistance to a cultural revitalization program. Or the possibility may not relate directly to the property affected. There have been a number of cases in which demolition of buildings has been accepted in return for the implementation of community revitalization plans, the purchase of facade easements, or the creation of rehabilitation revolving funds to encourage preservation of other buildings or neighborhoods.

Restate it. Try restating things, in the simplest terms possible:

> *"We insist that the Secretary of the Interior's Standards for Rehabilitation be met."*

> *"So you don't object to changing the building, but you want everything that's architecturally significant about the building preserved?"*

Explore implications. On the other hand, explore the implications of expansive statements:

> *"We'll guarantee that this project will do no damage whatever to any significant historic property."*

> *"You mean you're not going to do anything that could have any physical, visual, auditory, social—any kind of impact at all to any of these properties?"*

Try deconstruction. Break the problem down into its constituent parts:

> *"It seems like we have three problems here: visual impacts on the Old North Church, bulldozing the Magnificent Midden, and access to Spirit Peak. Can we look at each of these individually?"*

or

> *"It seems like there are different problems surrounding construction of the project and operations and maintenance. Can we look at each in turn?"*

or

> *"Each of the opponent groups has outlined its interests. Now can we look at each one by itself, pretending for the moment that none of the others exist? Then we can see what conflicts exist between addressing one set of interests and another."*

Document and move on. If points of agreement develop, record them, nail them down, and then move on. Conversely, if there are points that seem intractable, try setting them aside and working on issues where agreement may be possible. The intractable issues may evaporate as other things get resolved.

Be flexible. Don't get hung up on rules of procedure—even rules of proper ADR procedure. Adapt the consultation to the situation.

Recognize cultural variation. It may be inappropriate in a given cultural group for a young person to speak in the presence of his elders, or for meetings to begin without prayers, or for some things to be discussed by women in front of men. Some things may not be discussible in public at all. The person negotiating for the Indian tribe may not be able to commit the tribe to anything without consulting with the elders. Try to make sure you understand these factors going into the consultation, and design it to accommodate them.

Understanding such factors may require prior research—informal discussions with the group involved, perhaps advice or a study by a cultural anthropologist or sociologist. One group of practitioners in dispute resolution routinely conducts a social assessment on a community before launching a consultation program, to ascertain what groups should be brought to the table and what constraints there may be on their participation (Walker 1996).

Recognize political and legal realities. If consultation involves a federally recognized Indian tribe, it's important to make sure that it constitutes—or is preceded by—government-to-government consultation between the tribal government and the agency. In other words, don't expect the agency's consultant to be able to waltz in and start consulting with tribal elders before an appropriate line officer in the agency has consulted with the tribal government.

In the government context, recognize that negotiators may be constrained by positions taken by their superiors. On the other hand, don't take these kinds of constraints at face value. When the Corps of Engineers cultural resource manager says: "My colonel has instructed me not to consider that idea," it is perfectly within reason to suggest that this is a damned counterproductive position for the Corps to take, and if it wants to have a reasonable consultation, the colonel ought to rethink his position—and then to go on and discuss the idea while the Corps representative sits on his hands.

And recognize that there are legal limits on the authority an agency can grant to a group of consulting parties, and rules of the game that the group must follow. Under the Federal Advisory Committee Act of 1972 (FACA), an agency decision maker cannot give over his or her decision-making authority to an outside advisory group—the group must be advisory only. Under the same statute there are definite limits to how closed the meetings of such a group may be. However sensitive the issues to be discussed, however much the group may need to reason together in private, its meetings may have to be open to the public. Under FACA, in fact, the very formation of an advisory group is fraught with complexity, all to keep special interests from having undue back-door influence on federal decisions. Here is a place where, if you're representing a federal agency, you're going to *need* to talk with your lawyers. But tell them what you want to do, and don't take "no" for an answer without an explanation of *why* it has to be "no."

What's the Result of Consultation?

Consultation under Section 106 results in one of three things: agreement, termination, or project abandonment. The last option is never mentioned in the regulation, but it's always a possibility, and probably happens more often than people think. Some projects just aren't really very good ideas, and when confronted with problems, their proponents abandon them. But assuming the project's not abandoned, adverse effects end up being "resolved" either under a Memorandum of Agreement or after termination and issuance of ACHP comment.

Memorandum of Agreement

What an MOA Looks Like

Appendix IV is a model Memorandum of Agreement (MOA) for a hypothetical project. There's no particular magic to the format, but there is a logic to it.

The Title. The title should be designed to give the "cold reader" an immediate fix on what the agreement's about. It needs to contain the name of the action and the key players.

The "Whereas" Clauses. These clauses spell out the rationale for the agreement, and outline relevant actions that have led up to it, data supporting it, and so forth.

The Stipulations. These detail what will actually be done to resolve the adverse effect, who will do each thing, when, what standards will be employed, and so forth.

The Signature blocks. Signatures in these blocks represent agreement by the signatories and concurring parties.

Appendices. Appendices are often attached, providing things like detailed plans, standards to be followed, exceptions to standard practices, and systems for monitoring performance.

Heloise's Helpful Hints for MOA Writing

Writing MOAs and similar documents is an art in itself, and is the primary subject of a companion volume to this one, so in the interests of not undercutting my own sales, I won't go into detail here about how it's done. But I can offer a few basic suggestions.

VAUGHN'S FIVE Ws

Charlene Dwin Vaughn of the ACHP has outlined five "Ws" that should be represented in every MOA (Vaughn 1996), which I've paraphrased here:

What action is being proposed as a provision to mitigate or avoid adverse effects? Is it clearly described so that one does not need to interpret or "second guess" the intent?

Why: What is the purpose of the provision? Does it mitigate or minimize adverse effects?

Where will the proposed mitigation occur? Is the property to be affected identified by address, building type, archeological site designation, location within the APE, etc.?

Who has responsibility for implementing the provision, and are they to carry out the provision in consultation with any other parties? Does the agency or community have to obtain approvals from others before the provision is finalized or implemented?

When in project planning is the provision to be implemented? How long does the agency or community have to complete the terms of the provision?

If you're drafting an MOA, you ought to make sure that these questions are all answered in, or reasonably answerable from, the "Whereas" clauses, the stipulations, and the appendices.

There are a number of more specific things you should also keep in mind; these are derived largely from ACHP training material (cf. ACHP et al. 1996).

Remember the "cold reader." Don't forget that your MOA will probably be read and interpreted by people other than those who negotiate and draft it—by project managers, engineers, lawyers, judges. Write for them, not for yourself. Get a cold reader to review it; toss it over the partition to the wildlife biologist, hand it to your mother or your son.

Say what you mean, not what you think is "standard," or "acceptable." When I review an MOA and find some incomprehensible, pointless, counter-productive provision, and ask why it's there, it's not uncommon to learn that it's included because it's understood to be a "standard clause," or "something the ACHP wants to see." Nonsense. Include what's sensible, not what people want to see—unless, of course, there's a good reason for their wanting to see it.

Include all agreed-upon provisions. It is astounding how often something that's been agreed to—often a key thing—somehow just doesn't get included in the MOA. I got a call once from a federal cultural resource manager who wanted to know how he could get his agency not to renege on a promise to fund reburial of human remains from a Native American cemetery.

"What did they agree to do in the MOA?" I asked.

"Well, er, nothing," he said; *"it was a kind of side agreement with the SHPO."*

I imagine the bones are still kicking around a lab someplace.

Don't be too subtle. Say what's meant, what's agreed to, as directly and clearly as possible. I once drafted an MOA for a reservoir project where there was an important prehistoric rock art site next to where the dam will be. Everybody agreed that the proponent agency would take care of this site by funding construction of an interpretive center that would guide visitors around it and encourage them to take good care of it. But we weren't sure how the people higher up in the agency's organization, other than its archeologist who negotiated the agreement, would react to the idea, so we tried to slide the commitment past them by putting it in ambiguous language. The agency would "provide interpretive facilities," or words to that effect. Stupid. Policy at the agency changed, and management decided It wouldn't fund the interpretive center. "But the MOA says..." we argued. "Where?" asked management. "We figure our interpretive facility will be a sign and a brochure."

Check with a lawyer. Unless you have an unusually well-educated and thoughtful lawyer, to say nothing of one with the time to do it, don't ask your lawyer to write the MOA. If you ever see a product, it may well be indecipherable. But be sure to have one check it. A lawyer is like an auto mechanic; he or she can spot things that will be troublesome before they catch you on a snow-covered mountain pass.

Identify the undertaking clearly. Earlier, I've mentioned the African Burial Ground in New York City. When GSA and the ACHP drafted the MOA on the project that ultimately unearthed the Burial Ground (the SHPO, sensibly, withdrew from consultation because the MOA was so terrible), they simply referred to it as "the Foley Square Project." But the Foley Square Project involved construction on two separate city blocks—the "Courthouse Block" adjacent to the existing, historic federal courthouse, and the "Broadway Block" on (yes) Broadway. The MOA dealt almost exclusively with how visual and other impacts on the Courthouse would be dealt with; there was a sort of throw-away stipulation about archeology. When the Burial Ground emerged, the ACHP claimed that GSA didn't have an MOA covering it—hadn't complied with Section 106. "Sure we have," said GSA, "here's our MOA on Foley Square." "Yeah," said the ACHP, "but the Foley Square Project is construction on the Courthouse Block." *"Au contraire,"* said GSA, "it's construction on both blocks." "Sez you," rejoined the ACHP; "we don't see anything about the Broadway Block in this MOA." Eventually there had to be a new MOA, identifying the undertaking precisely, with reference to a detailed description. Much time and trouble would have been saved if the original MOA had done the same thing.

Assign duties only to signatory and concurring parties. So you plan to have the Washafornia State Museum take care of the artifacts from the data recovery project. Fine, but don't stipulate that it will do so unless the WSM has agreed to it, and either concurs in the MOA or signs some other agreement you can cite. You can't bind somebody who doesn't sign the agreement.

Where one of the parties has coercive authority over another party—for example, where FHWA holds the pursestrings on the Washafornia Department of Transportation, or the Corps of Engineers can issue or withhold a Section 404 permit, then you can stipulate that the coercive party will ensure that the coerced party will do what the MOA says. But even in this case it's a whole lot more congenial, and productive of long-term cooperation, if the coerced agrees to the MOA's terms.

Always provide a means of monitoring performance, and make these as explicit as possible. Standard language is available for this from GSA's "Environmental Call-In" web site, and I recommend it. Establish an annual, or periodic, review schedule, under which on a specified date the responsible agency will provide the other parties with a report on how things are coming along. The parties can then review the report and decide whether anything needs to be changed. If you don't provide for something like this, that enables the SHPO, THPO, ACHP, or other parties to say: "Hey, it's April 1st, where's your report?" it's easy for the MOA to get filed and forgotten, or for implementation of its terms to drift way off track without being caught. And this kind of drift can go in a number of different ways. I've seen situations where agencies wound up doing *more* than they'd agreed to, because everybody sort of lost track of what they were doing.

Old Guides and New

One of my last jobs at the ACHP in the late 1980s was to draft a publication called *Preparing Agreement Documents* (ACHP 1988). *PAD* laid out guidelines (some of them mentioned above) for agreement document writing, and provided standard-language stipulations. A lot of people still have and use *PAD*, but I don't recommend it. A lot has been learned since 1988, and a lot has changed. For example, we've learned that the provisions for periodic performance monitoring in *PAD* don't work. And NAGPRA's been enacted, making a lot of *PAD's* standard language about treatment of human remains irrelevant for projects on federal or Indian land. The ACHP and University of Nevada, Reno now have a class on agreement document writing, as does the National Preservation Institute. Until the companion volume to this book comes out, I recommend their syllabi in lieu of *PAD* (ACHP et al. 1996; NPI 1998). The appendices to these syllabi, which provide the standard formats and content for MOAs and their ilk, can be downloaded from GSA's Environmental Call-In worldwide web site (www.gsa.gov/pbs/pt/call-in/nepa.htm).

Termination and Comment

If an MOA isn't achieved—that is, if the agency, SHPO, or ACHP (or tribe in some cases) terminates consultation in accordance with the regulations—then the

ACHP renders a "comment" to the agency. The regulation goes into some detail about the termination process, but we don't need to here; it doesn't happen often, and in principle the same thing happens however it's done. Most historic preservationist practitioners go through life without ever having to deal with a termination and comment; if you have to, you can read the regulation.

What the regulation doesn't say is how ACHP comment is rendered. In fact, it's important to understand that the rendering of ACHP comment is not a staff function. Or more accurately, if it is carried out by staff, it's done with a lot of oversight by the Council itself—that is, by the 20-member panel of presidential appointees, agency heads, and others that comprises the actual Advisory Council on Historic Preservation. The comment may take the form of a letter signed by the chair, or it may be developed by a panel of Council members, or by the full Council sitting in review. Depending on the case (usually depending on its political visibility), the Council may hold public meetings, on-site inspections, and other information gathering or deliberative activities. The agency must assist the Council in carrying these out. However it's done, under the draft 1998 regulation the comment has to be rendered within 45 days after termination, unless the agency agrees to a different timetable. Under the 1986 regulation it's 60 days.

Under Section 110(l) of NHPA, the comment goes to the agency head. In other words, if the project is a highway, the comment goes to the Secretary of Transportation or the Administrator of FHWA—not to the regional FHWA staff or the state DOT that's really responsible for the project. If it's an NPS project it goes to the Secretary of the Interior or the Director of NPS. If it's a HUD project it goes to the Secretary of HUD, unless it's one where HUD has legally delegated its responsibilities to the local government, in which case it goes to the head of the local government. Also under Section 110(l), the recipient—the agency head—must document whatever decision is made (if any) once the comments have been considered, and he or she can't delegate this responsibility. Presumably the prohibition on delegation doesn't mean that the Secretary of Defense has to sit down at his or her own word processor and bang out a response to ACHP comments on an Army project, but it does mean that the responsibility can't just pass down the chain of command to the base commander. The Secretary has to be personally involved, and this involvement may have career implications for those responsible.

What does the agency have to do in response to the ACHP's comment? Nothing, other than to document its decision by preparing a summary of its rationale documenting consideration of the ACHP's comment, providing a copy of this documentation to the consulting parties, and making it available to the public.

People are sometimes surprised when they learn that, in the final analysis, the Advisory Council really is advisory; that its only ultimate authority under Section 106 is to render those comments that the agency is required to afford it the opportunity to provide. Citing this limited authority, some preservationists—

and some project proponents, for that matter, who are used to the more dictatorial powers of, say the Environmental Protection Agency under the Clean Air Act or the Corps of Engineers under the Clean Water Act—dismiss the ACHP, and the Section 106 process, as paper tigers. I don't think this is either reasonable or accurate. It's not reasonable because one has to understand that in creating Section 106, Congress didn't mean to make historic preservation superior to all other public interests; it merely meant to ensure that preservation concerns were duly weighed and balanced with other interests. It's not accurate because in fact few projects wind up going to the ACHP for comment; the great majority are worked through to agreement. Particularly since Section 110(l) was added in 1992, ensuring high-level consideration of ACHP comment, with a predictable trickle-down effect on those responsible for the action, agencies are reluctant to terminate consultation, so in the great majority of cases the process does result in agreement. Whether the agreements are good agreements is, of course, another matter.

Resolving the G-O Road's Effects

The Forest Service acknowledged that building through the Helkau Historic District would have an adverse effect on it. It proposed to mitigate this effect in three ways. First, it would place the road in such a way that it didn't take out any prayer seats or other specific locations where people carried out spiritual activities. Second, it would keep the shoulders of the road narrow, so people wouldn't be able to park and hop out to watch the funny Indians carrying out their rituals. Third, it would color the pavement brown to blend in with its surroundings.

The tribes pointed out that the Forest Service was, in effect, proposing to drive a road down the aisle of their cathedral, and allow 18-wheelers to rumble along it loaded with logs. Avoiding the pews on either side, coloring the road to match the floor, and keeping people from stopping as they trundled through didn't exactly take care of the project's effects. The SHPO and ACHP agreed with the tribes, and argued for a more drastic solution—rerouting the road altogether.

The Forest Service terminated consultation and the matter was referred to the ACHP. The ACHP's comment proposed that the Forest Service abandon several miles of the road and reroute it along another set of ridges, removing it not only from the Historic District but from its viewshed.

The Forest Service thanked the ACHP for its comment and decided to proceed as it had proposed, with the mitigation measures it had proposed. The tribes then took the Forest Service to court, charging violation of Section 106, NEPA, and other laws.

Discussion Question: What do you suppose the ACHP's position was on the Forest Service's compliance with Section 106? What do you suppose the court decided?

What's Usually Done to Resolve Adverse Effects?

What can the consulting parties agree to as ways to resolve adverse effects? Pretty much anything they want to, as long as it's legal.

What's Legal?

Is it legal to destroy a historic property? Absolutely, as far as federal law is concerned. It's not legal to destroy it without considering the matter—that's what Section 106 requires, and of course the way you consider it is by following the process set forth in 36 CFR 800. But once you've done that, you can destroy the property, subject to whatever agreement is reached under Section 106—and subject to any other legal authorities that apply.

Such legal authorities *do* exist, and constrain the flexibility of the Section 106 consulting parties a bit, determining some of the things that are characteristically agreed upon as revolvers of adverse effect.

Under Section 110(b) of NHPA, an agency can't destroy or damage a historic property, or assist anyone else in doing so, without first documenting the property. So at a bare minimum, an MOA has to provide for documentation. What kind of documentation, the level of documentation, and where the documentation ends up are all up to the Section 106 consulting parties. The legislative history of Section 110(b) makes it clear that the documentation to be done is whatever's appropriate to the type of property—it can be architectural or engineering drawings, historical research, oral historical research, archeological data recovery—whatever is appropriate. The level of documentation can range anywhere from super-detailed architectural drawings on acid-free paper and multi-volume archeological reports, to crayon sketches and polaroid snapshots—though I don't know of a case where the latter kind of documentation has been agreed to. Consulting parties *have* agreed to documentation in the form of videotapes, CD-ROMs, popular publications, and electronic databases. The only more or less absolute standard is that if the property to be damaged is a National Historic Landmark, then the NPS guidelines for Section 110 implementation as issued in 1988 (NPS 1988) specify that the standards of the Historic American Buildings Survey/Historic American Engineering Record (HABS/HAER) must be met, and that the results must be filed with the Library of Congress. However, the revised Section 110 guidelines issued by NPS in 1998 don't even deal with Section 110(b) (NPS 1998), so even this rule is rather up in the air.

If the MOA deals with archeological resources on federal or Indian lands, then standards that flow from the Archeological Resources Protection Act (ARPA; see below) must be met. This generally means that data recovery must be professionally supervised, follow an adequate research design, and the resulting information and material must be "curated" in accordance with pertinent regulations (36 CFR 79; see below). So you can't provide for an archeological site on federal or Indian land to be dug up by the local chapter of the Amalgamated

Graverobbers of America, with artifacts to be sold on the open market (some of us find this a bit restrictive, but there you are).

If the effects will occur on federal or Indian lands, then Native American ancestral remains and cultural items have to be dealt with in accordance with the Native American Graves Protection and Repatriation Act (NAGPRA; see below), and its implementing regulations (43 CFR 10). These require development and implementation of a "plan of action" (POA; see below) whose terms should be consistent with those of the Section 106 MOA—and the MOA must be consistent with the POA. You don't want to say in your POA that everything will be given back to Tribe X, and then in your MOA say that everything will go to the state museum.

What's Possible?

Beyond what's legally required or prohibited, anything goes, provided you don't stipulate murder, treason, environmental degradation, or some other illegal or manifestly offensive act. Some things that have been agreed to in MOAs include:

- Restoration or rehabilitation and adaptive use of buildings and structures

- Demolition and removal of properties that don't contribute to the historic or architectural significance of an area

- Transfers of development rights

- Redesign of projects to preserve specific properties, vistas, access points, landscapes, neighborhoods

- Relocation of buildings and structures

- Implementation of maintenance plans

- Design of projects like power lines to merge with the landscape and reduce visual effects

- Transfer of historic lands to Indian tribes, local governments, non-profit organizations

- Donation of easements on landscapes, facades, buildings, structures, and sites

- Development and implementation of community, neighborhood, and regional plans

- Creation of historic preservation revolving funds, or funds to support specific preservation-related purposes

- Establishment of design review procedures and groups to implement them

- Construction of museums, cultural centers, and curatorial facilities

- Installation and maintenance of interpretive facilities

- Public participation and education programs

- Intentional neglect and monitored deterioration

- Burial of archeological sites

- Creation of managed open space

- Visitor information facilities

Really, what the consulting parties can agree to is limited largely by their collective imagination. One MOA I wrote regarding impacts of a U.S. courthouse expansion on adjacent historic residential districts provided for the control of lawyers—to the extent of providing professional users of the courthouse with a brochure describing the historic and architectural qualities of the districts and encouraging the use of appropriate designs for converting residential buildings to law offices. Another provided for moving dozens of houses in a National Historic Landmark historic district to make way for an expressway expansion, and for donating them to the local public housing authority, which agreed to rehabilitate them and relocate them to vacant sites where they would stabilize the deteriorating district. There's no end to the possibilities.

What's Reasonable? Anzalone's Adages

It is possible, of course, for one or more of the consulting parties to go crazy and demand things that are completely off the wall. You need to remember that you're trying to mitigate impacts in the public interest, not to make points, punish your opponents, or throw your weight around. Ronald Anzalone of the ACHP has outlined some rules of thumb for judging whether what you're proposing is reasonable in terms of public benefit (Anzalone 1995).

Standard 1: Apply a combination of common sense, professional judgement, and civic responsibility.

Guideline: Sell the idea to yourself as if you were an intelligent, concerned, informed citizen (which *hopefully* you are!).

Standard 2: *Reject silly mitigation; subject all proposals to the "laugh test."*

Guideline: "...the American people are a very generous people and will forgive almost any weakness, with the possible exception of stupidity."
—Will Rogers, 1924

Standard 3: *Reject useless mitigation.*

Guideline: Understand what is *required* as well as the flexible application of such requirements, but do not propose or accept mitigating measures just to have some if there is no particular purpose served.

Standard 4: *Understand, explain, and justify mitigation.*

Guideline: Be prepared to try to explain your position and justify the expenditure of time, money, and other resources to—
  a) a spouse or close friend who's not "in the business;"
  b) your parents;
  c) Mike Wallace.

What's Required?

Anzalone mentioned "what's required," and one of the most frequent questions by people who are being asked to pay the bill is precisely that: "What *is* required?" The answer is pretty simple: not much. An MOA has to provide for documentation, because that's required by Section 110(b), but the kind of documentation it provides for is up to the consulting parties. It has to accommodate the terms of a NAGPRA POA if there may be Native American graves or cultural items involved on federal or Indian lands. Beyond these, there aren't any explicit requirements.

However, there are some general directions to guide the MOA negotiators. Section 110(d) of NHPA says that agencies are to conduct their affairs, to the extent compatible with their missions, in ways consistent with the purposes of the statute, and consider ways to advance those purposes. The purposes of NHPA are set forth largely in Section 2 (16 U.S.C. 470-1), in a statement of national policy. Some of the policies that are particularly germane to the content of MOAs are:

...to foster conditions under which our modern society and our prehistoric and historic resources can exist in productive harmony and fulfill the social, economic, and other requirements of present and future generations.

(to) provide leadership in the preservation of...prehistoric and historic resources...

(to) administer federally owned, administered, or controlled prehistoric and historic resources in a spirit of stewardship...

(to) contribute to the preservation of nonfederally owned prehistoric and historic resources and give maximum encouragement to organizations and individuals undertaking preservation by private means...

(to) encourage the public and private preservation and utilization of all usable elements of the Nation's historic built environment.

OK, all motherhood and apple pie, but if federal agencies are supposed to carry out their activities in a manner consistent with these policies, then these policies surely ought to be reflected in the MOAs they negotiate. So it's "required" that MOAs make some effort to foster conditions of productive harmony between historic resources and the modern world, provide for stewardship of federally owned resources, and so on. NEPA and other authorities point us in the same direction. In a nutshell, "taking effects into account" as Section 106 requires doesn't mean just saying "lookee there, we're knocking down that old building," it means considering and, if feasible, adopting means of treating historic properties in positive ways, or mitigating adverse effects on them. That's the overall "requirement." How the consulting parties on an MOA meet this requirement—depends.

Coordination with NEPA

Figure 8 shows the preferred way to coordinate Section 106 review with NEPA. Scoping is coordinated with scoping, identification, evaluation, and initial effect determination are coordinated with EA or DEIS preparation, and consultation to resolve adverse effects takes place as needed before the EA or EIS is finalized and the FONSI or ROD is issued. This way the public can be fully informed about the results of Section 106 review through its review of draft NEPA material, and the consulting parties under Section 106 can be fully informed of public views obtained by the agency through the NEPA process. Everything moves along smoothly, there's no redundancy, nothing falling through the cracks...

Of course, it doesn't always work this way. At least as often as not, the agency, or the SHPO, or the ACHP, or all concerned understand Section 106 to require such detailed information on properties and effects that it can't possibly be gathered when NEPA review is being done on a project's multiple alternatives. So Section 106 review gets put off until after a preferred alternative has been selected—even after the ROD's been issued or, even more dangerous,

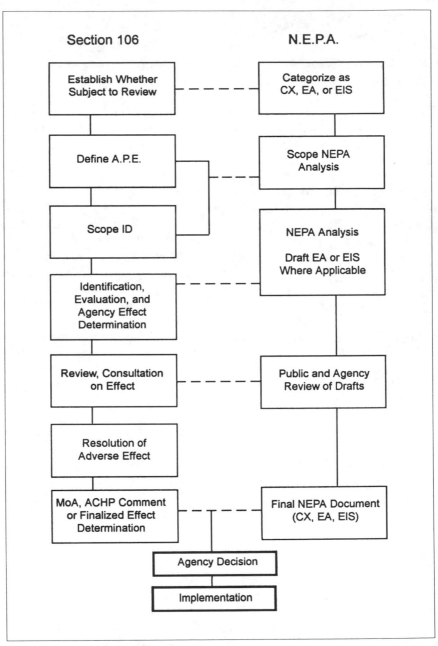

Figure 8. Coordinating Section 106 and NEPA.

the FONSI's been signed, specifying that there will be no significant impact when impacts on historic properties haven't even been determined. Obviously that's not what should be done, but as long as the identification, eligibility determination, and effect determination steps in Section 106 review seem to require so much highly detailed information, it's probably the way it's going to continue.

Discoveries

So, you've completed your Section 106 review, you've done, or are doing, whatever your MOA calls for (or maybe you've found that there are no historic properties subject to effect, or no adverse effect), and all of a sudden you run into something you hadn't bargained for. What do you do?

Anticipation

Let's begin by saying that you shouldn't encounter something you hadn't bargained for. During your Section 106 consultation and your NEPA analysis you ought to think about what might pop up, and bargain for it—develop procedures for dealing with it, and put these procedures in your MOA or whatever other agreement document you prepare. The regulation—both in its 1986 version and its 1998 draft strongly encourages this.

NAGPRA

The second thing to highlight is that if you're operating on federal or Indian land, and what you encounter is something that may be human remains or a Native American cultural item as defined by the Native American Graves Protection and Repatriation Act (NAGPRA, see below), then you have separate and distinct responsibilities under that statute and its implementing regulations. If you've really done your job right, you have a "Plan of Action" for dealing with such discoveries, and you can follow it. If you don't, you're going to need to stop what you're doing and open up consultation with relevant tribes, per the NAGPRA regulations.

No Plan, No NAGPRA

Let's suppose you don't have a pre-developed plan embodied in an MOA or something, and NAGPRA doesn't apply—say your project isn't on federal land, or the discovery has no chance of being related to an Indian tribe or Native Hawaiian group.

The 1986 Section 106 regulation was fairly straightforward about discovery situations. As is its wont, the draft 1998 draft complicates things a good deal.

Under the draft, if the undertaking hasn't been approved or if construction hasn't started, you go back and consult in the standard manner, to arrive at an MOA or obtain ACHP comment.

If the agency, SHPO or THPO, and any tribe or Native Hawaiian group that attaches significance to the discovery agree that the thing discovered is of value only for its "scientific, prehistoric, historic or archeological data," the subjects of the Archeological Data Preservation Act of 1974 (ADPA), then you can comply with that act in lieu of re-doing Section 106 review. This means, in effect, that you can conduct data recovery or get NPS to do so, paying them for the work, of course. But before you can do this, under the 1986 draft you have to consult with everybody listed above and get their agreement—a time-consuming business.

The third option—which is available under the 1986 regulation with rather fewer bells and whistles, and has been and doubtless will be the most often used—is for the agency simply to decide what it can do to resolve adverse effects, and notify the SHPO or THPO, tribe or Native Hawaiian group, and ACHP within 48 hours after the discovery. Those notified have 48 hours to respond, the agency takes the responses into account, and it implements whatever it decides to do.

So—you rip the aluminum siding off the undistinguished-seeming oldish building that you're about to demolish to expand the expressway, and find that it's Daniel Boone's log cabin. You've completed Section 106 review and have an MOA that doesn't deal with the building because nobody thought it was historic. What do you do?

You probably won't be able to get agreement that the cabin should be treated under ADPA, so you'll probably come up with your own proposal. You propose, let's say, to document the cabin and move it to the local city park where it can be restored and interpreted. You whip this plan out within 48 hours (during which time the draft regulation requires you to "make reasonable efforts to avoid, minimize or mitigate adverse effects"), and notify the SHPO and ACHP. If you're smart you'll notify other concerned parties, too, but the regulation doesn't require this except in the case of concerned Indian tribes and Native Hawaiian groups (we *can* imagine reasons why a tribe might be interested in Boone's cabin, [so] but let's assume they aren't).

The SHPO comes back within 48 hours and says "We think you ought to relocate the highway." The ACHP doesn't respond. At this point your agency can say: "Thank you very much, Ms. SHPO, but we're going to do what we planned to do in the first place." Or it can accede to the SHPO's direction, or it can negotiate. It's up to the agency, and if the agency so decides, it can move forward pretty promptly.

Of course, at this point you might have a lawyer for the Greater Appalachia Daughters of Dan'l' or the Tribes United to Destroy Evidence of Oppression knocking at your door pointing out that since you were only preparing the right-of-way, and construction had not really commenced, the regulation doesn't allow you to use the 48-hour provision, and you've got to go back into standard Section 106 consultation and address their concerns. There are some ambiguities in the language of the 1998 draft regulation that may or may not be resolved by the time this book is published; suffice to say that there may wind up being limitations on how broadly the discovery provisions can be invoked.

Incidentally, under the discovery provisions the agency can assume that a newly discovered property is eligible for the National Register without consulting anyone, though for obscure reasons under the 1998 draft it has to specify (to whom is not indicated) the National Register Criteria under which the property is assumed to be eligible.

NAGPRA Again

If you have the kind of situation we've just discussed, but NAGPRA does apply, then you have to do what's outlined above, but you need to coordinate it with NAGPRA compliance.

If 106 Has Not Been Completed...

The discovery provisions are not a substitute for regular Section 106 review. They can be invoked only for discoveries that occur after review has been completed. If you haven't done Section 106 and you discover something, you are way up a creek, and the only way you can legally paddle back down is by going through the full, regular 106 process.

Emergencies

If you're an agency that's likely to have to deal with emergencies, the regulation (and good sense) encourage you to develop procedures for dealing with their historic preservation implications. You're to do this in consultation with all the usual suspects, and the procedures have to be approved by the ACHP and/or embedded in a Programmatic Agreement (see below).

If you don't have procedures in place, and you're confronted with the need for an immediate response to a disaster or emergency declared by the president, a tribal government, or the governor of a state, then you're supposed to contact all the usual consulting parties and give them seven days to comment, if the agency official determines that this is feasible; if not, comment is to be invited during whatever time is available. These provisions are applicable only to actions taken within 30 days after the disaster or emergency has been declared.

Interestingly, the regulation in its 1998 iteration doesn't provide for the agency to do anything substantive at all. There's probably the assumption that the agency is going to do what it can to take care of historic properties, but there's no explicit requirement to this effect. The other serious problem with the emergency provision in the draft—and in the 1986 regulation—is that it doesn't apply to the run-of-the-mill, garden-variety emergencies that agencies deal with all the time. The bridge that's about to wash out, or the toxic waste spill—not declared an emergency by the president or governor, but demanding immediate action nonetheless. In what may be an attempt to deal with this, the 1998 regulation says that immediate rescue and salvage operations to preserve life or property are exempt from Section 106, but this seems likely to cause more problems than it will solve. The ACHP seems to be taking it upon itself to exempt agencies from an act of Congress—a dicey thing to do. Furthermore, the loophole it's creating seems like a big one, but of the wrong shape to accommodate most routine emergency situations. We'll see how it works.

Alternatives to the Standard Process

The 1998 draft regulation identifies several kinds of alternatives to the standard Section 106 review process—agency-wide program alternatives, exemptions, standard treatments to be described by the ACHP. Most of these are new and untried, and there's not much point in trying to discuss them now. In a few years we can see how they've shaken down. One alternative approach has been extensively tested, however, and merits a little discussion: the Programmatic Agreement (PA).

Programmatic Agreements

You're an official of the U.S. Bureau of Good Works, and Congress authorizes you to provide grants to orphanages for the repair of their buildings. The grants are to be awarded through State Good Works agencies, which will decide upon exactly which orphanages will get fixed up. Given that by the time it's known which buildings will be affected, you, the federal agency, will no longer be involved in the grants process (having turned the money over to the state), and given that most of the repairs will be pretty small-scale operations, how do you comply with Section 106?

You're a federal official responsible for the newly established kudzu eradication program, which is going to hire unemployed and homeless people throughout the South to dig up and burn the noxious plant that has been consuming the area since it was introduced some decades ago to control erosion. Your program may cause some rather surficial damage to archeological sites, but doesn't have much other impact potential. You have to maintain a high level of flexibility in deploying your forces, based on the level of unemployment and homelessness in different regions on a month-to-month basis. How do you comply with Section 106?

You're the Federal Alternative Power Authority, and you're reviewing a request by Sunshine Superco to license a solar power plant in Maine. The venture capital to support the project—including things like detailed historic property identification—won't be advanced by Sunshine's backers until it has all its federal licenses in hand. How can you comply with Section 106 without requiring the company to do studies without the money in hand to do them?

You're the Economic Development Officer for the City of East Westerly, and you've got Community Development Block Grant (CDBG) funds to support low-income housing rehabilitation throughout the city. HUD has delegated its Section 106 responsibilities to you. The program will involve dozens of small–scale rehab projects each year, each of which will be reviewed by the City Historical Architect. Standard Section 106 review seems unduly costly and pointless. But you've got to comply, so how do you do it?

These are the kinds of situations in which a Programmatic Agreement (PA) is appropriate. They're situations in which the standard Section 106 process just can't be done in a way that's responsibly coordinated with implementation of the program.

Under such a circumstance, the responsible agency (or local government, in the case of a CDBG program), the ACHP, some representative of SHPO-ness, and (in theory) other interested parties, including Indian tribes and Native Hawaiian organizations, sit down and try to work out an alternative way of meeting the basic requirements of Section 106 and other pertinent authorities. This alternative is embodied in a PA, which is signed by all the parties and then governs how the project is done.

I said that some representative of SHPO-ness has to be involved. That representative will be the SHPO if the action takes place in a particular state, a group of SHPOs if several states are involved, or the National Conference of SHPOs if the PA will have national effect. Some SHPOs claim not to be represented by the National Conference, and therefore argue that a PA executed by the Conference is not applicable in their states. This is a myth. SHPO participation in PA development, execution, and implementation is an artifact of the regulations, not a matter of right. The regulation says that the National Conference is the SHPO representative in nationwide PA matters, and that's simply the way it is, however much an individual SHPO may not like it.

PAs are negotiated and executed very much like MOAs—except that the ACHP must always be involved in consultation—and are subject to the same kinds of drafting principles. For more information than you'll ever want on PAs, see the "advanced" companion to this textbook. In brief, though, let's consider what kinds of alternatives we might set out under PAs for the four actions described above.

For the orphanage grants program, we might provide for the federal agency to delegate its Section 106 responsibilities to the state, which would then follow 36 CFR 800. We might exempt certain actions from review altogether, if they were thought unlikely to do damage. We might provide for expedited review of others, perhaps involving local preservation agencies. We might provide for those doing the projects to be trained in applying the *Secretary of the Interior's Standards for Rehabilitation*.

For the kudzu eradication program, we might provide for the eradicators to be trained in the identification of archeological sites, and for quick recordation and data recovery whenever one was found.

For the power project, we might have FAPA use background data and predictions about historic property distributions, developed as part of its NEPA review, in making its license decision, but defer detailed survey, evaluation, and treatment plan development until after the license is issued.

For the CDBG program, we'd almost certainly execute a very standard kind of PA, versions of which are working successfully in hundreds of cities, under which projects would require no review beyond that performed by the City Architectural Historian as long as the *Secretary of the Interior's Standards for Rehabilitation* were met.

Of course, there are pros and cons to all these kinds of options, and they would be the subjects of lively debate in PA consultation. What would finally be adopted would—what a surprise—depend on what the parties were willing to agree to.

Failure to reach agreement on a PA, unlike failure to reach agreement on an MOA, does not send the agency to get a final ACHP comment; nor does termination of a PA have that consequence. Instead, the agency must comply with the standard Section 106 process on individual actions under the program—individual orphanage rehabs, individual kudzu kleanups. No one really knows how one would do this under a program for which compliance with the standard process on individual actions didn't make sense in the first place.

Myths and Recommendations

For details on the pros and cons of PA development, and on how to develop one, see the advanced companion to this book, or take appropriate training. There's space here, though, to debunk a couple of widespread myths and offer a couple of recommendations.

MYTHS

It seems to be assumed in some quarters—though I've never had anybody explicitly state it—that a PA must more or less parrot or paraphrase the standard Section 106 process. This is nonsense. There's no point in a parrot PA; if the standard process works for you, why prepare an alternative? And paraphrasing not only is wasteful, it's dangerous, because when you start changing words without the intent to change meaning, you run the risk of doing the latter inadvertently—or at least tempt people to think that you *did* mean to do the latter. If you're drafting a PA and find it sounding a lot like the standard process, stop and think: do I really need this?

Some SHPOs and ACHP staff have suggested that an agency doesn't "deserve" a PA until it has shown that it can handle the standard Section 106 process. This is pretty silly; if the agency can handle the standard process, it probably doesn't need a PA. Conversely, the fact that it doesn't handle the standard process well may not mean that its officials are inherently evil, or stupid, it may just mean that the standard process doesn't work very well for their programs—the precise reason for doing a PA.

Some agencies seem to have concluded that a PA is always a good thing; PAs in some quarters have become faddish. Be careful about this. There's nothing in law saying you *have* to have a PA, and you ought to go to the trouble of doing one only if there's some value in it.

RECOMMENDATIONS

Be very careful about essaying development of a PA. Remember that it substitutes for the regulation; once it's in place, the regulation no longer applies, except to the extent the PA includes it by reference. So you're very likely inventing a whole new Section 106 process for your program. Be sure you're up to the challenge.

Don't make the PA more complicated than it needs to be. Perhaps the most common problem I've seen in PAs I've reviewed lies in getting carried away. What's needed may be some small surgical adjustment in the standard process—simplifying review of a class of actions that follows particular standards, assuming the eligibility of a given class of properties and getting on with determining how to deal with them—and people tie themselves into knots trying to redesign the universe around these minor adjustments. In most cases you're trying to *simplify* your compliance; don't make it more complicated.

Always, always, *always* provide for periodic reporting, monitoring, opportunities for course corrections. Your PA is going to be in place for awhile—often indefinitely—and you need to make sure that it works, and is responsive to changing conditions.

Guard against misinterpretation. Make the document as clear and understandable as possible, and provide ways for people to be reminded of (a) its existence, and (b) how to interpret it. A training component is often appropriate, and so may be some sort of provision for briefing new personnel—for example new commanding officers on a military installation where a PA guides planning.

Don't just follow an example. The fact that a PA was signed on somebody else's program doesn't mean that it's a good model for yours. We learn more about what works and what doesn't all the time, so an older PA is almost certainly inadequate by today's standards. And the circumstances that motivate agencies to develop PAs are unique; you can't easily apply a system that's appropriate in one case to another. Finally, PAs may be accepted when they're not especially good, and then they become enshrined in folklore as "successful" and people start using them as models. A classic example is a very complicated PA developed by the Forest Service to cover salvage logging after forest fires in California in the mid-1980s. The ACHP signed onto it with major misgivings, based on the Forest Service's assurance that it was something that would really work. It didn't. It was so complicated, so convoluted, that only one Forest ended up being able to follow it; the others stuck with the standard process. But the PA, having been signed, was assumed to have been successful, so when Hurricane Hugo downed a great deal of timber in South Carolina awhile later, the Forest Service there adopted it as a model. For reasons not entirely clear, the ACHP again signed off, but as far as I know the arrangement didn't work any better in South Carolina than it had in California. But now having been "successful" on both sides of the continent, it was naturally adopted when timber borers attacked the Southwest. This time the ACHP rejected the draft, to the Forest Service's great dismay, judging it impossible to implement. When I reviewed the Southwestern iteration it I was astounded at its incomprehensibility, and asked what a number of its provisions meant. It soon became apparent that nobody had any idea, but everyone assumed that the PA was the thing to do, since similar documents had been "successful" elsewhere.

Before you even start on the PA, establish clearly what you're trying to accomplish. The more explicit you can be about your goals, the easier it will be to stay focused and get a good product.

On the other hand, think about what you're *not* trying to do that you nevertheless need to take into account—the things that may facilitate or frustrate your PA's implementation. Step back and look at the real-world operational context in which your PA is going to have to work, and think about related issues that you may need to address.

And generally, think ahead; try to anticipate issues and make sure they're resolved, that you're not shooting yourself or someone else in the foot. For example—and this illustrates not only the need to think beyond your immediate need but also something of how broad and flexible a PA can be—consider the "World War II Temporaries PA," also known as "the World's Largest Demo–Memo."

In the late 1980s Congress directed the Department of Defense to do away with all its World War II temporary buildings. The military services, of course, have a fair number of these buildings—thousands, in fact, and there was much head scratching about how to do Section 106 on their wholesale demolition. Eligibility was a particular problem, since the buildings were built to standard designs and it was pretty hard to figure out why one might be more significant than another. This was clearly a job for PA-Man.

I got to draft the PA, and was (and am, for that matter) rather proud of it. It was pretty simple. It glossed the question of eligibility, simply assuming that all the buildings might be eligible. It accepted the fact that they were coming down, sooner or later—being in theory "temporary" and in view of Congress' direction. It provided for DoD to sponsor a major study of the contribution of World War II temporary architecture to the architectural history of the United States, and to document buildings representative of various types and designs. DoD was also to advertise with veterans' groups and others to see if anybody had really strong feelings about preserving a particular building or building group, and to consider these desires in deciding which ones to demolish when. With those things done, the services could demolish World War II Temporaries at will.

Whether you like this result or not (as it turned out, the Gulf War mobilization greatly slowed the demolition, but eventually, no doubt, all the buildings will be gone), I think you'll have to grant that it was an elegant solution.

A few years went by, and then the Air Force asked Pat Parker, by now an executive in NPS, to be a judge in a competition for an Air Force preservation award. One of the strong candidates was an installation that had taken a World War II temporary building, moved it to an appropriate location, and rehabbed it to serve as a museum on women in the Air Force. Not wanting to vote for a project that might be out of compliance with Section 106, Pat asked me what I thought. "Not a problem," I said, "there's this PA…" and then I went and looked, and realized that the only thing the PA permitted without regular Section 106 review was *demolition*. A rehab project had to go through the standard process. So I'd neatly made it easier for a military service to knock down a historic building than to keep it up. Stupid, and the direct result of not thinking through all the ramifications of the issues I was trying to address in the PA. Try to be smarter than I was.

Pre-Emptive Destruction

"Well," says Farmer Brown, irritated by all this fuss over some old building or bunch of artifacts that stands in the way of her federally assisted stock pond, "I think I'll just crank up my bulldozer and solve my problem." Can she?

Anybody who can drive a bulldozer can bulldoze, of course, but Farmer Brown may be jeopardizing her federal grant if she knocks over the old house or roots up the site. Section 110(k) of NHPA says that:

> Each Federal agency shall ensure that the agency will not grant a loan, loan guarantee, permit, license, or other assistance to an applicant who, with intent to avoid the requirements of section 106, has intentionally significantly adversely affected a historic property to which the grant would relate… (16 U.S.C. 470h-2[k])

Section 110(k) goes on to allow such a grant to be provided only if the agency, after consulting the ACHP, determines that some sort of justifying circumstances exist. So it's not an absolute prohibition on giving Farmer Brown her grant, but there's likely to be a considerable delay, a lot of questions asked, and, unless Farmer Brown can offer some awfully good explanations or pull some well-connected strings, she's unlikely to get money from Uncle Sugar.

Of course, the trick is to show that Farmer Brown *intentionally* knocked over the building, *with intent to avoid the requirements of Section 106*. Doing so or failing to do so usually turns on whether one can demonstrate that she knew what those requirements were. If she did, and wasn't bulldozing in her sleep, one has to assume that she knew what she was doing, and did it to avoid the requirements that she knew would otherwise obtain.

Section 110(k) can be usefully used to prevent people from doing damage to historic places. An Indian tribe I know, concerned about the proposed logging of a spiritual place by a company that was going to be seeking a federal permit to mine in the same area, wrote the company and copied the world alleging that the place was eligible for the National Register, that therefore Section 106 would require consideration of impacts on it during the permit process, and that therefore if the place was logged, arguably destroying its significance, the permitting agency would be prohibited from granting the permit by Section 110(k). The warning seems to have worked; the logging didn't take place.

Some Conclusions About Section 106

We've spent a lot of pages discussing the Section 106 process. If it all seems to you that it's pretty complicated, perhaps confusing, likely to be unduly time-consuming, I think you're right.

A lot of other people do, too, but most agencies and practitioners seem to accept it as given that it's the way it's got to be. This has results that I think are unfortunate.

One problem is that because Section 106 review is too complicated to be easily done early in planning, agencies tend to disconnect Section 106 and NEPA review. They put off the former until the latter is well advanced or even completed. In a study that I supervised in 1994, which looked at a large sample of EISs, we found that about 42 percent deferred Section 106 review until later—presumably until after the decision was made about how to proceed and the Record of Decision (ROD) was issued (King and Rafuse 1994). They'd say things like "cultural resource studies are not yet complete, but impacts on cultural resources will be mitigated pursuant to Section 106"—after which such impacts could be essentially dismissed. Only sixteen percent of the EISs clearly documented completion of Section 106 review prior to issuance of the FEIS and ROD.

The effect of deferral is to increase greatly the chances of conflict between development and preservation, and greatly *decrease* the chances of successful resolution, because by the time Section 106 is done, many alternatives have been eliminated and the agency is pretty well set on its preferred course of action.

Deferral results, I'm certain, from the complexity and property-specific character of Section 106 review as it's commonly understood. An agency often simply can't do the kinds of detailed studies and consultations that the regulation appears to demand when it's looking at a large number of alternatives under NEPA, so it puts things off until it can focus only on a single preferred alternative.

The 1998 draft regulation has a lengthy section supposedly encouraging and facilitating coordination between Section 106 and NEPA, but it's pretty much a sham. You can "substitute" your NEPA documents for certain Section 106 products (an MOA, for example), provided everything you do to get to the end of the NEPA process is consistent with the Section 106 regulation. This, of course, does nothing to solve the real-world problems that keep the processes separate.

The complexity of the process also generates high costs in money and time. These are often associated with activities that are of marginal relevance to the real issues of impact identification and resolution. Massive amounts of time can be spent arguing over the details of eligibility, or over precisely which examples of the Criterion of Adverse Effect apply.

The heavy focus of the regulation on the role of the SHPO has two unfortunate results at least. One is that agencies—assuming that the process is all about simply satisfying the SHPO—often feel no need to develop or use expertise of their own. Why pay for pricey experts of our own if we're going to do whatever the SHPO's experts tell us to do? Thus the responsible agency, which has the best chance of doing something intelligent about historic preservation early in and throughout the planning process, doesn't. Instead, Section 106 review becomes a rote matter for the agency—jumping through the hoop of "SHPO clearance."

The other result is that the SHPO is given great opportunity, and great temptation, to act in arbitrary and dictatorial ways, and to sweat the small procedural stuff rather than dealing with the large policy and substantive issues. Even if the SHPO doesn't do this sort of thing intentionally, it's easy for an agency or project proponent—particularly if they lack expertise of their own—to conclude that they're being jerked around by the SHPO, and respond accordingly. The SHPO then develops quite pragmatic reasons for thinking that the agency or proponent is antagonistic and not to be trusted, and so ratchets up the pressure, and the vicious cycle continues.

And while the agency and SHPO dance their intricate dance, everybody else can get shut out.

I hasten to say, first, that these problems have understandable historical roots. The strong emphasis on SHPO review made sense twenty years ago, when agencies and project proponents didn't have access to much expertise and the method and theory of environmental review in general weren't very well developed. But it's a different world today, and the ACHP doesn't seem able to understand this. I'll also hasten to say that during my tenure at the ACHP, I subscribed to its approaches and contributed to the problem. There were historical reasons for this, too, but I still regret it.

So what's needed? A thorough re-thinking of the process, I believe, going back to the basic requirements of the law and seeing how they could best be met given contemporary conditions. But as of this writing, it doesn't appear that this is going to happen, so we're all going to be stuck with the complexities I've outlined in such mind-boggling detail above. Good luck to us all.

Chapter 6

Other Cultural Resource Review Procedures

Introduction

Compliance with NEPA and Section 106 forms the core of practice in cultural resource management—NEPA because it's the umbrella law that structures how all environmental review is done, and Section 106 because it's got such detailed procedures, albeit applicable only to one kind of cultural resource.

NEPA and Section 106 aren't the only cultural resource authorities an agency needs to comply with, however, and therefore they're not the only ones a CRM practitioner needs to know about. And beyond legal authorities per se, there are aspects of customary practice that need to be understood.

Each of the legal authorities and aspects of practice we'll discuss in this chapter is central to some group of practitioners; there are people whose major practice is focused on NAGPRA, others who specialize in ARPA, others who deal exclusively with historical documents. I've meant no disrespect to any of these people by putting NEPA and Section 106 up front and giving them the most attention. It's NEPA and Section 106 that *most* CRM practitioners have to deal with *most* often, but the other authorities and practices are of equal or greater importance in their own contexts, and every cultural resource manager needs to know how to deal with them—and when to call in a specialist.

Let's begin by looking at a new and rapidly developing area of CRM practice and the statute and regulation that govern it—dealing with Native American graves and cultural items.

Native American Graves and Cultural Items

The Native American Graves Protection and Repatriation Act—with the sonorous acronym NAGPRA, is like a lot of other laws in being very well-intentioned, highly justified, and virtually impossible to make work. Its regulations, similarly, are grounded on excellent principles and struggle mightily to make sense of the statute, but wind up being so complicated that they'll probably be honored mostly in the breach.

NAGPRA was enacted in 1989 to correct a long-standing injustice. Since the eighteenth century at least, and particularly in the late nineteenth and twentieth, the bones, grave goods, and religious objects of American Indians and other native Americans have been treated by the majority society as objects of curiosity and scientific specimens. They have been dug up, stored, handled, analyzed, displayed and discarded with little or no consideration for their sanctity in the eyes of many whose ancestral communities created them, valued them, or claimed them as living members. They have been treated, in a word, with disrespect—for themselves and for those who ascribe cultural and spiritual value to them.

Spinning out of the Indian Civil Rights Movement of the 1960s, and as part of a world-wide resurgence of aboriginal power and cultural integrity, Indian tribes and other native American groups (Alaska Natives, Native Hawaiians) began to be increasingly vocal about the wrongs they had suffered at the hands of White society, and specifically at the hands of the U.S. government and the archeological community. Government offenses included not only the quaint 19th century U.S. Army practice of collecting parts of slain Indian for study and lodging in the Army Medical Museum, but also the support of archeological work that resulted in the exhumation of thousands of ancestral bodies. The tribes and such intertribal organizations as the National Congress of American Indians made their outrage known to Congress and the state legislatures. Results were varied at the state level (cf. Price 1991); at the federal level, the result was NAGPRA.

I tend to think that one should never let a lawyer write law, and NAGPRA is a good illustration of why this is so. It's very intricate, subject to lots of varying interpretations, loaded with balancing tests and shifts of the burden of proof back and forth between tribes on the one hand, and museums, agencies, and archeologists on the other. It's a wonder that it works at all, and I suspect that, to the extent it does, it works in spite of itself rather than because of it. As long as there's good will among the parties involved, NAGPRA provides a vehicle for cooperation. Let that good will break down, and it's going to be a different ballgame.

The bulk of NAGPRA deals with repatriation of human remains and what the statute refers to as "Native American cultural items." Repatriation, in simplest terms, means giving back. NAGPRA directs federal agencies and museums that have received federal funds to undertake a series of actions designed to result in giving back human remains and native American cultural items to the Indian tribes, Alaska Native Groups, and Native Hawaiian organizations, whence they came. That series of actions is pretty complicated, and subject to a good deal of interpretation.

The overall repatriation provisions of NAGPRA establish long-term, continuing responsibilities, and there is neither the space in this book nor the will in this author to discuss them all in detail. NPS and the University of Nevada,

Reno offer training specific to NAGPRA, and anyone who may be involved in the repatriation of remains and cultural items should avail themselves of this training. Most cultural resource managers dealing with projects and programs on the ground will encounter NAGPRA in a narrower context, which is what we'll address briefly here.

First let's dispose of a couple of myths.

Myth 1: NAGPRA Applies Only to Burials

There's a tendency to think that one has no potential NAGPRA problems unless one is likely to unearth a human burial. Not so. NAGPRA deals with burials, true, but it also deals with other "Native American cultural items." Such items include:

- Associated funerary objects—i.e., objects associated with a body;

- Unassociated funerary objects—objects that used to be associated with a body but no longer are;

- Sacred objects—objects needed for the practice of traditional religion; and

- "Objects of cultural patrimony"—defined as objects that have ongoing historical, traditional, or cultural importance central to the Indian tribe itself, rather than property owned by an individual tribal member.

This last term is especially open to interpretation. Clearly—and this is pretty certainly what Congress meant—a totem pole is an object of cultural patrimony. It was important to a group rather than owned by an individual (though there's room for argument here). But what about an unmodified rock that was regarded by a tribe as one of the First People, turned to stone for some sort of wrongdoing? What about a complex of grinding slabs used by a village? What about a tribe's whole arsenal of arrow points? Although the NAGPRA regulations (43 CFR 10) try to keep the definition of "object of cultural patrimony" pretty carefully bounded, questions like this are bound to come up.

So you're not out of the NAGPRA woods if you're unlikely to encounter burials; it depends on whether you may run into a wide range of cultural items, as well as on the interests of the relevant Native American groups and how aggressively they pursue them.

Myth 2: NAGPRA Requires Reburial of Human Remains

It doesn't. NAGPRA provides for repatriation to tribes and Native Hawaiian groups, who are taken to be the rightful owners of ancestral remains and cultural items. What they do with their property is up to them; they can put them in their own museums, rebury them, distribute them among households, put them out to return to nature, or for that matter sell them or grind them up for chicken feed. Of course, lots of groups want the remains of their ancestors, and sometimes their artifacts, returned to the ground, and there's nothing in NAGPRA to prohibit a federal agency (or anyone else) from helping them do so, but it's the tribe's call and the tribe's responsibility; it's not up to the agency.

We'll take a look at another myth in a moment. But first let's outline the two sections of NAGPRA that a cultural resource manager is likely to run into on a routine basis.

Section 3(c). Section 3(c) of NAGPRA says that you can't exhume, remove, or otherwise muck around with Native American bones or cultural items on federal or Indian land without a permit issued pursuant to the Archeological Resources Protection Act (ARPA), which has to have been coordinated with the tribe(s) or group(s) culturally affiliated with the remains, and which has to include provision for their disposition consistent with NAGPRA.

Section 3(d). Under Section 3(d) of NAGPRA, if a Native American cultural item is encountered inadvertently on federal land—during construction, for example—the party responsible for the project has to:

- *cease the activity in the area of the discovery, make a reasonable effort to protect the items discovered; and...*

- *notify, in writing, the...head of...(the) agency...having primary management authority...;*

- *Following the notification...,and upon certification by the...head of (the)... agency...that notification has been received, the activity may resume after 30 days of such certification. (25 U.S.C. 3002[d])*

In other words, the project manager must stop project work in the vicinity of the discovery, protect the items discovered, provide written notification to the agency head, receive certification from the agency head that notification has been received, and wait thirty days before recommencing work in the vicinity.

The NAGPRA regulations (43 CFR 10) provide a way to avoid the danger of enduring repeated 30-day (plus) work stoppages. In essence, 43 CFR 10.3 provides for the federal agency responsible for a project on federal or tribal lands to develop a pre-project "Plan of Action" (POA), for managing Native American cultural items that may be encountered during the project, and to follow the POA in lieu of stopping, notifying, awaiting certification, and delaying for 30 days every time such an item is encountered. In a nutshell, this section of the regulations requires federal agencies to:

- Notify tribes (or Native Hawaiian organizations) likely to be culturally affiliated with the items likely to be discovered, as well as any identifiable lineal descendants of those who produced or valued such items, of the likelihood that such items will be excavated, and of the agency's intent to develop a POA;

- Consult with such tribes and descendants; and

- After such consultation, prepare a written POA meeting standards set forth in 43 CFR 10.5, and implement the POA.

How to Develop a POA

The regulations go into considerable detail about how a POA is to be developed:

The Federal agency official must take reasonable steps to determine whether a planned activity may result in the excavation of human remains, funerary objects, sacred objects, or objects of cultural patrimony from Federal lands. (42 CFR 10.3[c][1])

The regulations don't spell out what these steps are, but they go on to require that:

Prior to issuing any approvals or permits for activities, the Federal agency official must notify in writing the Indian tribes or Native Hawaiian organizations that are likely to be culturally affiliated with any human remains, funerary objects, sacred objects, or objects of cultural patrimony that may be excavated. The Federal agency official must also notify any present-day Indian tribe which aboriginally occupied the area of the planned activity and any other Indian tribes or Native Hawaiian organizations that the Federal agency official reasonably believes are likely to have a cultural relationship... (43 CFR 10.3[c][1])

So the agency needs to identify tribes and others that may be culturally affiliated with any Native American cultural items that might be found on the lands subject to effect by the project, and notify them of its plans. Efficiency suggests that this be coordinated with the early stages of Section 106 review—APE determination and identification—and with the early stages of NEPA review (scoping, defining alternatives, describing the affected environment) as well.

Note that:

The notice must be in writing and describe the planned activity, its general location, the basis upon which it was determined that (Native American cultural items) may be excavated, and the basis for determining likely custody...

The notice must also propose a time and place for meetings or consultations... (43 CFR 10.3[c][1])

So you don't just send the tribe a letter saying "we plan to train pilots by bombing Blue Mountain," you've got to describe the proposed action, indicate how you determined who ought to be involved, and perhaps most importantly, propose a meeting or some other form of consultation.

What if the tribe doesn't respond to your written notice?

Written notification should be followed up by telephone contact if there is no response in 15 days. (43 CFR 10.3[c][1])

Who should be involved in consultation?

The consultation must seek to identify traditional religious leaders who should be consulted and to identify, where appropriate, lineal descendants and (tribes and organizations) affiliated with the (Native American cultural items)... (43 CFR 10.5[b][3])

Various kinds of information are to be exchanged...

During the consultation process...the Federal agency official must provide: (1) a list of all lineal descendants and (tribes or groups being consulted), and (2) an indication that additional information used to identify affiliation will be supplied upon request. (43 CFR 10.5[c])

During the consultation process...agency officials may request...
  Names and addresses of representatives
  Names and methods of contacting lineal descendants
  Recommendations on how...consultation...should be conducted
  Kinds of cultural items (to consider) (43 CFR 10.5[d])

Having consulted, the agency actually writes its POA, and the regulations go into great detail about what the POA must contain:

Following consultation, the...agency must prepare...a written plan of action... At a minimum, the plan of action must...document the following:
  1) The kinds of objects to be considered as cultural items...;
  2) The...information used to determine custody...;

3) The planned treatment, care, and handling of (Native American cultural items)...;

4) The planned archeological recording of the (Native American cultural items)...;

5) The kinds of analysis planned for each kind of object;

6) Any steps to be followed to contact Indian tribal officials...;

7) The kind of traditional treatment, if any, to be afforded the (Native American cultural items) by members of the Indian tribe or Native Hawaiian organization;

8) The nature of reports to be prepared; and

9) The disposition of (Native American cultural items). (43 CFR 10.5[e])

Whew! I don't know anybody who has actually prepared a POA in accordance with the regulations that covers all those bases. A lot of agencies have agreements with tribes, but as far as I know none of them meet the full standards set forth in the regulations. But obviously, agencies should have such POAs. Appendix V is a mock-up of a POA; as you can see, it's not a simple document.

Myth 3: The Tribe Must Concur in the POA

Although the tribe (or Native Hawaiian group, and lineal descendants) must be consulted during preparation of the POA, the agency is not required to obtain its concurrence where the POA applies to federal land.

Following consultation, the Federal agency official must prepare, approve, and sign a written plan of action. A copy of this plan of action must be provided to the lineal descendants, Indian tribes and Native Hawaiian organizations involved. Lineal descendants and Indian tribal official(s) may sign the written plan of action as appropriate. (43 CFR 10.5[e])

However, both NAGPRA itself (Section 3[c]) and 43 CFR 10.3(b)(2) require that Native American cultural items be excavated on tribal lands only with the consent of the appropriate Indian tribe. Practically speaking, then, tribal concurrence *is* required in POAs for projects on tribal lands.

POAs and Section 106

In most cases, a project that requires a POA under NAGPRA will also require review under Section 106, usually resulting in an MOA. An exception would be a research archeological excavation carried out under the Archeological Resources Protection Act (ARPA). Such excavations are exempt from Section 106 requirements as long as all the agency does is issue the permit. If the agency provides people, money, vehicles, equipment, then it's a different story.

A Section 106 MOA and a NAGPRA POA should be coordinated to make sure they don't contradict one another, but they shouldn't be one and the same document. The primary reason for avoiding such identity is that the two authorities give authority to different parties. Tribes are often involved in Section 106 review, but SHPOs are the ones an agency *must* consult. Under NAGPRA, however, it's tribes that the agency must consult, and SHPOs don't have any role at all. Nor, of course, does the ACHP. Trying to make your MOA and POA identical is probably only going to embroil you in argument over who can tell whom what to do.

But consistency between your Section 106 outcome and your POA is essential. You don't want to wind up saying in your MOA that you'll care for all the goodies in the local museum, while saying in your POA that you'll repatriate them to the tribe.

Graves and cultural items aren't the only things that are important to Native Americans on religious/cultural grounds, though in NAGPRA they have certainly found the most explicit sort of legal treatment. Religious practices themselves, and the places they are carried out, also have to be attended to, albeit in a rather more flexible way than do the subjects of NAGPRA.

Native American Religious Practices

Under the Establishment Clause of the First Amendment to the Constitution, the federal government should do nothing to prohibit the free exercise of Native American religions, but in fact, it has done a lot. During some periods in the past—including the rather recent past—tribes have literally been forbidden to practice traditional religions. Military force has been used to suppress religious practices like the Ghost Dance and the Sun Dance. Christian missionaries have been assisted in operating on Indian reservations, and virtually ran some of them in the past. Students at schools run by the Bureau of Indian Affairs (BIA) used to be prohibited from engaging in all kinds of traditional cultural activities, including religion. In recent times the use of peyote in traditional religious activities has been restricted. Starting in the late 1970s, the government began taking action to reverse such restrictions.

AIRFA

Recognizing the inequity of its past performance, in 1978 Congress passed what came to be known as the American Indian Religious Freedom Act (AIRFA). AIRFA is in fact a joint resolution of Congress, expressing as policy that the U.S. will respect and protect the right of Indian tribes to the free exercise of their traditional religions.

AIRFA doesn't actually tell agencies to do anything in particular, nor to refrain from doing anything. But the policy it sets forth has been argued about in court repeatedly, and, generally speaking, the courts have held that under

AIRFA, agencies should consult with tribes about anything that might affect their religious practices. The agency doesn't have to accede to a tribe's wishes, but it has to find out what they are and consider them. What the agency does or doesn't do in response to the tribe's concerns, of course, is constrained by the First Amendment; it can neither "establish" religion nor "prohibit" its free exercise.

Note that AIRFA does not require consideration only of impacts on religious *places*, though it is clearly relevant to how agencies consider such impacts under NEPA and Section 106. It addresses impacts on the *practice* of traditional religions. So under AIRFA an agency should consider, and consult about, the impacts of its actions on things like plant gathering for religious purposes, and on worship in areas that may not be historically rooted traditional cultural properties.

For the cultural resource manager, AIRFA is a call to recognize that religious practices, not just places, and certainly not just National Register eligible places, are "cultural resources" that need to be considered in planning. It also tells us that we need to make special efforts to involve Indian tribes in the planning process, through responsible, thoughtful, and culturally sensitive consultation.

Executive Order 13007

In contrast with the broad scope of AIRFA, Executive Order 13007 deals very explicitly with "sacred places." Although it provides another rationale for consultation with tribes, it's a rationale that's subject to a lot of potential misinterpretation. Or maybe correct interpretation; the motivations of this executive order's drafters remain rather obscure.

Issued by President Clinton on May 24, 1996, EO 13007 required five things of federal agencies:

1. Accommodate access to and ceremonial use of Indian sacred sites by Indian religious practitioners, where such accommodation is not clearly inconsistent with law or essential agency functions.

2. Avoid adverse effect to the physical integrity of such sites, subject to the same caveats.

3. Where appropriate, maintain the confidentiality of information on such sites.

4. Implement procedures to carry out the provisions of the order, including provisions for providing notice to Indian tribes of actions that might affect sacred sites or access to or ceremonial use of such sites in a manner that respects the government-to-government relations between the U.S. government and Indian tribal governments.

5. Provide a report to the president by May 24, 1997, addressing, among other things, any changes needed in law, regulation, or procedure to accommodate access to and ceremonial use of Indian sacred sites, to avoid adverse affect on such sites, and to facilitate consultation with tribes and religious leaders, including provision for the resolution of disputes.

The executive order contains a definition of "sacred site" that may well turn out to be mischievous, and is a classic example of what you get when you let policy documents be written by lawyers in swaddling clothes:

> "Sacred site" means any specific, discrete, narrowly delineated location on Federal land that is identified by an Indian tribe or Indian individual determined to be an appropriately authoritative representative of an Indian religion, as sacred by virtue of its established religious significance to, or ceremonial use by, an Indian religion; provided that the tribe or appropriately authoritative representative of an Indian religion has informed the agency of the existence of such a site.

Well, now…

• What does "specific" mean? A responsible definition, I think, would be that the site has to be a definite piece of real estate, not a whole class of properties. "Rocky Point," not "all sacred places in Washafornia." But what do you suppose it could mean to the folks who gave us the basis for *Pueblo of Sandia v. United States*.? You'll recall that in that case, the Forest Service wanted the tribes to provide maps with all spiritual places in Las Huertas Canyon marked with specific boundaries.

• What about "discrete?"

Again, one can responsibly take it to mean simply that the site has to have some kind of boundaries to discriminate it from the rest of the world, but it's easy to imagine a definition that would require a little red fence around the place, or a size no larger than a breadbox.

• Then there's "narrowly delineated."

Right—the more you pile these terms on top of one another, the more it adds up to "marked on a U.S.G.S. quadrangle with clearly defined and defensible boundaries." But it gets worse.

• What does "identified by an Indian tribe, or Indian individual…" mean?

Does the tribe or individual have to come up to the agency and volunteer the identification of the site? "Here's our list, Kemo sabe?" Obviously this kind of transfer of responsibility is what the Forest Service thought it could get away with at Las Huertas Canyon, and one is tempted to think that, having failed, they or others like them got to some dim bulbs at the White House or Department of Justice and had their way with them. It's completely inconsistent with the assignment of responsibility to agencies themselves by NEPA, NHPA, and various other statutes, but hey, what's a little inconsistency?

Of course, "identified by a tribe or individual" could be taken to mean "identified by a tribe or individual in response to an agency request, as part of the agency's consultation during the conduct of its planning responsibilities," but is there any reason to think agencies will do this? Perhaps, but not because of the wording of the executive order.

• And then, what does "appropriately authoritative" mean? Who's to decide? Are federal agencies going to get into vetting tribal representatives?

To their credit, in the work that federal agencies have been doing to prepare and now follow up on their reports to the White House, few if any seem to be taking advantage of the opportunities the executive order gives them to run roughshod over its presumed intent. Instead, most agencies at least seem to be interpreting the executive order in a manner consistent with NEPA, NHPA, and AIRFA, taking the responsibility on themselves to work with tribes to identify sacred sites, and then to figure out ways to manage them in such a way as to minimize physical impacts and impacts on access.

Note that a place can be a sacred site, subject to consideration under the executive order, and *not* be a historic property subject to consideration under NHPA. And while it has to be a piece of real property, the property itself is not the only subject for agency concern; it's access to the site, and its use for ceremonial purposes.

Government-to-Government, Fiduciary, and Treaty Relationships

In helping agencies implement Executive Order 13007, AIRFA, and all the other legal authorities that pertain to Indian tribes (NEPA, NHPA, etc.), a cultural resource manager needs at least a basic understanding of the special relationship that exists between the federal government and federally recognized tribal governments. A federally recognized tribal government is, of course, one whose official existence is recognized by the federal government. The Bureau of Indian Affairs (BIA) annually publishes a list of the several hundred tribes that are so recognized.

Tribes, of course, were sovereign nations on the North American continent before Euroamericans landed. For some centuries it was uncertain whether the natives or the invaders would gain the upper hand, or whether some sort of truce would emerge. By law today, federally recognized Indian tribes are still sovereign nations, to which the laws of the United States apply only as Congress explicitly determines. In many respects, the sovereign character of tribal governments gives them a superior position to those of states and local governments, which are subdivisions of the United States.

Federal agencies have to respect the "government-to-government relationship" between sovereign Indian tribal governments and the government of the United States. President Clinton usefully reminded agencies of this ongoing duty in a Presidential Memorandum of April 29, 1994.

What does this mean? Something pretty simple, but pretty powerful. As one tribal representative summed it up to me: "Your policy people talk to our policy people before your technical people talk to our technical people." Agencies are supposed to deal with tribal governments at an official, executive level. You don't send your archeologist out to chat with the tribal chairman, unless she's been invited. You don't send your consultant, or your engineer, or your lawyer. The line officer, that is, the official who's in the line of authority that descends from the president, is the one to make official contact—the park superintendent, the regional administrator. Staff can certainly set up consultation meetings, and they can follow up on them; the "technical people" can get together, once the "policy people" have agreed that it's appropriate for them to do so. But staff-level consultation isn't a substitute for executive consultation, and you don't send staff to talk with the tribal executive, unless you've been invited to do so.

The federal government also has a fiduciary, or trust, relationship with tribes, which is grounded in treaties not only with the tribes but with other nations—notably Great Britain, which sought to protect its Indian allies through the Treaty of Ghent at the end of the War of 1812. In effect, the federal government is supposed to look out for the interests of tribes. Where there's a question about how a law can be interpreted vis-à-vis tribal interests, it's supposed to be interpreted in favor of those interests. And government agencies are supposed to make their decisions in ways consistent with those interests, unless there is an awfully good reason to do otherwise.

And then, of course, there are specific treaties executed between tribes and the federal government or its colonial and imperial predecessors. In the typical treaty, the tribe ceded vast tracts of land to the U.S. in return for a reservation, food, other forms of support, and, particularly, peace. But often, specific rights were retained by the tribe—rights to fish or hunt, for example. And the rule that has generally guided the courts is, if a tribe didn't explicitly give up a right, then it retained it. So arguably, while a tribe may have given up the right to own huge chunks of land, and hence to farm it, log it, and have exclusive access to it, it did not give up the right to protect and use its spiritual places or protect the burial places of its ancestors unless it explicitly said it did in its treaty. More and more, tribes are making this sort of argument as a basis for exerting power over their ancestral resources beyond the boundaries of their reservations.

For all these reasons, you don't treat federally recognized Indian tribes as just another set of interest groups, just another part of the public. Individuals of Native American ethnic heritage are U.S. citizens, with all the rights attendant thereto, but they're also citizens of their own nations, and those nations have a special relationship with the U.S. government that has to be reflected in government dealings with them, in cultural resource matters as in all others.

AIRFA, the First Amendment, and the G-O Road

We left the case of the G-O Road, back in Chapter 5, with the Forest Service having decided to go ahead with the road through the National Register eligible sacred area, despite the objections of the tribes, the SHPO, and the ACHP. We asked the questions: What do you suppose the ACHP's position was on the Forest Service's compliance with Section 106, and what do you suppose the Court decided?

The ACHP took the position that the Forest Service had complied with Section 106, and testified in court to this effect. You'll recall that Section 106 doesn't require agencies to follow the ACHP's recommendations, only to take effects into account and give the ACHP a reasonable opportunity to comment. This the Forest Service had done, in accordance with the regulations.

The District Court threw out the Section 106 charge, as well as charges of violating NEPA and other statutes. It concluded that the Forest Service had consulted with the tribes, so AIRFA wasn't really an issue. The First Amendment, however, *was* a problem, and the District Court held that to build the road through the Helkau Historic District would violate the free exercise clause. It would, in effect, prohibit the tribes from the exercise of their religions. The case was appealed, and the Ninth Circuit Court of Appeals upheld the decision

The government appealed the case to the Supreme Court, which considered it and reversed the Appeals Court (*Lyng v. Northwest Indian Cemetery Protective Association*, 108 S. Ct. 1319 [1988]). At the time, the tests applied by the Court in determining whether the free exercise clause was violated were such that an action was determined not to be in violation if (a) it furthered a compelling government interest, and (b) it was the way of furthering that interest that was least restrictive on the practice of religion. The Court found, in a nutshell, first that the construction of the road through the District didn't actually prohibit the tribes from exercising their freedom of religion. They could still go up there and pray, they'd just have to dodge the trucks. The Court went on to hold that even if the rights of the tribes were inhibited, the government had a "compelling interest" in opening up the timber reserves of the interior. And since it didn't keep the tribes from practicing their religion, there really wasn't much of an issue about being the least restrictive means of furthering the government's interest.

Those who like to see the glass as half full for the tribes, rather than half empty, note that the Court expressed sympathy and respect for the tribal position, and indicated that the Forest Service was right to make efforts to mitigate its impacts. The bottom line, though, is that harvesting timber was held to be superior to tribal religious practice, and that running huge trucks through a sacred site was found not to keep people from practicing their religion. A troublesome decision, to say the least. And since *Lyng*, the Court has made it even harder to advance a free exercise clause argument, by establishing a new test. Under *Employment Division v. Smith* (494 U.S. 872 [1990]), "neutral and generally applicable" laws can be applied in ways that suppress religious practice, and the government doesn't need to advance a specific reason for refusing to exempt religious practices from regulation under such laws. Congress attempted to reapply the tests that were in effect at the time of *Lyng* by enacting the Religious Freedom Restoration Act (RFRA) in 1993, but the Supreme Court knocked it down as unconstitutional in 1997 (see Grimm 1997 for an excellent discussion of the pertinent case law).

So when push comes to shove, the First Amendment by itself offers thin support for the practice of traditional Native American religion. Taken together, though, the whole corpus of federal civil rights, religious freedom, environmental, and cultural resource law can make it very much in an agency's interests to pay close attention to such practices, and try to give them wide berth. In the G-O Road case, by the time the Supreme Court reversed and remanded the Appeals Court's decision, the timber land that once had been slated for logging had been designated as Wilderness and couldn't be logged, and the mills on the coast that would have turned its trees into lumber had mostly gone belly-up. Congress then capped things by prohibiting the Forest Service from ever completing the road. So the tribal religious practitioners now have a nice road to their sacred site. And the Forest Service in California, to its great credit, learned an important lesson, and now—in contrast with some other Forest Service Regions—has an exemplary program of cooperative forest management and cultural resource management with the tribes of the area.

Native Americans aren't the only ones who have cultural concerns about the environment, and not all such concerns are of a religious nature. The "environmental justice" movement, which deals with far more than cultural resources, provides a context in which a wide range of cultural resource issues can and should be addressed, as long as they're related to low income and minority groups.

Environmental Justice and Cultural Resources

Background

During the 1980s, it became increasingly apparent—particularly to residents—that nasty kinds of public facilities tended to be sited in neighborhoods and communities where most of the residents were minorities or didn't make much money. This probably occurred because property in such areas could be obtained cheaply and the residents tended not to make much of a fuss—or if they did, they didn't use the decision-making systems well enough to have much impact.

Whatever the reason, low-income and minority populations were taking it in the chin when it came to environmental impacts. In the 1980s, representatives of such populations began to make noise about it, and the "environmental justice" (EJ) movement was born.

EJ is based on a simple principle: that people shouldn't suffer disproportionate environmental impacts because of their ethnicity or income level.

EJ entered the environmental impact assessment game informally when practitioners recognized it as an issue and began to address it, occasionally, in EISs, EAs, and similar studies. When the Interorganizational Committee on Social Impact Assessment issued its *Guidelines and Principles for Social Impact Assessment* in 1993, one of the principles it espoused was that social impact assessors should "analyze impact equity" (NOAA 1994:18). But EJ became a formal part of environmental impact assessment when President Clinton issued Executive Order 12898 on February 11, 1994.

Executive Order 12898

The Executive Order directs each federal agency to:

...make achieving environmental justice part of its mission by identifying and addressing, as appropriate, disproportionately high and adverse human health or environmental effects of its programs, policies, and activities on minority populations and low-income populations in the United States and its territories and possessions, the District of Columbia, the Commonwealth of Puerto Rico, and the Commonwealth of the (sic: Northern) Mariana Islands.

It goes on to direct each agency to:

...conduct its programs, policies, and activities that substantially affect human health or the environment, in a manner that ensures that such programs, policies, and activities do not have the effect of excluding persons (including populations) from participation in, denying persons (including populations) the benefits of, or subjecting persons (including populations) to discrimination under, such programs, policies, and activities, because of their race, color, or national origin.

Further, it directs agencies to collect and analyze data on the comparative health and environmental risks borne by low-income and minority populations vis-à-vis the rest of the population, and to remove barriers to participation by such populations in the review of agency documents, public hearings, and other public participation activities.

In case this direction wasn't clear enough, the president accompanied it with a Presidential Memorandum directing agencies to analyze environmental effects on minority and low income communities as part of their NEPA analyses, and to provide means of mitigating "significant and adverse effects" on such communities "whenever feasible." The Memorandum also underscored the need to "provide opportunities for community input in the NEPA process" and to "ensure that the public, including minority and low-income community, has adequate access to public information…"

Executive Order 12898, like other executive orders, does not provide an independent basis for litigation—in other words, it can't be enforced in a court of law by itself. However, like all other executive orders, it is grounded in statutory law—in this case environmental law, civil rights law, and public administration law dealing with public information and participation, and these laws *do* provide causes for legal action.

In any event, the Executive Order gave a good deal of impetus to agencies to consider environmental effects on low-income and minority populations. The Environmental Protection Agency (EPA) and the Justice Department increased pressure on agencies to address EJ issues by creating units of their own to address the matter. EPA has been quite active in lobbying agencies to integrate EJ into their environmental analyses.

EJ and Cultural Resources

What does all this mean for cultural resource management? Consider a hypothetical example (but one based on a real case).

Out in the great State of Washafornia, there's a hilltop that's much like any other hilltop in the vicinity, except that about 15 years ago the members of a local Indian community set up a sweat lodge there. Generally speaking, they have sweats there every Friday night, with a fire, singing, drumming, and discussion of spiritual subjects, life lessons, and so on. The community is not a federally recognized tribe. It has no treaty rights to the area. The site is not an archeological site; no sweat lodge (nor anything else) stood on the site until 15 years ago. The Washafornia Department of Transportation (WashDOT) wants to build a highway that will take the hill away. What are its responsibilities?

The sweat lodge is clearly not old enough to be eligible for the National Register (one might try to make an "exceptional significance" argument for it, but good luck), so Section 106 isn't an issue. The community isn't a federally recognized tribe, so Executive Order 13007 doesn't come into play. But the community *is* a minority community, and it's quite probably low-income as well. So the Executive Order and the Presidential Memorandum indicate that WashDOT had better look closely at its impacts on the hilltop as part of its contribution to FHWA's NEPA analysis.

Is the impact on the community "high and adverse?" Is it "disproportionate?" As usual, it depends, and as part of their NEPA analysis WashDOT and FHWA are going to need to consider what it depends on. They'll need to consider, for example, what role the sweat lodge plays in the life of the community—is it one of a dozen, or the only one? If it's one of a dozen, are all twelve equally important? How does the community's use of this one compare with the ways it uses the other eleven? And does anybody else in the area have sweat lodges (in which case the impacts might not be "disproportionate" if WashDOT was knocking some of them out, too), or is it only the Indian group that has one? In short, the impact may or may not be high, adverse, or disproportionate, but to find out, WashDOT is going to have to analyze the role the sweat lodge plays in the culture of the community and the area.

Unlike NHPA, EJ is not strictly related to physical places on the land. Suppose, for example, that a community of Vietnamese immigrants harvests mushrooms on the Kindling National Forest, and the Kindling plans a fungicide program to wipe out the dread Fir Fungus. Or the residents of an African-American neighborhood fish for carp in Round Rock Reservoir, and the Corps of Engineers wants to raise the reservoir level in such a way that fish habitats will be affected. You get the idea.

So whether the impact turns out to be high and adverse or not, and whether it turns out to be disproportionate or not, the agency involved is going to have some analysis to do, and that analysis is going to involve addressing some sociocultural issues.

The Urge to Quantify

As we'll discuss in more detail a little later, there's a tendency in social impact assessment (SIA) under NEPA to seek easily quantifiable variables for analysis. This tendency has influenced how some people—including such authoritative entities as CEQ—have approached EJ analyses. To a considerable extent, practice in EJ analysis is evolving toward a consensus on the notion that one determines whether one may have an EJ problem, and hence whether one has anything to analyze, by looking at census data for the area where impacts will take place and determining whether the area is one in which lots of low-income or minority people live. If it is, then you may have a problem, and you'd better address it; if it's not, then you're in the clear. There's also a tendency to analyze impacts and community values as independent variables; you analyze air quality in terms of parts per million of this, that, and the other thing in the atmosphere, and if you're going to degrade the quality of the air above X point in an area where lots of low-income and minority people live, *and* if you're not going to degrade it as much in other areas, *then* you do an EJ analysis.

What's wrong with this? Well, first consider that impacts don't necessarily occur only where people live.

Almost nobody lives on the Kindling National Forest; those few who do are either Forest Service employees (mostly non-minorities, and however they may feel about it, not terribly low-income) or the owners of swank hunting cabins on inholdings. So census data are not going to indicate the potential for any EJ issues. But the spiritual leaders of the Motomac Tribe travel for days from their homes on the Barerock Reservation to access the high country on the Kindling to seek visions and make medicine. If the Washafornia Air National Guard (WANG) decides to carry out low-level training over the Kindling, with stealth bombers swooping down to carry out practice runs on the ridges, it's likely to drive a whole lot of antique religious practitioners into premature cardiac arrest. Clearly there's a high and adverse impact here, and just as clearly it's disproportionate, since nobody but the Motomac are carrying out spiritual activities on the ridges. This impact just isn't going to be detected, however, if the WANG doesn't get into EJ analysis unless census data indicate a resident low-income or minority population.

Viewing environmental impacts and EJ as independent variables is also a problem. Taking air quality as an example, an air quality expert, or the standards of the Quality of Air Commission (QAC), may indicate that the discharge of .0001 parts per million of gold dust into the atmosphere presents no human health or environmental problems. Ergo, there is no way that the discharge of such a level of dust by the Family Jewel Mine could have any impacts on anybody, low-income or minority or not. But suppose those Motomac religious practitioners up there in the high country of the Kindling NF believe that they must be able to see out across the adjacent valley to the hills on the other side in order to acquire their visions, and suppose further that *they* believe that .0001 ppm of gold dust in the air *will* impair their vision. Now, maybe they're nuts, or maybe they're not, but it is hardly consistent with the spirit of the Executive Order—which after all stresses the importance of involving low-income and minority people in analysis and decision-making—not even to examine the issue because the QAC in its Olympian wisdom doesn't think any impacts will occur.

So, where does all this lead us? EJ analysis is an evolving field, and cultural resource managers are only beginning to get seriously involved in it. But I think it's possible to lay out some common sense guidelines for considering the cultural aspects of EJ in environmental impact analyses.

CEQ has given us a start by issuing guidelines for the integration of EO 12898 compliance into NEPA analyses (CEQ 1997). Let's take a look at them from a cultural resources standpoint:

CEQ's Six Principles and Cultural Resources

CEQ's guidance outlines six principles that should guide NEPA review to ensure that EJ issues are considered. Somewhat abridged and paraphrased, they are:

- *Consider the human composition of the affected area, to determine whether minority populations, low-income populations, or Indian tribes are present... and if so whether there may be disproportionately high and adverse...effects on (such) populations...*

CEQ kind of fudges on whether it means "resident composition" when it speaks of "composition," and it recommends sources of data beyond mere census numbers for use in ascertaining composition, but nothing explicit is said about populations that use but don't live in the affected area. Nor is anything said directly about determining the affected area with reference to the views of those affected. "Indian tribes" seem to have been added to the list of populations as a wholly gratuitous political and rather counterproductive bow to tribal interests. Tribes aren't listed separately in the executive order itself, and are quite properly defined in CEQ's guidance as minority populations. Calling them out separately confuses things—are they minority populations covered by the order, or are they not? In any event, this guidance is pretty straightforward, if unenlightening: see if there are any EJ populations around, and if so, see if they're disproportionately highly adversely affected.

- *Consider not only direct impacts on the health and environmental quality of low income populations and minority populations, but indirect, multiple, and cumulative effects as well, including effects that are not within the agency's control or subject to agency discretion.*

The actual language of the guidance is a good deal more complicated than that, but that's the general gist. Very important direction: an agency should look not only at whether its particular project will poison the community, but whether it will contribute to an overall pattern of poisoning derived from multiple sources. In a more explicitly cultural example, an agency should be concerned not only about whether its particular project is going to drive all the Cambodian farmers out of the valley, or all the Jamaicans out of the neighborhood, but whether its project is part of a pattern of development that will have this effect.

- *Recognize that the cultural, social, occupational, historical, and economic characteristics of a low income community or a minority community may amplify the environmental effects of an action. Such a population may be more sensitive to such effects, and less resilient in adapting to them, than another community.*

Here, too, I've paraphrased a considerably longer and more complex piece of guidance—one that's particularly important from a cultural resource standpoint. It should be precisely the business of cultural resource managers to help agencies be sensitive to such characteristics.

- *Implement effective public participation strategies that seek to overcome linguistic, cultural, institutional, geographic and other barriers to meaningful participation, and that include active outreach.*

Consider this direction with reference to a case like *Pueblo of Sandia v. United States*. Think about the fact that a Native American community's traditional cultural practitioners may not have the money or free time to attend a whole lot of public meetings, and may not get or contribute much to them if they do attend. How about relocation of tribes to Oklahoma in the 19th century as a geographic barrier to meaningful participation in NEPA review of projects in Georgia?

- *Assure early and meaningful community representation in the process of NEPA analysis and review, recognizing that there may be diverse constituencies within a given community and seeking complete representation.*

It's often the case that the political leadership of a low income or minority community is made up of people who interact easily with the dominant society, usually because they've adopted substantial parts of the dominant society's value system. It's with this leadership that a government agency can most comfortably deal. CEQ is telling agencies that they've got to do better than that—they've got to seek "complete representation." Locating and assisting elements of a group that may not participate readily, or that may be discouraged from it by the group's leadership, should be a job for cultural resource managers, among others.

- *Where Indian tribes may be involved, make sure that interactions with tribes are consistent with the government-to-government relationship between the U.S. and tribal governments, the U.S. government's trust responsibility to tribes, and any pertinent treaty rights.*

Where an Indian tribe is the population involved, the need to seek complete representation has to be balanced with attention to the government-to-government relationship. If the tribal government says "work with us, and ignore those wacky traditionalists," the agency has to do the former, but it cannot do the latter, because the traditionalists are, after all, American citizens who are entitled to be heard. Helping an agency walk the narrow line between government-to-government consultation and openness to citizen participation can be an important job for a cultural resource manager.

EJ and NEPA Review

Some kind of EJ analysis should be done as part of every NEPA review—not just as part of an EIS.

CATEGORICAL EXCLUSIONS

In screening a project to see if it's a legitimate CATEX—that is, if no "extraordinary circumstances" exist that could drive it out of the CATEX category, you need to consider circumstances that could result in disproportionately high and adverse impacts on minority communities and low income communities.

SCOPING EAS AND EISS

The same, of course, goes for the analyses leading to EAs and EISs. In formal scoping for an EIS, and in informal scoping for an EA, an agency should ask itself, its research data and consultants, other knowledgeable parties, and the potentially affected community about whether impacts on low income or minority groups may occur. The composition of the resident community can be determined using Bureau of the Census (BOC) data and information from local social service agencies. The CEQ guidance says that low income populations should be identified with reference to the annual statistical poverty thresholds from the BOC Current Population Reports, Series P-60 on Income and Poverty, and that:

> (m)inority populations should be identified where either: (a) the minority population of the affected area exceeds 50 percent or (b) the minority population percentage of the affected area is meaningfully greater than the minority population percentage in the general population or other appropriate unit of geographic analysis. (CEQ 1997:19)

"Minority," by the way, is defined as:

> (i)ndividuals who are members of the following population groups: American Indian or Alaskan Native; Asian or Pacific Islander, Black, not of Hispanic origin; or Hispanic. (CEQ 1997:19)

People who use the affected area but don't live there may be harder to identify, since they will not appear in census data pertinent to the defined affected area per se. CEQ makes a bow toward identifying such groups, but isn't very explicit and doesn't give any direction about how to do it:

> In identifying minority communities, agencies may consider as a community either a group of individuals living in geographic proximity to one another, or a geographically dispersed/transient set of individuals (such as migrant workers or Native American), where either type of group experiences common conditions of environmental exposure or effect. (CEQ 1997:19)

Anthropologists, sociologists, and others who've researched the social and cultural characteristics of an area can be particularly important in identifying populations that may not be easily identifiable from census data. Scoping should certainly include consulting with such people, and of course with knowledgeable community organizations.

Public participation is a critical part of scoping, a key technique for identifying potentially affected populations, and a context in which a cultural resource manager's knowledge of cultural issues may be important. The CEQ guidelines list a number of ways to ensure effective participation, including the translation of significant documents, the use of facilities and locations that are local, convenient, and accessible, and the use of meeting sizes and formats that are tailored to the community or population. Scheduling meetings to avoid conflict with work schedules and community social events may be necessary.

The agency ought to use its cultural resource management or social impact assessment expertise to find out something about the affected community's communication styles and principles and design its public participation program with these in mind. People obviously won't participate if they feel they're being asked to do so in an inappropriate or offensive manner.

ESTABLISHING THE AFFECTED ENVIRONMENT

The shape, size, and character of the affected environment always varies depending on the resource type and impact type being considered. For EJ purposes, you need to think about where the proposed action could have impacts of any kind—physical, social, cultural, health—on people and their valued environments, and include these areas in the affected environment.

The CEQ guidance reminds us that:

the impacts within minority populations, low income populations, or Indian tribes may be different from impacts on the general population due to a community's distinct cultural practices. For example, data on different patterns of living, such as subsistence fish, vegetation, or wildlife consumption and the use of well water in rural communities may be relevant to the analysis. (CEQ 1997:12)

This is CEQ's most explicit acknowledgement of the fact that where one lives isn't the only measure of where one may be affected. The places where a community fishes, gathers, hunts, or draws water may be relevant—as may the areas where they carry out other cultural and religious activities.

ENVIRONMENTAL ASSESSMENTS

As discussed in Chapter 4, an EA examines the *intensity* of a project's environmental consequences, in their relevant *contexts*, in order to measure their significance and determine whether an EIS is necessary.

The interests of potentially affected low income communities and minority communities make up one of the contexts within which the intensity of impacts must be considered, because the regulations identify "affected interests" as such a context (40 CFR 1508.27[a]). In this context, an EA needs to consider measures of intensity like the following (based on 49 CFR 1508.27[b]):

- Both beneficial and adverse effects on aspects of the environment important to low income communities and minority communities.

- The degree to which the proposed action may affect the safety and health of such communities, and whether such effects are disproportional with those on the rest of the population.

- The degree to which the action may affect unique environmental characteristics valued by the affected communities, such as farm lands, recreation areas, traditional cultural properties and other historic places, and culturally valued neighborhoods or businesses.

- The potential for impacts to be controversial in the eyes of the affected community on environmental grounds.

- The potential for uncertain or unknown risks to the community, for example from the release of chemicals that may or may not have human health implications.

- The degree to which the action may set precedents for carrying out other similar actions in the potentially affected community, or in other similar communitties.

- The contribution the proposed action could make to cumulative impact on the affected community, including exposure to one or more chemical, biological, physical, or radiological agents across air, water, soil, or other environmental media over time, from single or multiple sources.

- The extent to which the action could affect historic properties or other cultural resources important to the potentially affected communities.

- Whether the proposed action could result in violation of a federal, state, Indian tribal, or local law designed to protect the potentially affected communities, or communities in general, from disproportionate adverse environmental impacts.

As you'll recall, 40 CFR 1508.14 says that economic or social effects by themselves aren't enough to require preparation of an EIS. But if economic or social effects are disproportionate and adverse, and linked to one of the measures of intensity listed above, then they may indicate the need for a higher level of analysis, including the possibility of preparing an EIS.

For example, suppose that a federal construction project in a city will drive up property tax rates to such extent that low income homeowners or businesspeople will be unable to remain in town. This wouldn't require an agency to prepare an EIS unless the socioeconomic effect of displacement by rising property taxes was related to environmental impacts like exposure to toxic materials or impacts on the community's cultural resource, even if the socioeconomic effect fell disproportionately on the low income or minority community. It would be appropriate to include measures to mitigate socioeconomic impacts in the FONSI, though, and to include measures to ensure that mitigation was completed. Where socioeconomic effects are disproportionate and related to one or more of the kinds of environmental impact types listed above, then an EIS may be necessary unless acceptable mitigation measures can be developed and included in the FONSI.

ENVIRONMENTAL IMPACT STATEMENTS

Of course, what goes for an EA goes for an EIS, too. EJ issues should be thoroughly and understandably addressed, in consultation with potentially affected communities. The CEQ guidance says that:

(w)here a potential environmental justice issue has been identified…, the agency should state clearly…whether, in light of all the facts and circumstances, a disproportionately high and adverse…impact on minority populations, low income populations, or Indian tribe is likely to result from the proposed action and any alternatives. This statement should be supported by sufficient information for the public to understand the rationale for the conclusion. The underlying analysis should be presented as concisely as possible using language that is understandable to the public and that minimizes use of acronyms or jargon. (CEQ 1997:13)

Cultural resource managers should have a lot to say about how an affected community can be brought into participation in the analysis underlying an EIS (or EA), and about how information should be presented so it will be understandable. Preliminary information and findings should be shared with potentially affected communities, in a manner sensitive to cultural differences and modes of communication.

ALTERNATIVES

The CEQ guidance says that:

(a)gencies should encourage the members of the communities that may suffer a disproportionately high and adverse…effect…to help develop and comment on possible alternatives to the proposed agency action as early as possible in the process. (CEQ 1997:13)

This is very important guidance, and presents another context in which cultural resource management practice can be fruitfully employed. Many "traditional" cultural resource managers who work in Section 106 review are pretty familiar with the consultation and negotiation that take place there, often enough in a cross-cultural context. This sort of familiarity with dispute resolution can be usefully applied to encouraging potentially impacted communities to work with agencies in exploring alternatives. Helping a traditional community not only understand what environmental impacts a project may have, but work with the project proponent to define impacts and explore alternatives to avoid them is a truly satisfying kind of practice (cf. Parker and King 1987).

MITIGATION OF ADVERSE EFFECTS

Mitigation measures should, of course, be developed in consultation with affected communities and groups, and should provide for their ongoing participation in a cooperative framework as the mitigation measures are carried out. CEQ reminds agencies to:

> ...carefully consider community views in developing and implementing mitigation strategies. (CEQ 1997:14)

What might some mitigation measures be? As always, it depends, but here are some examples from one of my own experiences—mediating an environmental dispute over a proposed airport in Micronesia:

- Redesigning warning lights to reduce impact on a sacred mountain;

- Redesigning a dredge area to permit continued access to reef resources;

- Inclusion of a moorage place for village boats;

- Establishing an adjudication panel to settle disputes over land and natural resources;

- Creating a fund to support a village agricultural cooperative;

- Accelerating sewerage service construction to make up for lost over-water sanitation facilities;

- Permitting temporary access to such facilities across the construction site;

- Control of noise and dust impacts; and

- Archeological data recovery carried out by the villages. (Parker and King 1987)

RECORD OF DECISION

CEQ recommends that agencies distribute their RODs to affected communities, designing such documents to explain impacts, decisions, and mitigation measures:

> *...in non-technical, plain language for limited-English speakers. Agencies should also consider translating documents into languages other than English where appropriate and practical.* (CEQ 1997:14)

So, in a nutshell, Executive Order 12898 provides strong direction to agencies to consider cultural, along with other, kinds of impacts on low income communities and minority communities, including Indian tribes. Cultural resource managers have important roles to play in EJ analysis—particularly, I think, in balancing a tendency by other environmental practitioners to deal only with easily quantifiable variables and to treat affected communities as sources of data rather than as collaborators in environmental analysis.

Beyond environmental justice, and beyond low-income and minority groups, there's a whole sociocultural environment out there that needs to be addressed in impact assessment and other aspects of management. Let's turn to that environment and how it's dealt with.

Social Institutions, Ways of Life

Background

Oddly, the aspects of culture to which most people feel most intrinsically attached have the least explicit treatment in law. The social institutions, ways of life, belief systems, that make communities and neighborhoods and social groups what they are, are not the subjects of any specific laws, executive orders, rules, or regulations. This is probably because they're so soft and squishy, so hard to define explicitly—though few would deny their importance.

What am I talking about? The *Guidelines and Principles for Social Impact Assessment* define this class of cultural resource as:

> *...the ways in which people live, work, play, relate to one another, organize to meet their needs and generally cope as members of society, (as well as) the norms, values, and beliefs that guide and rationalize their cognition of themselves and their society.* (Interorganizational Committee 1993; NOAA 1994:1)

In other words, the social and cultural dimensions of the environment, which may or may not be related to such things as chunks of land, buildings, and neighborhoods.

How can there be a "cultural resource" that's not property-based? Consider the example of providing satellite television service to remote villages in Alaska. The satellite dishes will sit on chunks of ground, and so do the houses of the people who'll watch the TV, but we've missed the major sociocultural impact of providing the service if all we do is make sure the dishes don't plop down on archeological sites. The major impact of bringing Hollywood's latest fare to small, kin-based societies in the arctic is on their family structure, their values, their forms of interaction. These are all "cultural resources" in the sense of being resources on which people rely for at least psychological sustenance, and often physical sustenance as well, but they have only incidental property referents. This is the kind of resource—albeit almost never referred to as a "cultural resource"—with which social impact assessment (SIA) is supposed to deal, and it's a kind of resource that people can feel *very* strongly about.

Most study of impacts on this kind of resource is done under NEPA's broad umbrella, though sometimes laws dealing with specific programs are a bit more directive. The Magnuson Fishery Conservation and Management Act, as amended (18 U.S.C.A. 1801 et seq.), for example, requires consideration of economic and social impacts of systems for limiting access to fisheries. The Outer Continental Shelf Lands Act, as amended (43 U.S.C.A. 1331 et seq.) requires analysis of the impacts of resource development activities on "the physical social, and economic components, conditions and factors which interactively determine the state, condition, and quality of living conditions, employment, and health."

A concern about "intangible" aspects of culture is also expressed in the American Folklife Preservation Act (AFPA; 20 U.S.C. 2101), which created the American Folklife Center to "preserve and present American folklife." However, the AFPA only authorizes the *collection and presentation of information* about folklife; it doesn't have a NEPA-like or Section 106-ish requirement that agencies consider folklife in planning, so folklife matters tend to remain marginal to the enterprise of cultural resource management.

In 1980, in an amendment to NHPA, Congress directed the American Folklife Center and NPS to prepare a report on "...preserving and conserving the intangible elements of our cultural heritage such as arts, skills, folklife, and folkways" (16 U.S.C. 470a note) The result of this study was a report that recommended, among other things, that the federal government:

> *indicate the full range of cultural resources included under the protection of the law by defining cultural and historic resources to include historic properties, folklife, and related traditional lifeways.* (Loomis 1983:74)

Largely for want of a clear and well-organized constituency, this never happened, and it's probably a good thing. An effort to associate folklife and folkways with historic properties in law probably would have resulted in the creation of something like a National Register of Folklife Resources. This, I think, would have been an utter disaster. We have enough trouble with a National Register of Historic Places, without trying to divide up and register something as fluid and dynamic as folklife.

So impacts on sociocultural institutions, ways of life, and similar soft social factors are considered in NEPA-based environmental review, and occasionally under other authorities. This consideration tends to be pretty haphazard, however. There are guidelines for SIA under NEPA, (cf. Branch et al. 1983; Burdge and Colleagues 1994; Finsterbusch and Wolf 1981; Taylor, Bryan, and Goodrich 1990), but none is in the form of regulation or other official government direction.

The Guidelines and Principles for SIA

The closest thing we have to official direction is something I've cited several times already, the *Guidelines and Principles for Social Impact Assessment*. The *Guidelines and Principles* were prepared by an "Interorganizational Committee on Guidelines and Principles for Social Impact Assessment" in 1993; the Committee was made up of representatives of the Rural Sociology Society, the American Psychological Association, the American Sociological Association, the American Anthropological Association, the Society for Applied Anthropology, the Agricultural Economics Association, and the International Association for Impact Assessment. The *Guidelines and Principles* have been published in a number of venues, perhaps most conveniently in a short stand-alone 1994 booklet by the National Oceanic and Atmospheric Administration (NOAA 1994).

I described the *Principles* in Chapter 4. The *Guidelines* are a bit more extensive, and are usefully organized around the steps in the NEPA process, as follows:

1. Public Involvement—Develop an effective public involvement plan to involve all potentially affected publics.

This guideline goes on to discuss ways to do this, many of which we've touched on already. It makes the point that public meetings by themselves are inadequate, and recommends surveys as a first step in developing an ongoing public involvement program.

2. Identification of Alternatives—Describe the proposed action or policy change and reasonable alternatives.

This guideline goes on to recommend that information be collected on each alternative with respect to the stages of planning, implementation or construction, operation and maintenance, and decommissioning or abandonment. With respect to each stage and alternative, information should be developed on population characteristics, community and institutional structures, political and social resources, individual and family changes, and community resources.

3. Baseline Conditions—Describe the relevant human environment/area of influence and baseline conditions.

The *Guidelines* recommend baseline studies of human relationships with the biophysical environment, historical background, political and social resources, culture, attitudes, and social-psychological conditions, and population characteristics.

4. Scoping—*After obtaining a technical understanding of the proposal, identify the full range of probable social impacts that will be addressed based on discussion or interviews with numbers of all potentially affected.*

Scoping, this guideline says, should include:

...reviews of the existing social science literature, public scoping, public surveys, and public participation techniques. It is important for the views of affected people to be taken into consideration. Ideally, all affected people or groups contribute to the selection of the variables assessed...

5. Projection of Estimated Effects—*Investigate the probable impacts.*

The *Guidelines* list a series of methods that can be used to project effects. The comparative method compares the proposed project with previous similar projects and their effects. The "straight-line trend" method projects change into the future based on existing trends. The "population multiplier method" links change in population size to changes in other variables. Scenarios are used to construct hypothetical futures and consider their implications. Expert testimony is obviously a key method, employing expert advice. Computer modeling can be applied to a variety of other models. Finally, one can calculate "futures foregone," for example, what will be given up in terms of future land uses or social benefits if this river valley is flooded or that bridge is built.

6. Predicting Responses to Impacts—*Determine the significance of the identified social impacts.*

The *Guidelines* note that this is "a difficult assessment task often avoided," but it is obviously important. Since SIA is about human responses to environmental change it is vital to project what these responses will be. So the proposed action will increase property tax rates. Will this actually drive out low income families, or will they stay because of comparably higher property values? Comparison with previous like cases and interviews with affected groups can provide the basis for this sort of projection.

7. Indirect and Cumulative Impacts—*Estimate subsequent impacts and cumulative impacts.*

The *Guidelines* acknowledge that such impacts are "difficult to estimate precisely" but stress the importance of trying to predict them.

8. Changes in Alternatives—*Recommend new or changed alternatives and estimate or project their consequences.*

The *Guidelines* do not envision the impact assessor to be a passive collector of data. She or he is supposed to provide constant feedback to planners, providing recommendations about changes and their effects.

9. Mitigation—Develop a mitigation plan.

The *Guidelines* discuss mitigation in some detail, promoting a sequence of priorities ranging from avoiding adverse effect altogether through compensation for unavoidable adverse effects.

10. Monitoring—Develop a monitoring program.

The *Guidelines* here encourage full participation by the affected community in getting mitigation and monitoring plans "in writing" so they can be enforced. (NOAA 1994:11-18)

However...

The *Guidelines and Principles* provide a good deal of common sense advice about how the sociocultural aspects of the environment should be dealt with in environmental review. Unfortunately, though, they aren't very thoroughly attended to in a lot of SIA studies. As discussed in Chapter 4, SIA is often warped into "Socioeconomic Impact Assessment," and emphasizes economic and other easily quantifiable variables to the exclusion of all else. This doesn't need to be the case—indeed the *Guidelines and Principles* point in quite another direction—but it often *is* the case. This sort of narrowing of SIA's focus, which allows so much of culture to fall through the cracks between quantifiable economics and land-based historic properties, is something that cultural resource managers can and should struggle with, and the *Guidelines and Principles* are a useful weapon to use in that struggle.

Cycling back into the specific concerns of historic preservation, we need to consider several authorities that require attention to historic places in our central cities.

Urban Historic Districts

NHPA was enacted in substantial part because of rampant demolition in the nation's urban centers, occasioned by the generally misguided assumptions of urban renewal. Discouraging federal agencies from knocking down the center cities didn't stop people and capital from fleeing to the suburbs, however, and it soon became apparent that the government ought to do what it could to stabilize and stimulate the nation's central business areas (CBAs). Since many CBAs contain lots of historic buildings, often comprising historic districts, and since clearly, the best way to preserve such properties is to keep them in active use, interests in CBA stabilization and historic preservation have tended to coincide.

The Public Buildings Cooperative Use Act

Back in 1976, the Public Buildings Cooperative Use Act (40 U.S.C. 601a and 611; PBCUA) was enacted, including a requirement that the General Services Administration (GSA) give preference to the use of historic buildings to fill federal space needs. The idea was to fight agency flight to the suburbs, and instead use the fulfillment of federal space requirements to leverage downtown economic development via the rehabilitation of historic buildings.

Under the PBCUA, GSA began to give a 10% preference to offerors of historic buildings when it sought to lease space to fill agency needs. In other words, if I offer a non-historic building for $100 and you offer one for $109, all else being equal, you win. GSA feels that this preference has been generally effective in directing federal investment into historic buildings. Others disagree.

Executive Order 12072

In 1978 , with similar motivations, President Jimmy Carter issued Executive Order 12072, directing that preference be given to siting federal offices in CBAs. Although historic preservation wasn't central to this order, its intent was much the same as the PBCUA—to use the federal workforce to help stimulate downtown economic development.

Section 110(a)(1) of NHPA

Preservationists tended to be dissatisfied with the vigor with which GSA pursued its PBCUA responsibilities, so in the 1980 amendments to the NHPA, Section 110(a)(1) was added, and amended in 1992 to include the following direction:

Prior to acquiring, constructing, or leasing buildings for purposes of carrying out agency responsibilities, each Federal agency shall use, to the maximum extent feasible, historic properties available to the agency.

Section 110(a)(1) is pretty directive. As long as it's "feasible"—which presumably means practical, economically sensible, and consistent with the agency's mission and mandates—any federal agency *shall* give preference to the use of historic properties. This requirement speaks not only to GSA but to all federal agencies, and it's a mandatory provision, not just a "should do."

Agencies have pretty much ignored Section 110(a)(1).

Executive Order 13006

One might think that the response by preservationists would have been to lobby and litigate to get agencies to change their ways under the existing law, but instead, the National Trust and others pushed President Bill Clinton for another executive order. Executive Order 13006, issued on May 21, 1996, directed all agencies to give preferential consideration to the use of historic buildings in historic districts in central business areas. If such buildings couldn't be found to suit the government, then compatible new construction within historic districts was to be the next choice, followed by use of historic facilities *not* in historic districts.

So we have two statutes and two executive orders which collectively drive the federal government toward using historic buildings in historic districts in central business districts to fill their needs for offices and other spaces. Although the primary impact of all these requirements is on GSA, they affect other agencies as well, either directly when an agency does its own real estate transactions, or through GSA when GSA serves as an agency's real estate agent.

Altogether, these laws and executive orders give historic preservationists a potentially powerful set of tools to use in encouraging agencies to reuse urban historic buildings and historic districts. Enthusiasm should be tempered with an appreciation for a couple of realities, however.

First, the government isn't required to use historic facilities if they don't serve an agency's program needs. If the agency's employees won't fit in the building, or if its use would greatly inconvenience the public, or if the agency does things (e.g., some kinds of laboratory work) that are incompatible with the facility or the neighborhood, the government doesn't have to use a historic property.

Second, it's generally up to the agency to define what its program needs are, and a lot of agencies and their employees don't want to be in old buildings, or downtown. A lot of them prefer nice new buildings in the suburbs, with lots of parking space. So there's some tendency, on the part of some agencies, to structure their program needs in such a way as to ensure that they *can't* be satisfied with historic facilities in central business areas. Where GSA is the government's agent and has the will (by no means a universal condition), it can try to jawbone its client into flexing its requirements, but in the final analysis if the client then wants to jettison GSA and go to a commercial agent, it can do so. The agency itself is then subject to most of the same legal requirements as GSA is, but it may be willing to take its chances.

Third, there are some other legal requirements that more or less directly conflict with the historic/downtown requirements. The Rural Development Act of 1972 (42 U.S.C. 3122) directs agencies to give preference to siting in *rural* areas. Executive Order 11988—another Carter-era executive order—directs that agencies not contribute to development of floodplains. There are extensive guidelines, issued originally by the now-defunct Water Resources Council and now implemented under the oversight of the Federal Emergency Management Agency (FEMA), that prescribe a rather complicated eight-step review process for any federal project that might contribute directly or indirectly to floodplain development (WRC/FEMA 1978). Although not technically regulations, the guidelines are cast in quite directive language, and agencies tend to follow them with some rigor. Historic center cities, of course, are often in floodplains, and FEMA—rightly, given the serious environmental, social, health, safety, and economic implications of floodplain development—tends to be something of a junkyard dog when it comes to hounding agencies about compliance. As a result, Executive Order 11988 rather severely constrains how responsive agencies can be to Executive Order 13006 and its cohort of related authorities.

What most cultural resource managers need to know about the PBCUA, Section 110(a)(1), and Executive Orders 12074 and 13006 is that they exist, that they generally promote the use of downtown historic buildings in historic districts by federal agencies, and that there are a number of ways agencies avoid vigorous compliance with them, for good reasons and bad. If you find yourself involved in a potential real estate transaction by a federal agency, you need to know about these provisions.

Parenthetically, these four laws and executive orders, together with the Rural Development Act and Executive Order 11988, also exemplify a tendency in the federal government that makes it increasingly difficult to do anything about anything. With the best of intent, Congress enacts laws, and presidents issue executive orders, that are not always consistent with one another and that sometimes work directly at cross purposes. Laws are seldom repealed, executive orders are seldom withdrawn. Instead, new laws are passed and orders issued, whose relationships with those that went before often seem to have gone unconsidered. Federal agencies can spend a great deal of time and effort trying to resolve the contradictions that result, instead of getting along with implementing anything in the real world. It's easy to "blame the bureaucrats" for this, but it's really not the bureaucrats' fault; it's the nature of the beast with which bureaucrats struggle every day.

Authorities like Executive Order 13006 and Section 110(a)(1) of NHPA have two theoretically symbiotic purposes—to stimulate economic development and to encourage preservation of historic buildings and structures and the districts in which they stand. Wherever they exist, in urban areas or rural, historic buildings have special needs. There's a very well developed body of practice involved in the treatment of these resources, with its own special standards and methods. There's no way to do full justice to these here, but let's have an overview.

Historic Buildings and Structures

A building, in National Register parlance, is a construction designed to hold people or activities. A house, a barn, a courthouse, a grocery store, a church. A structure is something that's designed for some other purpose—a tunnel, a mine shaft, a power plant, a fortification, a road, a bridge. Ships and aircraft are also classified as structures. These categories have permeable boundaries, of course; a fortification and a power plant house activities. And the function of a construction can change through time; a power plant can be converted into offices, a silo can become a hotel. People have been known to argue over whether something is a building or a structure, but only if they don't have much else to do.

What sets buildings and structures apart from other kinds of historic properties is that they are entirely (or almost entirely, as in the case of a sod house or a structure built into a cave) human constructions that exhibit design features reflecting their times and functions and the thought processes of those who designed and built them. Unlike many sites and districts, they are also rather discretely bounded; they have walls, floors, roofs. And in many cases they are occupied and can continue to be occupied, or reoccupied, to meet contemporary needs. The kinds of things we do with and to buildings and structures reflect these characteristics. We document their design elements, and we try to preserve these elements while facilitating their continuing use or reuse.

One of the major tools used in facilitating continuing use and reuse is a set of standards issued by NPS on behalf of the Secretary of the Interior, and every cultural resource manager needs to know about them.

The Secretary of the Interior's Standards for the Treatment of Historic Properties

The Secretary of the Interior, through NPS, has long promoted standards for doing various good things with historic buildings and structures. In 1992 these were gathered together into a rather muddy little brochure called *The Secretary of the Interior's Standards for the Treatment of Historic Properties*. The title is inaccurate; the standards are really for the treatment of buildings and structures. The inaccuracy results from their authorship by NPS's architectural gurus, who have never really internalized the fact that there are properties out there that *aren't* buildings and structures.

But the Standards, and the plethora of guidance that backs them up, are helpful and generally common-sensical, if you just substitute "buildings and structures" for "properties" throughout.

The Standards address four kinds of treatment: *preservation, rehabilitation, restoration,* and *reconstruction.* An obvious fifth—demolition—is not entertained.

PRESERVATION

"Preservation" means something different in the Standards than it does under NHPA. Section 301(8) of NHPA defines "preservation" very broadly, to include everything from identification to documentation—consistent with the scope of the statute itself—and explicitly including "rehabilitation" and "restoration," which the "Standards" *contrast* with "preservation." But let's not quibble. The Standards define preservation as:

...the act or process of applying measures necessary to sustain the existing form, integrity, and materials of an historic property. (NPS 1992)

Under the Standards, then, preservation means keeping the building or structure in its existing form, preserving its integrity, respecting its materials. It "focuses upon the ongoing maintenance and repair of historic materials and features."

There are eight Preservation Standards:

Standard 1: A property shall be used as it was historically, or given a new use that maximizes the retention of distinctive materials, features, spaces and spatial relationships...

So you use a barn as a barn, or you can probably get away with using it as a farm museum, but if you want to convert it into office space, you probably can't call it preservation under the definition given in the Standards. You *can* call it preservation under NHPA Section 301(8), of course, and people seem able to live with this ambiguity.

Standard 2: The historic character of a property shall be retained and preserved. The replacement of intact or repairable historic materials or alteration of features, spaces, and spatial relationships that characterize a property shall be avoided.

So you've got to leave the place pretty much alone, although...

The limited and sensitive upgrading of mechanical, electrical, and plumbing systems and other code-required work to make properties functional is appropriate within a preservation project.

So you can bring the building or structure up to code and keep it there, as long as the work you need to do is "limited" and "sensitive" to its historic fabric.

Standard 3: Each property shall be recognized as a physical record of its time, place, and use. Work needed...shall be physically and visually compatible, identifiable upon close inspection, and properly documented for future research.

This standard is a tricky one, because it seems to say two contradictory things. On the one hand, anything you need to do should be "physically and visually compatible" with existing fabric, but on the other, it should be "identifiable upon close inspection." So if you have to replace some badly deteriorated woodwork, let's say, it ought to look and feel just like the old woodwork, but close inspection by somebody who knows his or her stuff should reveal that it's not of the same vintage as the original. And the work should be documented so the future scholar doesn't have to rely entirely on her or his own senses.

Standard 4: *Changes to a property that have acquired historic significance in their own right shall be retained and preserved.*

There's a beautiful four-story U.S. Courthouse in Old San Juan, Puerto Rico, built in 1914 with a grand entrance facing the sea. In 1941, a rather ugly addition was built, wiping out the entrance and extending several more stories into the unclouded Caribbean sky. When the Courthouse needed fixing in the 1990s, a proposal was floated to demolish the addition. There was violent and successful opposition to this proposal, because the addition—a visual landmark in Old San Juan, if a less than distinguished one—had acquired its own historical significance.

Standard 5: *Distinctive materials, features, finishes, and construction techniques or examples of craftsmanship that characterize a property shall be preserved.*

This standard is pretty obvious, but often takes a good deal of research to apply. You have to determine what the distinctive features, finishes, and construction techniques are, and they may not be obvious, particularly if the building has undergone a lot of changes over the years—changes which, themselves, may have achieved historic significance and therefore not be things you can strip away willy-nilly. And sometimes preservation can be a very costly affair, particularly if the examples of features in question weren't meant to survive for very long.

Standard 6: *The existing condition of historic features shall be evaluated to determine the appropriate level of intervention needed. Where the severity of deterioration requires repair or limited replacement of a distinctive feature, the new material shall match the old in composition, design, color, and texture.*

Adherence to this standard, of course, has to be balanced against making sure that people in the future don't mistake today's replacement for yesterday's original. If half your wall light sconces are deteriorated beyond repair, you're going to want to replace them, and you ought to copy the existing sconces—make them look essentially identical with the originals. But somehow or other you also need to make sure that careful examination will allow someone to distinguish the old from the new. Why? Architects will tell you that it's a matter of honesty.

Standard 7: Chemical or physical treatments...shall be undertaken using the gentlest means possible. Treatments that cause damage to historic materials shall not be used.

The second sentence of this standard may be a tall order. Arguably any treatment that alters the surface (or subsurface) of any piece of architectural fabric causes some damage. But generally it's pretty obvious that this is a sensible, very important, standard. No doubt you've seen those brick walls in your local brew pub, nice and clean and rough-surfaced. They've been sandblasted, which has removed the hard surface of the brick. They look fine now, but in a few years, or decades, or perhaps centuries, depending on what they're exposed to, they'll deteriorate and eventually the wall will fall down. Sandblasting—or blasting with pretty much anything—will also destroy surface details, for example sculptural elements. So you don't want to do it, ever. Water and a soft-bristle brush are the recommended cleaning agents for most kinds of historic architectural fabric; sometimes detergent of various kinds is OK, and there are some acceptable chemical treatments, but (of course) it depends, on the material, the gunk that you're trying to remove, the environmental conditions, and so on. One thing doesn't depend, however; there is—well, as far as I know there is—*no* circumstance under which sandblasting is a good idea.

Standard 8: Archeological resources shall be protected and preserved in place. If such resources must be disturbed, mitigation measures shall be undertaken.

This sop to archeology is found in each set of standards. Like a lot of the standards, it contains a mild internal contradiction. Are we to preserve and protect in place, or are we to mitigate? In real world terms, though, what it means is that as we're bringing our preserved building or structure up to code, and have to upgrade its utilities or clean up its landscaping, we ought to be careful about whatever's in the ground, and plan for data recovery if we're likely to disturb something. That something may be something associated with the building or structure itself—the remains of a demolished wing or bay, an old cistern, a privy pit—or something unrelated but important, like a prehistoric site or the buried ships that lie under waterfront commercial rows in New York, San Francisco, and other cities.

REHABILITATION

The Standards for Rehabilitation may be the most important of the lot. Rehab is:

...the act or process of making possible a compatible use for a property through repair, alterations, and additions while preserving those portions or features which convey its historical, cultural, or architectural values.

The idea behind NHPA and other historic preservation authorities is not to fossilize historic buildings and structures in their original conditions, but to keep them alive, as parts of modern life. Living things have to change, and rehab is the means we have of making necessary changes while retaining the basic characteristics that make the place important.

The rehab standards are particularly important because a developer has to meet them in order to qualify for certain investment credits on his or her federal income tax. "Tax Act" work was big business for preservation-oriented architects during the first Reagan administration, when the credit was very liberal. Congress then tightened up the requirements, and today there are fewer Tax Act projects. But the tax credits still generate a good deal of rehabilitation, and each project must be reviewed by the SHPO, under NPS oversight, to make sure the rehab standards are met.

Rehab is not perfect preservation; something's always lost. But that's life. What rehab can do is to keep a good old building standing and functional, serving a purpose. It can extend the life of the investment the building represents. Rehab permits "adaptive use"—that is, the use of a building or structure (or, in theory, another kind of historic property) for something other than the use for which it was originally intended, without completely sacrificing the characteristics that reflect its original use, or that otherwise make it important.

There are ten rehab standards:

Standard 1: *A property shall be used as it was historically or be given a new use that requires minimal change to its distinctive materials, features, spaces, and spatial relationships.*

Very similar to Preservation Standard 1, but a bit softer, more permissive of change. Now, what constitutes "minimal change? How much change is too much? It depends, of course, and it often and perhaps inevitably depends on a lot of highly subjective factors. Perhaps including the side of bed on which a reviewer arises in the morning, or how much he had to drink the night before. There are lots of horror stories about SHPO and NPS reviewers of rehab projects getting terribly sticky about some things and being loose as a goose about others, with no apparent rationale for the difference. Some people seem to feel that, since architecture is an art, the reviewer of architectural issues should have a whole lot of artistic license in accepting or not accepting things based on gut feelings. Perhaps, but the reviewer or planner in a CRM context should remember that she or he is dealing directly or indirectly with the taxpayers' money, and it's to those taxpayers that we have to be responsible.

Standard 2: *The historic character of a property shall be retained and preserved. The removal of distinctive materials or alteration of features, spaces, and spatial relationships that characterize a property shall be avoided.*

This reads a lot like Preservation Standard 2, but it's subtly different. Where the preservation standard talks about avoiding replacement of *historic* materials, the rehab standard talks about avoiding removal of *distinctive* materials. This may seem like hairsplitting, but the difference between all historic materials and distinctive materials is a considerable one. Say we've got an old office building with a lot of woodwork, including some really nice woodwork in the public spaces and some pretty boring woodwork in the offices. All of it is historic, and if we're preserving the building we're going to need to respect it all. But if we're rehabilitating the building, we may decide that the woodwork in the public space is what's really distinctive, and the garden variety woodwork elsewhere can go, or be substantially altered.

Standard 3: Each property shall be recognized as a physical record of its time, place, and use. Changes that create a false sense of historical development, such as adding conjectural features or elements from other historic properties, shall not be undertaken.

Here the contrast with the equivalent preservation standard is a bit starker. We're still recognizing the building or structure as a record of its time, place, and use, but rather than insisting rigorously on compatibility with, but distinctiveness from, existing fabric, we're simply saying: "don't lie." Don't slap a false front on your old store to turn it into the Deadwood Saloon. Don't stick phony muntins between the panes of your double-glazed aluminum frame windows to make them look like they have old timey multiple panes.

Standard 4: Changes to a property that have acquired historic significance in their own right shall be retained and preserved.

This one is precisely the same as its preservation equivalent, and has to be interpreted in the same way.

Standard 5: Distinctive materials, features, finishes, and construction techniques or examples of craftsmanship that characterize a property shall be preserved.

This one, too, is identical with its preservation counterpart, and has to be taken to mean the same thing. In practice, though, it tends to be interpreted with more flexibility.

Standard 6: Deteriorated historic features shall be repaired rather than replaced. Where the severity of deterioration requires repair or limited replacement of a distinctive feature, the new material shall match the old in composition, design, color, texture, and, where possible, materials. Replacement of missing features shall be substantiated by documentary and physical evidence.

Oddly, this standard actually seems more absolute than its preservation equivalent, which does not flatly prescribe repair rather than replacement. It's not meant to be, though. The distinction that's attended to is that the preservation standard demands rigorous evaluation to "determine the appropriate level of intervention needed," the rehab standard simply says you ought to repair rather than replace. The research requirement is less strenuous. The fact that the Standards routinely say "thou shalt" or "thou shall not" when they mean "thou oughta" or "thou shouldn't" was pointed out to NPS when the Standards were rewritten in the late 1980s, and NPS acknowledged that they didn't mean precisely what they say. NPS wanted to speak firmly, and did, but in practice, a rule of reason applies. In the case of Standard 6, the existence of this rule is indicated by the obvious contradiction between the first and second sentences. If you were *always* to repair rather than replace, there would be no need for matching new material with old. The actual rule is that you should repair rather than replace unless it's just flatly unreasonable to do so, whereupon you should make sure the replacement matches the original.

Note that Preservation Standard 6 says nothing about using matching *material* in replacement, but Rehabilitation Standard 6 does. This is probably because the NPS standard setters couldn't imagine the designer of a preservation project replacing, say, wood-frame windows with vinyl-clad, but they could well imagine it of a rehab project designer. Note, too, that the rehab standard says you match materials "where possible." While it's arguably almost *always* "possible" to replace something with the same material as the original—to replace "in kind"—the way this language tends to be interpreted is to mean "where feasible." Real-world factors like availability, cost, and effectiveness are considered.

But such considerations need to be justified. It's very easy for a building manager who wants to improve energy efficiency to tumble for triple-glazed windows in aluminum frames, without exploring the costs and benefits of alternatives like interior storm windows. Very often, when these costs and benefits are accurately calculated, it turns out to be far more cost-effective, and just as energy-effective, to repair and upgrade the existing windows, rather than to replace them.

Standard 7: *Chemical or physical treatments...shall be undertaken using the gentlest means possible. Treatments that cause damage to historic materials shall not be used.*

Same as the preservation standard, with the same rationale. It's no more desirable to let the wall of a rehabilitated building fall down because of sandblasting than it is to let the wall of a preserved building collapse from the same cause.

Standard 8: Archeological resources shall be protected and preserved in place. If such resources must be disturbed, mitigation measures shall be undertaken.

Same as the preservation standard, same rationale, same implications.

Standard 9: New additions, exterior alterations, or related new construction shall not destroy historic materials, features, and spatial relationships that characterize the property. The new work shall be differentiated from the old and shall be compatible with the historic materials, features, size, scale and proportion, and massing to protect the integrity of the property and its environment.

This one is unique to the Rehab Standards, for obvious reasons. One does not do new construction as part of a preservation project as defined in the Standards (though of course, one could do so on a preservation project as defined in NHPA).

This standard prescribes a narrow path that an architect has to walk in designing a new-construction component of a rehab project—a new wing on a building, say, or a new floor, or a new building in a complex of old ones. On the one hand the architect is to "differentiate" the new work from the old; on the other she is to make sure the two are "compatible in terms of "materials, features, size, scale and proportion, and massing." It's a path with very subjective boundaries; architects can argue endlessly about whether one of them has achieved a good result on any given project.

Suppose you're dealing with a Victorian ironfront commercial building, and you need to provide access for the disabled. Suppose the only economically feasible way you can do this without really mucking up the building is by adding an outside elevator shaft. What do you make this shaft look like?

The Standard indicates that you don't try to make it look like a little skinny Victorian ironfront standing next to the original building, and I think most people would agree that this would look pretty stupid. But suppose you can kind of tuck it in against a wall of the building and extend a facade a little bit to disguise it? The Standard discourages this, too, because you're not "differentiating" the new from the old. But reasonable people might ask who cares, if the relationship between the old and the new is a visually pleasing one. The answer is usually that wrapping the new in so it looks like part of the old is not an "honest" solution, and that it may confuse people in the future. Take that for what it's worth.

On the other end of the spectrum, some architects will lean so strongly toward differentiating between the old and the new that they'd build a plain concrete box to house the elevator, or maybe something of anodized aluminum. The Standard discourages this, too, because this solution isn't "compatible with the historic materials, features, size, scale and proportion, and massing to protect the integrity of the property and its environment."

What the Standard encourages is something that really does tend to be pretty pleasing when you see it—a new building or wing that doesn't pretend to be old, but that echoes the existing building in interesting, subtle ways. The color's similar, though probably not identical. If the original is made of brick, so is the new, or perhaps it's not but it doesn't contrast shriekingly with the brick. Windows are in line with those in the original, and of about the same scale. It's not grossly out of proportion with the original. One of the things that makes such a solution pleasing to the eye, I think, is that it obviously takes intelligence to design, and it requires a certain amount of intelligence to interpret and appreciate. It adds something more than just an elevator shaft to the built environment. Anybody can copy something, and anybody can build something that doesn't respect its environment. Designing something that isn't a copy, but does respect what's around it, requires some thinking, and it's pleasant to experience the result of such thinking. So in some ways, the best thing about this Standard is not what it says, per se, but that it encourages thoughtful design that enriches the visual environment. And it also encourages some wonderful arguments among architects.

Standard 10: *New additions and adjacent or related new construction shall be undertaken in such a manner that, if removed in the future, the essential form and integrity of the historic property and its environment would be unimpaired.*

This standard, also unique to the Rehab Standards, is pretty straightforward. You ought to build your addition so that if and when it's taken down, the original building or structure is still there, without big holes in it.

There's a classic example at the Old Post Office in Washington, D.C., where the ACHP has its offices. A glass passage has been added connecting commercial spaces on the lower floors with an adjacent commercial area. The passage links to the old building through a window, and just sort of snuggles up against the wall around the window without piercing it. If it's ever taken down, all that will have to be done is to re-hang the sashes in the window opening, and maybe rebuild the frame, and no one will be able to tell that the glass connector was ever there. Of course, if this doesn't happen until the connector has achieved historical significance in its own right there will be other problems to confront.

RESTORATION

Restoration is:

...the act or process of accurately depicting the form, features, and character of a property as it appeared at a particular period of time by means of the removal of features from other periods in its history and reconstruction of missing features from the restoration period.

Had GSA taken down the 1941 addition to the Old San Juan Courthouse, and rebuilt the grand entrance, this would have been restoration.

Restoration Standards 1, 2, 3, 5, and 6 are virtually the same as their equivalent Preservation Standards, except that they focus on the period to which the property is restored rather than to all pertinent historic periods. Restoration Standard 8 is the same as Preservation Standard 7 (Use gentle methods), and Restoration Standard 9 is the same as Preservation Standard 8 (Be nice to archeology). Restoration Standard 4, rather than requiring preservation of changes to the property that have acquired historic significance, provides for such changes to be documented.

Restoration Standards 7 and 10 are peculiar to this set of standards. Standard 7 requires documentary or physical evidence to support replacement of missing features from the restoration period, and prohibits the creation of:

...a false sense of history...by adding conjectural features, features from other properties, or by combining features that never existed together historically.

Standard 10 points in the same direction, rather elegantly stating that:

Designs that were never executed historically shall not be constructed.

Both standards discourage speculation and frivolity, and promote honesty. If you don't know and can't prove that the McDuck Bank Building had twelve-over-twelve windows in its heyday, you don't make it so when you restore it—or if you do, because you've got to put *something* in the window openings, you don't represent them as what used to be there. If the bank never had a money bin (in which one can dive around like a porpoise or toss coins up and let them hit you on the head) you don't build one to match Walt Disney's vision.

RECONSTRUCTION

Reconstruction, according to the Standards, is:

...the act or process of depicting, by means of new construction, the form, features, and detailing of a non-surviving site, landscape, building, structure, or object for the purpose of replicating its appearance at a specific period of time and in its historic location.

Reconstruction is something that *can* be applied to properties other than buildings and structures, though it isn't very often. Generally speaking, for obvious reasons, it's things that were once constructed, such as buildings and structures, that get reconstructed.

Most of the Reconstruction Standards have no counterparts among the Preservation, Rehabilitation, and Restoration Standards. Reconstruction is rarely enough done that we will not devote much space to discussing the Standards here, but in brief:

Standard 1: Reconstruction shall be used...when documentary and physical evidence is available to permit accurate reconstruction with minimal conjecture, and such reconstruction is essential to the public understanding of the property.

In other words, don't do it unless you need to and can do it accurately.

Standard 2. Reconstruction...shall be preceded by a thorough archeological investigation...

Archeology should be used to provide physical evidence of what the property was like, and archeological sites—including those related to the thing being reconstructed, and other sites (e.g., a prehistoric site underlying Fort Clint Eastwood)—shouldn't be unnecessarily mucked up. One thing that is sometimes forgotten in planning reconstructions is that the archeology needs to be done far enough in advance of design to allow the data from the archeology to influence planning. Too often, designs are developed with a considerable degree of conjecture, and then archeology is done only to "salvage" data that implementing the design will destroy.

Standard 3: Reconstruction shall include measures to preserve any remaining historic materials, features, and spatial relationships.

This really isn't much different from Standard 2. If there is anything original there—in the ground or elsewhere—it ought to be preserved.

Standard 4: Reconstruction shall be based on...accurate duplication...rather than on conjectural design or the availability of different features from other historic properties...

If you can't prove that Fort Clint Eastwood's walls were seventeen feet high and made of redwood logs, you don't build them to that height, of that material, or if you do (because you have to build them to *some* height, out of *something*), you explain that you really don't know quite how high they were, or what material was used to build them. And you don't haul in old buildings from Forts Lee Marvin and Danny Glover to add to Eastwood's ambience.

Standard 5: A reconstruction shall be clearly identified as a contemporary re-creation.

Put up a sign. Don't fool the public.

Standard 6: Designs that were never executed historically shall not be constructed.

If Fort Clint Eastwood didn't have a tower from which the troops could watch for attacking Indians, you don't add one because the fort in "Buffalo Soldiers" on TV had one and it really looked neat.

How Do the Standards Relate to Compliance?

Some architects follow the Standards simply because they're good advice, for historic buildings and, for that matter, in general. But for the most part, the Standards are employed in order to comply with one of several legal authorities.

THE TAX CODE

If you own the McDuck Bank Building and preserve it as an operating bank, rehab it as a bed and breakfast, or restore it as a museum of banking, then if you want to take a preservation tax credit on your federal income tax, you have to show the Internal Revenue Service that your work meets the pertinent Secretary's Standards. To do this, you've got to show that the project was reviewed and approved by the SHPO, with the blessing of NPS. Many historical architects make their living designing or consulting on the design of tax code-supported rehab projects, and others spend their lives reviewing such designs on behalf of SHPOs or NPS.

SECTION 106

If you're going to use, say, Community Development Block Grant funds from the Department of Housing and Urban Development through your local government to rehab the McDuck Bank Building, then if you want to get a determination of "no adverse effect," you're going to have to meet the Standards. You have to do this in consultation with, and document the agreement of, the SHPO, or go to the ACHP for its agreement.

Some people subscribe to the myth that a project done under a Section 106 MOA must also meet the pertinent standards. It's nice if it can, but it's not necessary. Remember that an MOA is done on measures to mitigate the adverse effects of a project. We're acknowledging that there may or will be adverse effects, and we're finding a way to resolve the effects. There's no requirement that the way chosen be consistent with any particular standards, as long as it's not illegal.

Example: a low-income housing provider who was part of a development project at an abandoned Air Force base had, he believed, been burned by cost-overruns resulting from review under the Tax Code. He refused to participate in the project if the MOA on transfer of the base out of federal ownership required that the Standards be followed. Rather than lose his participation, and in view of the character of the buildings, we executed an MOA that had the developer use the Standards as guidance, but not be strictly bound by them. Whether you like this solution or not, it was legal.

Technical note: If you refer to the Secretary's Standards in a Section 106 document—or any other document, for that matter, that you expect people to follow—don't refer to them simply as "the Secretary's Standards." There are a whole lot of Secretary's Standards—for Archeology and Historic Preservation, for the documentation of historic watercraft, and, who knows, probably for the classification of infirm raptors. Give a complete citation, such as *The Secretary of the Interior's Standards for Restoration, National Park Service 1992*. Remember the "cold reader," and don't assume that he or she will know which Standards to which you're referring.

SECTIONS 110(A)(1) AND 111, PBCUA, AND EO 13006

For all practical purposes, you have to follow the pertinent standards to comply with Section 110(a)(1) of NHPA—which promotes use of historic properties by federal agencies as long as such use is consistent with their preservation (as defined in NHPA). You also have to follow them when carrying out the comparable provisions of the Public Buildings Cooperative Use Act, and when preparing a building for adaptive use under Section 111 of NHPA (see below). Executive Order 13006, which promotes the same kind of preferential use of historic buildings and structures in historic districts, explicitly requires that rehabilitation and new construction be "architecturally compatible with the character of the surrounding historic district or properties."

HSRs, HBPPs, and Similar Plans

Agencies that manage a lot of historic buildings, like GSA, NPS, and the military services, tend to have regulations and procedures requiring or at least promoting the development and use of management plans that effectively apply the Secretary's Standards where they're needed. NPS pioneered the form with what it called a "Historic Structures Report" (HSR); the HSR model was picked up by GSA and other agencies, and adapted in various ways.

The term "Historic Structures Report" doesn't exactly make one think instantly of a plan, and that's not surprising, because an HSR didn't start out to be primarily a plan. It was a description and evaluation of a building or structure, used as the basis for figuring out how to manage it. But the basic idea was to identify the building's significant characteristics, and it was a natural step to link those characteristics with prescribed treatments. This in effect made the HSR a plan.

But because HSRs started out being largely descriptive and evaluative, they tend to involve a lot of up-front research, and hence a lot of investment before you get a product that can actually be used. Dissatisfaction with the high up–front costs of the HSR led GSA, with the Georgia Institute of Technology, to develop the Historic Building Preservation Plan (HBPP). Doing an HBPP involves a relatively quick and dirty descriptive and evaluative study that leads to breaking the building up into *zones* designated for various kinds of treatment. A "preservation zone" should be maintained intact, a "rehabilitation zone" can be rehabilitated. In a "free zone" one can have one's way with the space. Within each zone, *elements* like wall lights, elevator doors, and woodwork are identified and assigned "treatment ratings" based on significance and condition. The zones and elements are linked to standards, grounded in the Secretary's Standards. Certain zones and elements are to be preserved, others restored, others rehabbed, while others can be blown away (cf. Georgia Tech. 1993).

Other agencies have similar kinds of plans. The Corps of Engineers, for example has guidelines for "proactive maintenance plans" (PMP) for historic buildings and structures (Rushlow and Kermath 1994).

Plans like this make a great deal of sense as ways to rationalize the use of standards like those of the Secretary, so you're not giving things more attention than they deserve but are highlighting those aspects of a building or structure that really need care. The problem, as with many plans, is getting them used. It's awfully easy to put a plan on a shelf and ignore it. There have also been problems with linkages between things like HBPPs and Section 106 compliance. Ideally, if a GSA building manager is following his or her HBPP, he or she ought to be in compliance with Section 106, but of course this isn't the case if the HBPP hasn't been reviewed in accordance with the Section 106 regulation. This isn't the kind of thing that's easy for a building manager to deal with, along with the zillion day-to-day problems he or she has to juggle.

The development of things like HSRs and HBPPs is another major aspect of practice for many historical architects. It's an area where there's a lot of room for creative work to develop plans that are practical, effective, and user friendly. Obviously, it's an area in which computer applications make a lot of sense, and the HBPP in particular is designed to be a computer-based plan. However, there's still a lot of unevenness in system availability and computer literacy across the federal establishment, and available applications are developing a good deal faster than they can be used as bases for plans. There's a great deal of growth potential for cultural resource managers with good computer skills, strong interests in architectural preservation, and ability to handle complex, multivariate systems.

Adaptive Use

If an agency can't continue to use a historic building for its original purpose, then Section 111 of NHPA requires that it pursue alternative uses, including "adaptive use." Adaptive use is simply using a building designed for one purpose to serve another. Converting the warehouse to office space, the grain silo to a hotel, the old house to a restaurant, the church to an arts center, the lighthouse to a bed-and-breakfast, the fire lookout to a campsite, the mill to a mall. For federal agencies, adaptive use often requires the development of partnerships with others, and the use of mechanisms like outleasing, cooperative agreements, and co-management. Section 111 adaptive use arrangements have to be worked out in consultation with the ACHP, and are subject to Section 106 review. They usually involve application of the *Secretary of the Interior's Standards for Rehabilitation* to maintain the architectural integrity of the structures involved, though the statute itself does not explicitly require that such integrity be preserved.

Documentation

When a building or structure can't realistically be kept in continuing use, or adapted for a new use, there's nothing in federal law to keep it from being demolished or allowed to fall down, providing compliance with two legal authorities is achieved. The agency has to consider the effects of its proposed action under Section 106. In this context the review and planning requirements of various related authorities, such as NEPA and NHPA Sections 110(a)(1) and 111, have to be addressed. This review, of course, may lead to selection of an alternative that keeps the building standing. If the decision is to demolish, though, then the second legal requirement kicks in; under Section 110(b) of NHPA the property must be documented.

Some people think that documentation is all you ever have to do with a historic building—that, for instance, it's all you have to consider under Section 106. This is resoundingly not so. Alternatives that will keep the building standing and in active use obviously have to be considered in order to be consistent with the purposes of NHPA as required by its Section 110(d). Documentation is what we do as a fall-back, when other alternatives have failed, or as a sort of addendum.

The granddaddy of documentation programs in the United States is the Historic American Buildings Survey (HABS). HABS is one of the only—perhaps *the* only—remaining holdover in government from the "make work" programs of the Franklin Roosevelt administration, that helped pull the U.S. out of the Great Depression. HABS put out-of-work architects to work documenting historic buildings around the country, preparing detailed architectural drawings and filing them in a special collection at the Library of Congress. When the Historic Sites Act was passed in 1935, it gave NPS the rationale to continue HABS indefinitely, and it did.

In the late 1960s and early 1970s, HABS began to get increasingly involved in recording engineering features, facilities, structures, and even processes. This obviously required some rather different bodies of skills and techniques, so eventually it became the focus of its own program—the Historic American Engineering Record (HAER). HABS and HAER have remained closely linked, and are jointly administered as the HABS/HAER division, program, office, group, or whatever the prevailing nomenclature is at NPS during this particular phase of the moon.

HABS/HAER has pretty rigorous documentation standards (summarized in NPS 1983), though these are not monolithic. There are very rigorous standards and not so rigorous standards, which can be applied depending on the perceived significance of the building, structure, or other facility. The HABS/HAER staff at NPS advises agencies about which standards to use and how to interpret them in particular circumstances. HABS/HAER also does its own documentation work, in cooperation with various academic institutions.

Documentation to HABS/HAER standards and filing the results with the Library of Congress is one way to document an historic building or structure, but it's not the only way. SHPOs, Indian tribes, local governments, statewide organizations, and other groups have their own standards and procedures that can be employed. According to the NPS guidelines for implementing Section 110(b) of NHPA (NPS 1988), it's up to the parties consulting under Section 106 to decide what sort of documentation will be done on a threatened property, and what will be done with the results (but see NPS 1998, which revises the Section 110 guidelines and no longer provides direction on Section 110[b]). Many Section 106 MOAs spell out alternative documentation standards, though some simply provide for the responsible agency to contact HABS/HAER and do as they're told.

From buildings and structures we can turn our attention to the ground, and look at the authorities that are dearest to the hearts of many who are used to calling themselves cultural resource managers—archeological sites.

Archeology

The federal government controls a vast number of archeological sites on public lands throughout the country, and it holds many more in trust for Indian tribes on tribal lands. As discussed in Chapter 4, the Antiquities Act of 1906, the nation's first generally applicable cultural resource management law, was aimed at protecting these sites. By the 1970s, however, it had both become inadequate and been declared "unconstitutionally vague," so a new legislative initiative was launched that resulted in the Archeological Resources Protection Act.

The Archeological Resources Protection Act (ARPA)

ARPA regulates access to archeological resources on federal and Indian lands. Uniform regulations issued cooperatively by the Department of the Interior (43 CFR 7), the Department of Agriculture (36 CFR 296), the Tennessee Valley Authority (18 CFR 1312), and the Department of Defense (32 CFR 229) govern ARPA implementation.

ARPA's regulations define "archeological resource" as:

> ...any material remains of human life or activities which are at least 100 years of age, and which are of archeological interest. (43 CFR 7.3[a])

"Of archeological interest" is then defined as:

...capable of providing scientific or humanistic understandings of past human behavior, cultural adaptation, and related topics... (43 CFR 7.3[b])

The definition of "material remains" is similarly broad, encompassing everything from architecture to waste products.

ARPA in essence forbids anyone from excavating or removing an archeological resource from federal or Indian land without a permit from the responsible land managing agency. It also forbids the sale, purchase, exchange, transport or receipt of any resource removed in violation of ARPA or any provision flowing from any other law. Violators face substantial fines and jail sentences if convicted, plus confiscation of what they've dug up and what they've dug it up with (including vehicles, boats, etc.).

ARPA implementation has been ably addressed by Hutt, Jones, and McAllister (1992). Any cultural resource manager who expects to deal with ARPA or its violations in any detail at all should carefully study what they have to say. Training in ARPA enforcement is available from NPS and the Federal Law Enforcement Training Center (FLETC). There's been quite a bit of ARPA prosecution since the law was enacted, and there are now law enforcement officers and prosecutors who specialize in it. Cultural resource managers have important roles to play in ARPA administration, but you need to be careful not to go beyond your competence. Crime scene investigation is a specialized field in its own right, and ARPA investigators don't need well-intentioned amateurs mucking up their evidence. And some diggers of artifacts in violation of ARPA are armed and dangerous. The basic rule, if you see what you think is an ARPA violation in progress, is: take notes and report what you've seen to the authorities, but don't try to intervene.

Whether ARPA is a wise statute is subject to debate, though it's not debated much in professional archeological circles. Some avocational archeologists and most artifact collectors and artifact dealers have rather less enthusiastic views of the law than do most professionals, for obvious and sometimes not-so-obvious reasons. One of the latter is a question about whether criminal prosecution is the best way to deter or redirect destructive behavior. Another is justified unhappiness about lumping "mom and pop" artifact collectors with commercial diggers and manifestly deranged vandals of rock art into a single outlaw category (King 1991). But whether one likes it or not (and professional archeologists, almost to a person, do), ARPA is the law of the land, and there's a substantial body of practice that's developed around it in which a cultural resource manager who's so inclined can become expert.

For most of us, ARPA is relevant on a day-to-day basis because its permitting standards apply to whatever we may agree should be done to an archeological site on federal or Indian land under Section 106, NEPA, or another authority. The standards are not terribly onerous, though they can be interpreted in needlessly draconian ways and can be kind of silly if carried to their logical conclusion. The permittee must meet professional qualifications (43 CFR 7.8[a][1]), but this doesn't mean, as it's occasionally construed, that every individual on the applicant's team has to meet them. Recovered material and data must be housed in an institution that meets specified standards (43 CFR 7.8[a][6]; see also 36 CFR 79). The work must be done for scholarly and/or preservationish reasons (43 CFR 7.8[a][2]). The recovered resources remain the property of the United States in perpetuity (43 CFR 7.6[a][5]), and can be disposed of only when they've lost archeological interest and hence become non-resources—thus, archeological resources are about the only kind of resource that the government can *never* dispose of.

There's a widespread belief that federal agency employees and contractors don't need ARPA permits. In fact, they do, but their contracts and position descriptions are, in effect, construed to be their permits. Such documents must, of course, meet the standards that ARPA and its regulations set forth (43 CFR 7.5[c]).

If all a federal agency is doing is issuing an ARPA permit, it doesn't need to go through Section 106 Review (43 CFR 7.12), but if it's providing any other form of entitlement or assistance (funding, trucks, shovels, etc.) then it needs to do Section 106. The kind of thing that is subject to Section 106 review—putting in roads, cutting trees, and the like—isn't construed to be excavation and removal of archeological resources, so it's not subject to ARPA permitting, but of course it is subject to other permit requirements and the environmental review requirements that go along with them (43 CFR 7.5[b][1]).

Indian tribes with possible interests in resources to which a permit pertains must be notified by the relevant land manager, and given an opportunity to consult about the work. Where the work will be done on tribal land, of course, the tribe has to give its permission. Under NAGPRA, ARPA permits must be coordinated with culturally affiliated tribes.

Archeologists in the 1970s weren't concerned only about the removal of archeological resources from public lands by individuals. There were also all those federal, federally assisted, and federally licensed projects that were wasting sites on lands both public and private. To deal with these, archeologists turned to another oldish law, the Reservoir Salvage Act of 1960, and sought to bring it up to date.

The Archeological Data Preservation Act of 1974

When the Corps of Engineers came home from World War II, Congress assigned it the job of building dams in the Missouri River drainage, and later elsewhere in the nation, for purposes of flood control and power generation. Recognizing that the reservoirs that would rise behind these dams would inundate thousands of archeological sites, NPS and the Smithsonian Institution set up the Missouri River Basin Program, later the River Basin Salvage Program.

The purpose of the program, of course, was to carry out rapid "salvage" excavations of archeological sites before they were swallowed up by the rising waters.

By 1960 the Smithsonian had pulled out of the program, but Congress, in the Reservoir Salvage Act, gave NPS the authority to request appropriations to support it. For the next decade and a half, NPS supported the bulk of archeological salvage in the country on a few million dollars a year. But only reservoirs qualified for salvage (FHWA began to fund salvage on the Interstate Highway System in the 1960s, but it was a pale shadow of NPS's program). A few other projects had salvage components, but as federal involvement in agriculture, urban renewal, and other land modifying programs increased during the Eisenhower and Kennedy administrations, federally supported archeological destruction became rampant.

It was during this period, of course, and in response to the same stimuli, that the NHPA was created, but few archeologists recognized its potential. Instead we focused on amending the Reservoir Salvage Act to broaden its scope and increase its funding. The result, after five years of work led by Arkansas' redoubtable Bob McGimsey, was the "Moss-Bennett Act" (after its sponsors). Never given a formal title by Congress, Moss-Bennett came to be known as the Archeological Data Preservation Act of 1974 (ADPA) or the Archeological and Historic Preservation Act, and by several other names.

ADPA does three major things. First, it directs all agencies to report to the Secretary of the Interior if any of their projects may cause the loss of "significant scientific, prehistorical, historical, or archeological data." Second, it gives them the choice of recovering threatened data themselves or asking Interior to do it for them, and third, it authorizes them to transfer up to one percent of the cost of a project to Interior to support salvage if they request that Interior do it. Interior, of course, is represented by NPS.

ADPA today is something of an anachronism, since it is largely redundant with Section 106 review. As a result, it tends to be honored in the breach with one significant exception. It is often used as an authority for the conduct of salvage, and, less frequently, for the transfer of funds to NPS to do salvage, when agencies discover archeological sites *after* Section 106 review has been completed. It is also one of the authorities that NPS uses to produce an annual report to Congress on the status of the "national archeological program."

ADPA could have a life of its own in that it applies, in theory, to things other than National Register eligible properties. Its reference to "scientific, prehistorical, historical, or archeological data" gives it at once both a broader and narrower scope than NHPA. Narrower in that it doesn't relate to many kinds of historically and culturally significant properties (most buildings, for example) that are significant for more than the information they contain. Broader because scientific, prehistorical, historical, and archeological data are present in more than properties eligible for the National Register. On the whole, though, the scope of ADPA is taken to be narrower than that of NHPA, and it's used—when used at all—to justify funding data recovery from National Register eligible archeological sites.

ADPA is also responsible for the abiding myth that an agency can spend only the equivalent of one percent of its project cost on archeology, or on all of historic preservation—and for the opposing myth that agencies are obligated to turn over one percent of the cost of each project to archeologists. In fact, what the law does is to authorize the *transfer* of up to one percent *to NPS* (with provisions for waiving the limit where necessary). An agency can spend as much or as little as it wants (or as the consulting parties under Section 106 decide) on data recovery if it funds the work itself rather than going through NPS. And ADPA by no means creates a one percent entitlement for archeology.

Most cultural resource managers will encounter ADPA in two contexts. If you're in a federal agency, every year you're likely to be called upon to contribute data for NPS's annual report to Congress. You may also find occasion to transfer money to NPS to do data recovery in discovery situations. Be sure to remember that ADPA is *not a substitute for Section 106 review*. If you discover something during a project, you need to follow the discovery provisions of 36 CFR 800, and you can invoke those provisions only if you've completed Section 106 review on the project. ADPA simply gives you a mechanism for carrying out the plan you develop for handling the discovery under the Section 106 regulation.

The Curation Regulation

36 CFR 79, *Curation of Federally-Owned and Administered Archeological Collections*, is an NPS regulation, applicable government-wide, that governs the "curation" of federally owned archeological material and data. If you check your dictionary you're unlikely to find "curation;" if it's an English language word it's of very recent origin. It means caring for artifacts and data in a curatorial facility. The regulation, which NPS was authorized to issue by Section 101(a)(7)(A) of NHPA citing itself, ADPA, and ARPA, establishes standards for curatorial facilities that house federal collections, and procedures by which federal agencies are to ensure that their collections are properly housed in such facilities.

36 CFR 79 is important because when we do archeological excavations for federal agencies, we need to be sure that the resulting data and materials are properly housed in institutions that meet the regulation's standards. This can be a costly, time-consuming effort, but it's clearly worthwhile. There's not much point in doing data recovery if we're not going to take proper care of the data.

On the other hand, there's a certain amount of irony in the strict standards imposed by Part 79—and indirectly by ARPA, which specifies that federal collections (except material repatriated under NAGPRA) must remain the property of the federal government. As the former Federal Preservation Officer for GSA once pointed out in a speech in the spectacular New York Custom House (an NHL), GSA has the authority to sell a building like the Custom House as long as it's standing, but if it demolishes it and then digs up its fragments, it will have to keep them in perpetuity.

Moving on, let's look at the law pertaining to one particular kind of archeological site that's been singled out by Congress for special attention: the waterlogged remains of wrecked watercraft.

Shipwrecks

I might as well acknowledge at the start that I'm prejudiced about shipwrecks—or to be a bit more gentle, I have some definite opinions, which tend to diverge from those of "mainstream" CRM. My biases will show in this discussion; I can't help it. The best I can do is to try to be explicit about it.

Shipwrecks are a pretty neat kind of cultural resource, and they're surrounded with a great deal of mystique. Some of them contain treasure, and a lot more of them are assumed to. They are often hard to get to, and dangerous. Their exploration often requires fancy, high-tech gear. They lie in an unusual, often beautiful, fragile, environment that's not entirely friendly to air-breathers. They almost invariably are where they are because of some human tragedy, which may be expressed in their physical characteristics or in historical or oral historical data about them. Finally, each represents a parcel of stuff that was snatched out of the terrestrial world in a single event. As a result, each represents—as archeologists are fond of saying—a "time capsule" reflecting its times and the society that launched it on the waves.

So perhaps it's no wonder that underwater archeologists view the subjects of their study virtually as religious objects.

Another result of being where they are, and what they are, is that human involvement with shipwrecks traditionally is governed by Admiralty law, an esoteric body of theory and practice dealing with the regulation of ships at sea. Grounded (as it were) on the fact that a ship represents a considerable human investment that should not lightly be given up to nature, Admiralty law encourages the salvage of shipwrecks, and it has little truck with historic and archeological values. Under Admiralty law a salvor can "arrest" a wreck and obtain exclusive salvage rights to it, with only such controls as the Admiralty court chooses to impose. Where a salvor arrests a historic wreck, the court will sometimes require the salvor to salvage the wreck with some kind of archeological controls, sometimes not. Since archeological controls tend to increase the time and money that must be invested in salvage (though they arguably also increase the value of the products), salvors have at best a mixed record of accepting such controls. This has led to some fairly egregious examples of shipwreck destruction by salvors which, in turn, has caused maritime archeologists to view salvors, as a class, pretty much as the Devil incarnate. Underwater archeologists are prone to categorically denying the possibility that commercial salvage and good archeology can ever, conceivably, cohabit comfortably. While this view tends to have experience on its side, it's experience that's been shaped by archeologists as well as by salvors. Underwater and historical archeologists have strongly discouraged one another from participating in commercial salvage ventures, thus leaving the salvors to their own devices.

In any event, dissatisfaction with Admiralty law, and with the conflicts between Admiralty law and the laws of certain coastal states (notably Texas) that tried to impose draconian controls on commercial salvage, led archeologists in the 1980s to promote passage of a new federal law. After a great deal of negotiation, this statute was enacted as the Abandoned Shipwrecks Act of 1988 (ASA: 43 U.S.C. 2101-2106).

The Abandoned Shipwrecks Act (ASA)

To be an abandoned shipwreck under the ASA and guidelines for its implementation issued by NPS (NPS 1990b), a wreck has to be that of a vessel, including its cargo, whether intact or scattered, that has been abandoned—that is:

> ...to which title voluntarily has been given up by the owner with the intent of never claiming a right or interest in the future and without vesting ownership in any other person." (NPS 1990b:50120)

For this reason U.S. Naval vessels are not covered by the act—the Navy never gives up the ship. Similarly, vessels of the Confederate Navy are not covered; they passed to the U.S. Government when the Confederacy surrendered, and are now administered by GSA. For that matter, all warships are entitled to sovereign immunity from the act, and remain the property of the nations in whose names they are commissioned (NPS 1990b:50121). If you're not a nation with a warship, however, you don't have to sign a paper to "voluntarily" abandon your ship; if you don't take action to mark and remove it after it goes down, you are taken to have abandoned it (NPS 1990b:50120).

The wreck also has to be on or in submerged lands of the United States, as defined in the Submerged Lands Act (43 U.S.C. 1301), and it has to meet one of two other tests. Either it has to be on the National Register or determined eligible for it, or it has to be "embedded" in the sea bottom or a coraline formation.

ASA asserts U.S. ownership of all wrecks meeting these criteria, thus removing them from the salvage-oriented purview of the Admiralty courts. It then promptly signs title to them over to the states within whose waters they lie, except in cases of submerged public lands—that is, lands administered by the U.S. or to which the U.S. holds fee title, with some exceptions—and Indian lands (lands held in trust for Indian tribes and individuals).

It is then up to the states to manage wrecks, and access to them, with attention to the nonbinding guidelines issued by NPS (NPS 1990b).

So, if you want or need to do something with a shipwreck, you first need to find out if it's on public or Indian land. If not, then find out if it's a warship; if so you have its commissioning government or its successor to deal with. If not, and it's on the submerged lands of the U.S., then you deal with the state.

There's a myth that the ASA forbids the commercial salvage of shipwrecks. It doesn't, and in fact assumes that both public and private sector salvage will occur. The NPS guidelines do their very best to limit salvage by going into great detail about the controls that should be applied to it (NPS 1990b:50131-35), but the bottom line is that, subject to state regulation, commercial salvage *is* permitted. Of course, states regulate salvage to varying degrees, so there are states where it *is* effectively forbidden.

The excavation of shipwrecks may be subject to legal requirements other than those of the ASA. Wrecks on public and Indian land are subject to the provisions of ARPA, and any federal permit to work on a wreck is subject to NEPA and Section 106. It's not uncommon for a salvor, whether public sector or private, to need a permit from the Corps of Engineers (under Section 10 of the Rivers and Harbors Act or Section 404 of the Clean Water Act) to discharge dredged material. In such a case, the salvor will be subject both to whatever the state requires under the ASA and its own laws, and the terms of the Section 106 agreement the Corps works out with the salvor, the SHPO, the ACHP, and other interested parties.

Cultural resource managers get involved with shipwrecks as public servants responsible for managing them or for managing access to them, and as contractors for public and private sector interests. It's in the latter role—as contractors for commercial salvors—that one swims into turbulent water. The underwater archeology community tends to give a very cold shoulder to those who have truck with salvors; they are regarded as flirting (at least) with the Devil. To punish such people and the salvors for whom they work, organizations like the Society for Historical Archeology won't let them give papers at their meetings. No doubt many commercial salvors tremble in their wet suits over this. In any event, if you want to work with a commercial salvor, there's certainly no law against it, and no logical reason why you can't do perfectly good research in the public interest, but you're likely to become a pariah, so be forewarned.

Shipwrecks are often equated, by their fervent protectors, with historical documents, because they can tell such detailed stories about the past. But what are the legal authorities that deal with "real" historical documents—on paper and other media?

Historical Documents

The importance of historical documents has been recognized since the beginning of the Republic and before, and documents—as represented by the Library of Congress—were the first kind of cultural resource in which Congress invested legislation and money. Today, two statutes of government-wide applicability provide for the preservation of historical documents of different kinds.

The Federal Records Act

The Federal Records Act (FRA; 44 U.S.C. 2101-2118, 2301-2308, 2501-2506, 2901-2909, 3101-3106, 3301-3324) isn't ordinarily thought of as a cultural resource management statute. Certainly, though, historical documents are cultural resources, and the FRA is intended to make sure that such resources, when produced by or in the possession of the federal government, are properly managed.

The FRA is also one of the few—really the *only*—cultural resource law that carries fines and jail sentences with it. Violation of the FRA can put a federal official in jail for up to three years, and saddle him or her with a fine of two thousand dollars, or both. However, the FRA is routinely violated by federal agencies—including such ostensibly historically-oriented agencies as NPS and the ACHP.

The FRA covers all kinds of "records"—books, papers, maps, photographs, "machine-readable" material and other documentary materials—as long as they're made or received by a federal agency in the transaction of the agency's business. Its central purpose is to preserve evidence of the government's organization, functions, policies, decisions, operations, and activities, as well as basic historical and other information.

FRA implementation is overseen by the National Archives and Records Administration (NARA), which has a very extensive set of regulations (36 CFR 1222–1238). At their core, these regulations require agencies to establish internal procedures for compliance, set up retention and disposal schedules, and manage their records accordingly. Agencies do this, although compliance on paper and compliance in reality are rather different things. The Navy, for example, has FRA procedures that total about a thousand pages (SECNAVINST 5212.5C), but when I was hired a couple of years ago to do a CRM class for a closing Navy base whose personnel had found lots of old files stuffed away in its corners, nobody on the base seemed ever to have heard of the procedures, and everyone seemed rather awestruck to learn that they existed. I also found that the Navy's whole records management program was supervised by one rather beleaguered-seeming lieutenant at the Washington Navy Yard. And that's the Navy—a highly organized, by-the-book sort of operation. I think it's safe to say that the FRA is often honored in the breach.

The Navy's Records Disposal Manual (SECNAVINST 5212.5C, which stands for Secretary of the Navy Instruction #5212.5C) can give us an example of how FRA is supposed to work. It divides the world of records up into a host of categories, and for each of these prescribes "retention standards." Here are some examples:

Naval Reserve Officer and Enlisted Strength Reports: Destroy when 2 years old or when purpose is served, whichever is earlier.

Correspondence, messages, and reports pertaining to personnel casualty incidents: Permanent. Transfer to WNRC when 3 years old, offer to NARA when 25 years old.

Routine monthly weather observations from naval units: Transfer monthly to Fleet Numerical Meteorology and Oceanography Detachment (FLENUMMETOCDET), Asheville, NC for periodic transfer to the National Climatic Center.

Captured documents: Permanent. Transfer to NARA after intelligence evaluation or 25 years after cessation of hostilities, whichever is later.

There are hundreds of such categories, each with its own standard. Some standards, like the first one quoted above, provide for prompt destruction of records that nobody thinks will have historical value. Others provide for temporary retention, others for retention forever. Permanent records are typically retired by the operational office or unit to an agency management center, and eventually to NARA for management by the National Archives at a NARA-approved repository or a Federal Records Center.

What does this mean for the cultural resource manager? If you're in an agency, you're probably producing records that may themselves become historical documents, and you ought to be responsible enough to posterity to manage them according to your agency's FRA procedures. So you'll need to find out what these procedures are. There should be somebody in the organization— probably a secretary—who's assigned the function of Records Management Officer. This person *should* be able to advise you.

If you're a contractor, or an agency employee, or staff to a SHPO, a local government, a tribe, or a local organization, you may encounter situations where records are threatened by some kind of proposed action. In the Navy base instance mentioned above, the base—a high-tech weapons testing facility—was closing, and would be transferred out of federal ownership. The Navy had found piles and piles of old lab notebooks, files on experiments, and the like stuffed in lockers, heaped up under lab benches, and so forth. What to do with them?

In theory, the thing to do in a case like this is to find out what the agency's records management policy is, and dispose of the records in accordance with it. But if the records are old, and the people who produced them have passed on to other jobs or to the big cubicle in the sky, more research may be required. It may be very hard to figure out what categories to assign things to. To be in compliance with the FRA, agencies ought to think about and budget for this kind of thing just like they think about and budget for doing Section 106 review or cleaning up toxic wastes, but my impression is that this doesn't often happen, and a lot of important records go into the dumpster as a result. There's a well-known horror story about the Forest Service, when its headquarters moved from the main Agriculture Building in Washington to the old Auditor's Building across the street. Supposedly, a whole lot of records from the days of Gifford Pinchot, who started the Service back in Teddy Roosevelt's administration, wound up in a dumpster, where they were luckily rescued by a collector of historical documents—who then sold them back to the Forest Service. At about the same time, the Department of Veterans' Affairs dumped a whole passel of old veterans' files—really old ones, with a lot of papers signed by a long-extinct president named Lincoln—which have made something of a splash in the records collecting community. Don't let this happen to you; someday *somebody's* going to go to jail for this sort of thing.

Besides whoever is responsible for records management in your agency or your client's agency, NARA has regional archives whose staff can be consulted, and it puts out various publications about records management (cf. NARA 1989, 1992).

Section 112 of NHPA

Section 112 of NHPA also address records—in this case, records of historic preservation work:

> *Each Federal agency that is responsible for the protection of historic resources, including archeological resources pursuant to this Act or any other law shall ensure...*

> *Records and other data, including data produced by historical research and archeological surveys and excavations are permanently maintained in appropriate data bases and made available to potential users pursuant to such regulations as the Secretary shall promulgate.* (NHPA Section 112[a][2])

The responsibility imposed by NHPA operates separately from that imposed by FRA, but the two should be coordinated. In essence, records of historic preservation work are always permanent records, and should be managed accordingly under FRA. In carrying out or contracting for historic preservation work—and other kinds of cultural resource management work, too, though the responsibility to do so isn't as clearly established—a cultural resource manager should make sure that permanent retention of records is provided for.

Finally, what about historical objects that aren't documents, aren't of archeological origin, and aren't Native American cultural items?

Artifacts

Oddly, there is no overall law dealing with the preservation of historic but not-strictly-archeological objects. Various agencies have internal procedures of their own. For example, in the Navy the preservation of historic objects is coordinated by the Office of the Navy Historian, who reports to the Chief of Naval Operations (CNO). OPNAVINST 5730.13 directs naval units to report "items of historical interest" to the Historian. The Historian's own instruction, tersely entitled NAVHISTCENCUAINST 11100.1, identifies items of historical interest as those associated with combat, capture, achievement, notable events, technical uniqueness or significance, heroism, humane efforts, human interest, and sponsorship of unit activities by others. The Historian's tiny staff works with naval units to identify specific objects of interest and arrange for them to be cared for. Most other large agencies have programs that are more or less similar, but aside from selective work by the Smithsonian there is no government-wide requirement to manage historical objects.

For the cultural resource manager, this means being knowledgeable about the collections management policies and procedures of one's agency or client, and doing the best one can with them.

The Clara Barton Problem

As this book was laboring its way through the computer, an incident happened in Washington, D.C. that illustrates a gap in protection of cultural resources, through which important stuff can fall. The General Services Administration had inherited a building from the Pennsylvania Avenue Development Corporation (PADC), and proposed to demolish it. The building had been constructed before the Civil War, but had long since lost its integrity through replacement of its facades, so it was determined not eligible for the National Register. Hence, no further review was required under Section 106.

As the building was being prepared for demolition, a contractor's employee came upon a painted signboard in an attic room. The signboard announced the presence of the Missing Veterans' Bureau, under the direction of Miss Clara Barton, and the papers seemed to have been associated with the work of the famous Civil War-era nurse in locating lost Union soldiers and their resting places for grieving families. The signboard was turned over to NPS historians, who scoured the room and found documents confirming that Barton had indeed operated out of the building toward the end of the war. Apparently Barton had simply locked the door and walked away when she got better digs in 1865, and the room hadn't been opened since. Obviously the room and its contents are of great historical interest and interpretive value; the building now is going to be saved and restored.

The only reason the signboard was turned over in the first place was that its discoverer was the personal friend of the superintendent of a nearby unit of the National Park system. Otherwise, it might well have been lost, together with the documents and the room.

The documents, which may turn out to be of considerable historical interest, were not federal records (except by virtue of their unknowing acquisition by GSA), so there was no reliable way one could expect them to be managed under

FRA. Neither they nor the signboard were strictly archeological resources, so they weren't managed under ARPA. Most importantly, they weren't identified during the identification phase of the Section 106 process, which focused on the character of the building, not of its contents.

Earlier we identified a gap between historic preservation and social impact assessment through which many sociocultural resources may fall. Here's another one—smaller and more esoteric, but nonetheless important—that ought to be closed.

To guard against future Bartonesque situations, GSA has issued guidance to its field offices recommending that special efforts be made to identify and manage documents and artifacts, arguing that such materials have to be considered under FRA, NHPA, and particularly the Archeological Data Preservation Act (ADPA). Perhaps this will help, but it's no substitute for a government-wide effort.

We need a systematic approach to identifying and preserving threatened documents and objects that are not of an archeological nature, and we don't have it. A responsible cultural resource manager should be on the lookout for such materials, though, and not be limited by the specifications of the National Register and other federal institutions.

One Last Historic Preservation Authority: Executive Order 11593

It's hardly the best, but I've saved Executive Order 11593 until last because I haven't known quite what else to do with it. Executive Order 11593 is something of an anachronism today, but it was extremely important when President Nixon issued it in 1972.

When NHPA was enacted in 1966, Section 106 required agencies to consider the effects of their actions only on properties *included in* the National Register. Naturally, the response by agencies was to keep properties from being nominated to the Register, while the response by project opponents was to nominate properties right and left. Executive Order 11593 neatly solved this problem by directing agencies to survey their lands to find and nominate historic places to the National Register. More importantly, in the meantime NPS was directed to issue guidelines for determining the eligibility of properties for the Register, and agencies were to determine the eligibility of unevaluated properties as part of their Section 106 work. If a property was eligible, it was to be treated as though it were on the Register. These provisions were eventually incorporated into NHPA itself, and into the Section 106 regulations, so the executive order is largely irrelevant today. It occasionally crops up as a rationale for insisting that agencies nominate everything they own to the National Register, or as a basis for insisting on surveys to identify all eligible properties, but the argument for such continued applicability is rather thin, I think. The Executive Order directed agencies to complete their surveys and nominate everything to the Register by 1974. Nobody made it (although it was rumored that the Tea Tasting Commission did, which may or may not be true). Does this leave agencies with a continuing responsibility to identify all historic properties and nominate them to the Register? If so, why is it that Congress in 1980 incorporated the "nominate all properties" requirement into Section 110(a)(2) of NHPA and then removed it in the 1992 amendments? I don't think the executive order has much relevance today, but it still exists, people sometimes cite it, and for historical reasons if for no other, it's good to know that it exists.

Having looked at authorities and aspects of practice that focus on particular kinds of resources, we also need to consider authorities that apply to special kinds of projects, or special kinds of lands—and equally, consider what authorities *don't* apply.

Special Situations

Ongoing Land Management

Cultural resource managers in land managing agencies have a number of laws, regulations, and policies to deal with that their compatriots in other kinds of agencies do not. Some of these are specific to the agencies, and others spring from the character of the lands the agencies manage. Only a land management agency can effectively engage in ecosystem management, for example, so it is to agencies like BLM and the Forest Service that ecosystem management policies mostly apply.

Land management agencies are especially responsible for administering some of the laws we've discussed above—ARPA, for example—and there are also some provisions of NHPA that apply particularly to them. Notably, under Section 110(a)(2) of NHPA, each such agency is responsible for having a program that ensures, among other things:

> ...that historic properties under the jurisdiction or control of the agency are identified, evaluated, and nominated to the National Register; (and)

> ...that such properties under the jurisdiction or control of the agency...are managed and maintained in a way that considers the preservation of their... values in compliance with section 106... (NHPA Section 110[a][2][A]and [B])

Although technically these provisions apply to all agencies, only agencies with historic properties under their jurisdiction or control (i.e., agencies that administer land and structures) can carry them out.

So land management agencies have ongoing responsibilities to identify and manage historic properties. A few things need to be noted about these responsibilities.

Identification and evaluation. Identification and evaluation under Section 110(a)(2) can be a rather more leisurely, long-term, and therefore multi-phased activity than can comparable activities under Section 106. Without a specific project schedule to attend to, an agency need not try to identify everything of historical significance on a particular timetable. As a result, identification work under Section 110(a)(2) tends to be given a rather low priority for funding, and cultural resource managers pretty much have to get used to that. It's a good idea to work up plans for identification projects and have them on hand in case your agency needs to spend up leftover money at the end of the fiscal year.

If you're a contractor, you may be puzzled by why a client offers you a scope of work for a Section 110(a)(2) survey that's different from the one you'd have for a Section 106 survey. You may be charged only with identifying historic buildings, or only landscapes, only archeology, or only traditional cultural properties. Or you may be assigned to do only background research, or sample fieldwork. The reason for this, of course, is that the agency isn't trying to locate *everything;* it's moving along, identifying the stuff that it thinks has the highest priority, with years and years ahead of it, and little enough money to identify the rest.

Nomination. Every agency's program has to provide for nomination to the National Register, but there's no requirement that everything be nominated, or that nomination proceed on a particular timetable. As noted above, Congress explicitly removed the requirement to nominate all historic properties when it amended NHPA in 1992—recognizing that agencies have lots of ways to keep track of, and manage, historic properties without going to the expense and trouble of nominating them. A wise agency nominates things when it serves some purpose, and doesn't invest its scarce fiscal resources in nominating because it's nice to do.

Management and maintenance. What an agency does to manage and maintain historic properties under its jurisdiction depends on the nature of the properties and what's happening to them that needs management. It may be routine maintenance of old buildings, stabilization of archeological sites, giving assistance to an Indian tribe to manage the plant and animal resources of a gathering area—a wide range of possibilities. The allusion in Section 110(a)(2) to Section 106 reminds us that neglecting management and maintenance is an adverse effect under the Section 106 regulations, that management and maintenance activities can help mitigate impacts on historic properties, and that even such activities, benign as they may seem, require review under Section 106.

Transportation Projects

Where a federally assisted transportation project is involved—that is, one assisted by an agency of the U.S. Department of Transportation (DOT), then the agency has to comply with Section 4(f) of the DOT Act (49 U.S.C. 303)—the act that created the Department. Section 4(f) says that:

The Secretary of Transportation may approve a transportation program or project requiring the use of publicly owned land of a public park, recreation area, or wildlife and waterfowl refuge..., or land of a historic site...only if:

1) there is no prudent or feasible alternative to using that land; and

2) the program or project includes all possible planning to minimize harm to the park, recreation area, refuge, or historic site resulting from the use. (49 U.S.C. 303)

The courts have found that any National Register property, and any property determined eligible for the National Register, is an "historic site" for purposes of Section 4(f). They've also crafted the concept of "constructive use," which holds, in essence, that if you affect a property in such a way as to potentially alter its use, you've used it. As a result, virtually any adverse effect under Section 106 of NHPA is a Section 4(f) use. Note, too, that while 4(f) applies only to use of publicly owned land in a park, recreation area, or refuge, it applies to anybody's land in an historic site.

So Section 4(f) imposes a pretty draconian requirement on transportation agencies: they can't have an adverse effect on a historic property unless there's no prudent or feasible alternative.

There's a whole body of practice involved in conducting Section 4(f) analyses—not only of impacts on historic properties, of course, but on parks, recreation areas, and refuges. Such analyses are carried out in coordination with NEPA studies.

Because Section 4(f) applies when there will be an adverse effect under Section 106, but (arguably at least, and according to regulations of the Federal Highway Administration) doesn't if there's no adverse effect, transportation agencies tend to try to move heaven and earth to avoid findings of adverse effect. This has made them very vigorous users of the "Research Exception" in the 1986 Section 106 regulation. If this exception goes away in the revised regulation it will be interesting to see how transportation agencies adjust, though it appears that there's plenty of room for them to do so.

In coordinating Section 4(f) with Section 106 review, it's important to keep things in sequence, because Section 4(f) sets up a very rigid hierarchy. You first determine whether there's a prudent and feasible alternative. If there is, you use it. If there's not, you explain this in your 4(f) documentation and go on to develop and implement "all possible planning to mitigate harm." This means that in Section 106 review you want to be careful not to get deeply into negotiation about mitigation measures until you've thoroughly explored alternatives that will avoid adverse effect—i.e., "use"—altogether; otherwise you can really muddy the 4(f) process. Ideally the 106 consultation ought to get to the point of reaching a conclusion about avoiding adverse effect and then, if there appears to be no way to avoid it, Section 106 review should be put on hold while the agency makes a preliminary 4(f) finding about "prudent or feasible alternatives" and gets public response. Then Section 106 review can continue, taking the public response into account, either to explore alternatives the public has raised or to identify and agree on mitigation measures. This sort of coordination is outlined in Figure 9.

One other point about Section 4(f). It applies to "transportation programs and projects," but that doesn't quite mean "all projects that have to do with transportation." Nor does it quite mean "only the construction of transportation facilities." On the one hand, a road built by the Forest Service to haul logs is not subject to Section 4(f) because it's not done by the DOT. On the other hand, a Coast Guard permit to build or remove a bridge *is* subject to Section 4(f) because the Coast Guard is part of DOT.

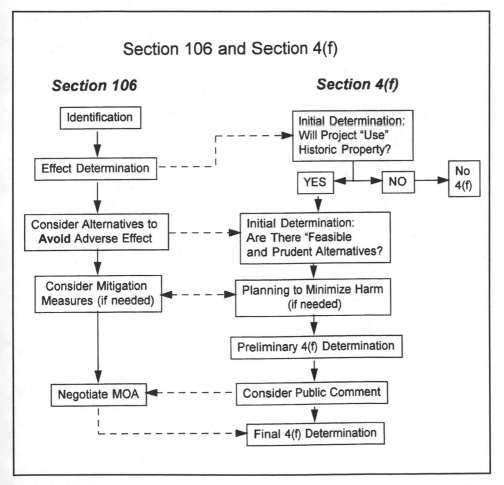

Figure 9. Coordinating Section 106 and Section 4(f).

Other Agency-Specific Laws

Section 4(f) is probably the best known law dealing (in part) with cultural resources that's specific to a particular group of agencies, but there are many others—too many to begin to discuss here. Federal land management agencies have their own organic legislation—for example the Federal Land Policy and Management Act (FLPMA) for the Bureau of Land Management—which often contain (as FLPMA does) direction about aspects of CRM. Laws pertaining to particular lands or resources—a new National Park, a wilderness area, a wild and scenic river—often contain specific direction about cultural resources particular to the area or interests involved. Assistance agencies are sometimes told by Congress to use their money to advance particular purposes that have to do with cultural resources.

Unless Congress says so, none of these agency-specific, land-specific, or program-specific laws supersedes NEPA, NHPA, and the other general-purpose authorities, but cultural resource managers who work for or with agencies to which they apply need to know about them, and figure out how to deal with them. And those seeking to influence the behavior of an agency need to know about them, too. In some cases they may be far more influential than the general-purpose laws.

Indian Tribal Lands and Programs

One could write a very large and complicated book on CRM as it applied to Indian tribes, and one such book in fact exists (Klesert and Downer 1990). Suffice to say that whenever one is dealing with any of the CRM laws and programs on tribal land, or in a manner that may affect the interests of a federally recognized tribe, then one has some more or less specific, special things to consider, such as tribal sovereignty, the need for a government-to-government relationship, the government's trust or fiduciary responsibility to tribes, and any specific (or not so specific) treaty rights. We've touched on some of these issues above; just remember that they're always there when you're operating on or near tribal lands, or with tribes on other lands, or when you may affect resources important to tribes, including cultural resources. They may or may not seriously affect the way you do business, but you've always got to consider them.

Projects Without Federal Involvement

If there's no federal involvement in a project or program, then the federal cultural resource laws don't apply, and if you're a citizen trying to influence the project or program, you can't use these laws to do so. However, there are two caveats to consider.

One is that the arm of the federal government is pretty long. Putting up cell phone towers requires permission from the Federal Communications Commission. Putting in an automatic teller machine requires the permission of the

Federal Deposit Insurance Corporation. Many projects require permits to cross federal lands. And so forth. So don't assume that a project doesn't have federal involvement just because there's no sign on the job site saying "Project of Suchandso Agency." Inquire of your local planning agency, or the SHPO, ACHP, or other pertinent agency, or your Congressman. And don't belabor the City Council or County Planning Commission about violating NEPA or Section 106; it's not their problem (unless they're using federal money or need a federal permit themselves). It's the federal agency's responsibility to comply with the laws and regulations, so they're the ones you want to belabor.

The other caveat is that there are many states that have "little NEPAs" and "State 106s" of various kinds, or that have unmarked grave laws, Indian burial laws, repatriation laws, archeological laws, and so on. Many local governments have historic preservation ordinances and their own programs of environmental review. Exactly what these laws, ordinances and programs say and do—and the extent to which they're followed—range all over the map, but they may be there and they may be helpful. Don't assume that you've got no tools to use at all just because there's no federal involvement.

International Actions

NEPA's applicability to U.S. agencies operating outside the United States is the subject of continual debate and court challenges. Thus far, it has been taken to apply in certain unusual circumstances (e.g., in Antarctica) but generally applies to domestic actions. Section 106 of NHPA quite explicitly applies only in the fifty-nine entities that are "states" for purposes of the act. Most of the other cultural resource laws also apply only in a domestic context.

But most other countries have environmental laws, and sometimes various kinds of cultural resource management laws, of their own that U.S. agencies operating within their borders must (usually, and in theory) follow (cf. Stipe 1982; R. Wilson 1987; Wilson and Loyola 1981). The effectiveness of these laws varies widely. In Latin American countries, for example, there are severe prohibitions on messing about with el patrimonio nacional, but these don't seem to apply to many governmental projects.

The U.S. Department of Defense a few years ago issued something called the "Overseas Environmental Baseline Guidance Document" (OEBGD, which some pronounce "ObyGod!"), which directed the military services to follow either the host country's environmental laws or the pertinent U.S. laws, whichever were more stringent. Other agencies have more or less similar policies, but how well any of them are followed is hard to say (cf. CEHP 1994a, 1994b).

There's also a considerable body of international pronouncement on cultural resource matters. Not laws, generally not very binding on anybody, but expressions of international intent, usually in the form of "Conventions" and "Recommendations" by the United Nations Educational, Scientific, and Cultural Organization (UNESCO) and other international bodies. Conventions actually *do* bind governments once they formally become party to them. For example, there's the *"Convention on the Means of Prohibiting and Preventing the Illicit Import, Export and Transfer of Ownership of Cultural Property"* (UNESCO 1976), which deals with how to control international trafficking in antiquities. The U.S. is a party, and is bound by its terms, resulting in the occasional arrest of international traffickers and the confiscation and return of stolen antiquities. Recommendations are not binding, but often lay out useful principles that can be used when jawboning an agency or a government, or to guide development of a plan or scope of work. The *"Recommendation Concerning the Safeguarding and Contemporary Role of Historic Areas"* (UNESCO 1976) and the *"Recommendation Concerning the Safeguarding of the Beauty and Character of Landscapes and Sites"* (UNESCO 1962) offer policy recommendations that would certainly make for a better world if they were followed. They can be drawn upon in CRM practice—internationally and domestically—as just what they are: the best recommendations of the concerned international community about how cultural resources should be managed.

Many private corporations and some government agencies are having their environmental protection programs certified as meeting appropriate standards under ISO 14000 (ISO 1995; Sayre 1996)—a standard established by the International Organization on Standards, with which agencies and companies comply voluntarily. Some national governments are looking to ISO certification as a means of exerting environmental controls over corporations operating within their boundaries; some stockholder groups are looking to it as a way of ensuring corporate responsibility toward the environment, and some companies and agencies see it as an important demonstration of such responsibility and hence as a marketing tool. ISO 14000 is an entirely process-oriented standard, but some of the processes it espouses, like having systems in place to attend to the environmental concerns of those around one's place of business, can have useful implications for cultural resource management—both internationally and in the domestic context.

Part Three

Bringing It All Together

Chapter 7

Comprehensive Cultural Resource Impact Assessment

By this time it will doubtless be no surprise that I think agencies ought to analyze the effects of their actions on cultural resources in coordination—addressing all kinds of resources, all the pertinent legal requirements, and all kinds of impacts in a comprehensive manner. I don't expect this to happen any time soon, and practitioners certainly can't be blamed for not doing such comprehensive analysis if the job descriptions and scopes of work under which they operate don't allow it. But if by chance you're in charge of preparing a scope of work, or designing a cultural resource impact assessment, here's what I suggest you do.

This chapter is organized following the model of a typical chapter in Larry Cantor's *Environmental Impact Assessment* (Cantor 1996), to facilitate its use in conjunction with that popular textbook. A typical Cantor chapter begins with basic information and concepts, outlines pertinent laws and other authorities, and then outlines basic steps in the assessment process. Having covered the first two items in great detail above, we'll begin here with the "basic steps."

Basic Steps in Comprehensive Cultural Resource Impact Assessment

Ideally, compliance with the cultural resource legal authorities through impact prediction and assessment should be a coordinated, integrated process that addresses all legal and regulatory requirements. Combining the requirements of the three major regulations, and all the laws, results in the following steps.

1. Scoping

During formal scoping for an EIS, or informal scoping for an EA, a concrete effort should be made to determine what cultural resource issues—if any—will need to be addressed in analysis. If NEPA scoping is not performed—that is, if the action is categorically excluded from detailed NEPA review under the agency's NEPA procedures—it may still have to be reviewed under Section 106 or other cultural resource laws, because all the laws and executive orders are independent of NEPA.

The Section 106 regulations require several analytical steps that logically should be performed during scoping.

The first of these is to determine whether the action is an "undertaking" that is subject to review under Section 106 (one that is not may still require review under other cultural resource authorities). In essence, an action is subject to review under Section 106 if it is to be done by or for a federal agency, will receive federal assistance, or is subject to federal review and regulation, and if it is the *kind* of action that has the potential to affect historic properties. Thus, constructing a new building or rehabilitating an old one is subject to review because if any historic properties are involved they are likely to be affected, but purchasing office supplies is not subject to review because it cannot affect historic properties.

The next step is to determine the project's "area of potential effects" (APE). The APE comprises the area or areas where the undertaking may affect historic properties, should any such properties subsequently be found to exist. All kinds of potential effects should be considered in determining the APE: physical, visual, auditory, direct, indirect, cumulative, etc. The APE is the area (or areas) to which Section 106 analysis will relate.

The last scoping step under Section 106 is what the 1998 draft regulations actually call "scoping," or in the 1986 version, "assessing information needs"— that is, determining what kinds of information should be gathered as a basis for Section 106 compliance. This is done through background research into the area's history and prehistory, previous studies done in the area, and so on. It also involves consultation with the SHPO or THPO, potentially concerned Indian tribes, local governments, and other possible stakeholders.

The NAGPRA regulations require an early determination as to whether the proposed action might result in unearthing "Native American cultural items"— that is, human remains, associated and unassociated funerary objects, sacred objects, and objects of cultural patrimony of an Indian tribe—on land under the control of a federal agency or tribe. If such impacts are possible, then the agency should identify Indian tribes or Native Hawaiian groups who might have ownership rights in such items, and consult with them about developing a "Plan of Action" (POA) for managing the impacts.

The other cultural resource laws do not have specific regulatory schemes that deal with impact analysis, but logically, during scoping under NEPA an agency should ascertain whether there are likely to be issues with Native American sacred sites (EO 13007) or religious practices (AIRFA), the cultural concerns of low-income and minority populations (EO 12898), historical documents (FRA), historical, scientific, or archeological data (ADPA), and other cultural resources (NEPA itself), through background research and consultation.

In summary: during scoping for an EIS, or its equivalent for an EA, or reviewing a project that is categorically excluded under NEPA, the agency should determine whether it has cultural resource review responsibilities, and if so it should establish the geographic area(s) in which it will carry out analysis and initiate consultation with stakeholders to identify key issues.

Some cultural resource issues may be too sensitive for public disclosure. This is often the case, for example, with the concerns of Indian tribes about impacts on sacred sites and religious practices. As a result, it's important to remember that under the NEPA regulations, scoping is *not* just a public meeting. Consultation with tribes and others who may be concerned about impacts on cultural resources sometimes should be initiated *before* general public scoping meetings are carried out.

2. Identification of Cultural Resources

Based on scoping, the next step in analyzing impacts on cultural resources is to try to identify the resources that may be affected.

Depending on the situation, a wide range of cultural resource types may need to be addressed, including:

- Historic properties—that is, places included in or eligible for the National Register of Historic Places by virtue of their historical, archeological, architectural, engineering, or cultural significance. Buildings, structures, sites, and generally non-portable objects (e.g., signs, street furniture) can be historic properties, as can "districts" made up of multiple individual properties. "Prehistoric" archeological sites (that is, those dating from periods before written records) may be historic properties. Historic properties are the focus of Section 106 review.

- Native American cultural items: human remains, associated and unassociated funerary items, sacred objects, and objects of cultural patrimony that may be related to an Indian tribe or Native Hawaiian group. These are the subjects of NAGPRA.

- Archeological resources, which are usually historic properties but occasionally are not. Under ARPA, an archeological resource is an archeological site, feature, or artifact that is over 100 years old; ARPA applies only on federal and Indian lands.

- Archeological, historical, and scientific data, the subject of ADPA— usually found in or in association with archeological resources and historic properties, but may exist independently.

- Native American religious practices, the subject of AIRFA. These may or may not be related to specific places such as sacred sites.

- Indian sacred sites on federal land, the subjects of Executive Order 13007. These may or may not be historic properties and/or archeological resources, and may or may not contain Native American cultural items.

- Cultural uses of the natural environment (e.g., subsistence use of plants and animals, ceremonial or other religious use of places, plants, animals, minerals), which must be considered under NEPA.

- Community cultural norms, values, and beliefs, and their expressions in the ways people work, play, relate to one another, organize to meet needs, and generally participate in society. This kind of resource, which may or may not involve historic properties or some other kind of resource, or use of the natural environment, is the subject of Social Impact Assessment (SIA) under NEPA. Special attention should be given to the sociocultural values of low-income populations and minority populations, in accordance with Executive Order 12898.

- Historical documents, whose management by federal agencies is the subject of the FRA.

Like other environmental planning activities, identification of cultural resources should be an interdisciplinary effort. Specialists typically needed in identification include planners, historians, architectural historians, landscape historians, archeologists, cultural anthropologists, and sociologists. Sometimes one person may combine multiple specialties.

A mistake that many agencies fall into is that of assuming that historic properties are the only kind of cultural resource that has to be addressed, and that a single kind of specialist—usually an archeologist—is sufficient to address all such resources. A good scoping effort should tell you what kinds of expertise are actually needed.

A related common mistake is to assume that the same kind of identification effort must be carried out throughout the area of potential effects defined under the Section 106 regulations. In fact, the kind of identification work that is needed depends on the kind of resource that is expected and the kinds of effects that are likely. In an area where only visual effects are likely, for example, there is seldom any need to do an archeological survey. But a study to identify places of visual or architectural value, and cultural activities that might be affected by changes in the visual environment, would be quite appropriate.

It is very important to carry out identification in consultation with stakeholders, who after all are often those who know about and ascribe value to cultural resources. The SHPO or THPO must be consulted under the Section 106 regulations, and Indian tribes or Native Hawaiian groups must be consulted under NAGPRA. Low-income and minority groups must be consulted under Executive Order 12898, and tribes must be consulted under NHPA, AIRFA, and Executive Order 13007.

Kinds of studies that are often necessary to identify cultural resources include (but are not limited to):

- Background studies of local history, prehistory, geography, ecology, ethnography, and culture, and the identification of and consultation with stakeholders, as a basis for generating predictions about cultural resources that may be present in different areas of potential effect.

- Surveys of architectural and engineering resources, including buildings, structures, and districts made up of buildings and structures, carried out by qualified architectural historians, historians, and where the social values of possible districts may be important, sociologists or anthropologists (Derry et al. 1985).

- Identification of cultural landscapes—that is, landscapes that are either built to reflect cultural norms (e.g., parks and parkways) or whose character reflects unplanned relationships between human culture and the biophysical environment (e.g., a traditional farming landscape: see Keller and Keller 1987; McClelland et al. 1990).

- Archeological surveys to identify prehistoric and historic archeological sites (see King 1977a), carried out in close cooperation with descendant communities.

- Traditional cultural property surveys, to identify places (including natural places) that have significance in the cultural traditions and lifeways of communities (see National Register 1990).

- Studies of impacts on living sociocultural systems such as neighborhoods, low-income and minority groups, other ethnic groups, religious practitioners, and other groups, and on their uses of the natural environment (cf. Bickman and Rog 1997; Interorganizational Committee 1993; Stoffle 1990).

- Surveys to identify and evaluate historical documents or artifacts that may be affected by an action like base closure (cf. Odegaard 1990; Miller 1990; Warnow 1982).

The level of detail at which identification has to be done is often a problem for coordinating review under NEPA and Section 106. NEPA, of course, is to be complied with at an early stage in planning, and requires analysts to give more or less equal treatment to multiple alternatives. Section 106 is supposed to be complied with early in planning, too, and should include consideration of alternatives. However, the level of detail that is often understood to be necessary for Section 106 purposes, and insisted upon by SHPOs or THPOs, may require more fieldwork than it is feasible for an agency to do when it is examining numerous alternative project sites. As a result, agencies sometimes defer Section 106 review until after they have selected a preferred alternative, and even after they have completed NEPA review with a FONSI or ROD. This narrows the range of mitigation options they can consider under Section 106, while tainting the NEPA documentation with incomplete data. Revised Section 106 regulations proposed by the ACHP in 1997 will permit "phased" identification of historic properties, which may help alleviate this problem.

3. Determinations of Significance

Historic properties are the only kind of cultural resource for which a rigorous significance determination process is prescribed in regulation. If a property meets the National Register Criteria (36 CFR 60.4) it is eligible for the National Register and impacts on it must be considered under Section 106. If it is not eligible, impacts do not need to be considered under Section 106, but they may need to be considered under other authorities.

Practically speaking, however, the significance of each kind of potentially affected cultural resource has to be determined. How this is done is up to the analyst, with the sole exception of historic properties.

Some historic properties are already listed in the National Register, or have already been determined eligible; these can be easily identified through consultation with the SHPO or THPO. Previously unidentified properties that may be historic are evaluated by the agency, in consultation with the SHPO and others, by applying the National Register Criteria to each property.

To compare a property to the National Register Criteria often takes a lot of research, and a good deal of information. This is the major reason that Section 106 review is generally understood to require very detailed identification work. As mentioned above, this can lead an agency to defer completing Section 106 review until after an alternative has been selected, and NEPA review has effectively been completed. This is unfortunate, because it leaves a whole class of cultural resource incompletely addressed in NEPA review, and by the time historic properties *are* addressed, it may be too late to do much about impacts on them.

In some cases it is possible to "jump over" the step of evaluating particular properties against the National Register Criteria. This is especially important with regard to Native American sacred sites that may be eligible for the Register, because traditional religious practitioners are often uncomfortable with providing information to outsiders about what makes such places significant. Where the agency, SHPO or THPO, and other parties participating in Section 106 review agree, it is possible simply to assume that properties are eligible for the Register, without explicitly mapping or describing them, and then jump on to figuring out what effects the project will have. Of course, even to determine what effects will occur requires at least a general understanding of what kinds of historic properties are likely to exist in the area of potential effects. Archeologists are ahead of most other cultural resource specialists in developing "predictive models" to indicate which subareas of an APE are likely or unlikely to be archeologically sensitive (cf. Judge and Sebastian 1988), but some kinds of projections or predictions can usually be made with regard to all kinds of cultural resources.

In those rare cases in which historical documents may be affected by an action and need to be evaluated, the responsible agency's procedures for implementing FRA may provide a useful guideline, but consultation with professional historians and archivists, and with the regional office of the National Archives and Records Administration (NARA), is highly recommended.

With cultural resources other than historic properties and documents, consultation with knowledgeable parties (e.g., archeologists with regard to archeological resources, Indian tribes with regard to resources relevant to them) and other stakeholders provide the primary means of assessing significance.

4. Assessing Effects

Again the Section 106 regulations are the most specific about how effects are to be measured. With respect to historic properties, the regulations set forth "Criteria of Adverse Effect" that agencies are to apply, in consultation with SHPOs or THPOs, pertinent Indian tribes, and others.

Subject to various procedural checks and balances, if the agency finds that there will be no adverse effect, and the SHPO or THPO concurs, the agency documents this fact and can proceed with the action. Some determinations of no adverse effect may be "conditioned" upon measures to ensure that there will in fact be no adverse effect; such a "conditional no adverse effect" determination is much like a mitigated FONSI in concept, though a "CNAE" does not necessarily equal an "MFONSI" or vice-versa.

If there will be adverse effects on historic properties, then the agency moves on to the next step in the process—seeking ways to mitigate the adverse effect.

There are no similarly specified procedures for determining effects on Native American cultural items, Native American religious practices, community sociocultural values, and other kinds of cultural resources. The *Guidelines and Principles for Social Impact Assessment* provide useful guidance with respect to community values, however, and these can be generalized to address a whole range of cultural resources. The *Guidelines and Principles* list both quantitative (straight-line trend projections, population multiplier methods, computer modeling) and non-quantitative (comparative method, scenarios, expert testimony) methods. While quantitative methods are useful as elements of most impact analyses, analysis of impacts on cultural resources is usually at base non-quantitative. The value of cultural resources, and hence the severity of impacts on them, lies largely in people's perceptions, and is seldom amenable to rigorous quantification. Attempts to quantify, in fact, often obscure the real character of effects.

In a NEPA context, effects are often measured against the definition of the word "significantly" found at 40 CFR 1508.27. This definition is useful as far as it goes, but does not provide much very specific guidance. Generally, the severity of impacts on cultural resources is something that must be determined based on expert judgement and consultation with stakeholders.

As with any other kind of environmental attribute, cultural resources can be affected in a wide variety of ways, for instance:

- Physical damage or destruction through demolition, excavation, land modification, etc.;

- Alteration of the visual environment where this environment has cultural value—for example, alteration of a culturally valued viewshed;

- Alteration of the auditory environment where this is relevant—for example, generating noise in the vicinity of an American Indian sacred site where quiet is of great importance);

- Introducing things into the environment that are incompatible with the resource's cultural value—for example, increasing traffic through a culturally valued neighborhood, or driving up property values in such a neighborhood so that low-income people can no longer live there;

- Neglect of a resource that an agency is charged with protecting—for example, letting a federally owned historic building fall down, or letting an archeological site get eroded away or vandalized;

- Transfer of property out of federal ownership in such a way that damage to cultural resources can result—for example, selling a surplus federal installation without restrictions to preserve its historic properties.

5. Seeking Mitigation Measures

The Section 106 regulations refer to this stage of analysis as "resolving adverse effects," but the measures considered are essentially those set forth in the definition of "mitigation" at 40 CFR 1508.20:

- Avoiding the impact altogether

- Minimizing impacts

- Rectifying impacts

- Reducing or eliminating impacts over time

- Compensating for impacts

The important factor required by the Section 106 regulations—and also, with respect to a narrower range of parties, by the NAGPRA regulations—is that mitigation measures are to be sought in consultation with various stakeholders. The Section 106 regulations give centrality of place in the consultation process to the SHPO or THPO, but also require consultation with tribes, Native Hawaiian groups, local governments, property owners, applicants for permits and licenses, and a broad range of other parties, ultimately including the public in general. The NAGPRA regulations require consultation with tribes or Native Hawaiian groups that may have affiliations with Native American cultural items subject to disturbance by the action. Other cultural resource-related authorities, such as AIRFA and Executive Orders 12898 and 13007, also call for various kinds of consultation.

Consultation is a flexible process, involving whatever it takes to seek agreement on mitigation measures. There is a vast literature on effective means of consultation, in the context of public participation in decision-making and alternative dispute resolution.

Consultation is not all an agency needs to do to seek mitigation measures, of course. Additional analysis may be necessary both to refine judgements about effects and to explore specific mitigation measures. Consultation often leads to, and is dependent upon, the conduct of such analyses. For this reason among others, it is important to give the consultation process the time it needs to reach a reasonable conclusion. None of the regulations impose specific time limits on consultation or on other actions involved in determining mitigation measures.

Consultation is subject to the limitations imposed by the Federal Advisory Committees Act (FACA), which in essence seeks to ensure that federal agency decisions are made in the open, without undue influence by special interests. FACA limits the extent to which an agency can make its decision dependent upon binding negotiations with particular groups, and its requirements must be carefully attended to in planning and carrying out consultation.

Where an EIS is being prepared under NEPA, consultation about mitigation measures should take place primarily during the public review period between the DEIS and the FEIS, so that it can be informed by public comments on the DEIS. Where only an EA is prepared and a FONSI is the likely outcome, consultation should be completed before the FONSI is issued, since it may result either in mitigation measures to be included in the FONSI or in the decision that an EIS has to be prepared.

6. Establishing and Documenting Mitigation Measures

Assuming mitigation measures are agreed upon, the various regulations require that they be documented in various ways.

Mitigation measures with respect to historic properties are set forth in Memoranda of Agreement (MOAs) under Section 106. MOAs are executed by the agency, the SHPO or THPO, and other stakeholders, subject to ACHP oversight. For some large-scale projects, and for certain federal programs, where impacts cannot be accurately foreseen before the federal decision must be made, Programmatic Agreements (PAs) are executed.

With respect to Native American cultural items, means of handling such items must be set forth in Plans of Action (POAs) that meet specific criteria set forth in the NAGPRA regulations (43 CFR 10.3 and 10.5). POAs are based on consultation with affiliated tribes or groups, but do not necessarily have to be signed by their representatives. As with Section 106, the NAGPRA regulations allow for programmatic approaches to compliance; an agency can enter into a Comprehensive Agreement (CA) with a tribe or group about how cultural items are to be handled. A CA must be signed by the relevant tribe or group to make it binding.

Other kinds of cultural resources are not the subjects of such detailed procedures, but are sometimes addressed in some manner in Section 106 MOAs. An MOA on a project that will have impacts on the overall socioeconomic character of a community, for example, may include such measures as historic preservation revolving funds and other forms of assistance to local property owners and businesses. MOAs dealing with impacts on Native American sacred sites sometimes contain provision for compensatory actions such as providing land to a tribe for cultural use, or helping fund a cultural center of some kind. Agreements of this kind can also, of course, be developed independent of Section 106 and NAGPRA.

Whether based on an agreement or not, mitigation measures are often set forth in, or as attachments to, FONSIs. Where this is done, it is important to be sure that the measures actually reduce the impacts of the action to a nonsignificant level. It is obviously illogical, at least, to say that an action has "no significant impact" when in fact it has impacts that various parties agree—perhaps grudgingly—are acceptable given specified mitigation measures.

This is a special problem with regard to historic properties, because many SHPOs and others in the historic preservation field do not understand much about NEPA, and tend to ignore it in carrying out Section 106 review. Section 106 does not require that impacts on historic properties be mitigated, only that the agency take its effects into account. This is done, in part, through consultation with SHPOs and other stakeholders, but often the result of consultation is not what anyone would regard as full mitigation of effects. For example, it is not uncommon for an MOA to provide only for documenting a historic building before it is destroyed—not because anyone thinks this reduces the impact of demolition to an insignificant level, but because it is the only thing everyone can agree to. It clearly makes no sense for an agency to translate the existence of such an agreement into the basis for a FONSI, but this is often what happens.

The other NEPA contexts in which mitigation measures are commonly set forth are in EISs and in RODs. In these contexts there is more flexibility about what is proposed, because the agency doesn't have to meet the test of reducing impacts below the level of significance.

However it is done, it is very important that mitigation measures be put in writing and that the agency clearly and formally commit to carrying them out. This is one of the great strengths of the Section 106 process—it results in clearly binding agreements. The other cultural resource authorities (other than NAGPRA) do not provide specifically for such agreements, but there is nothing to keep an agency and concerned stakeholders from entering into them as parts of review under NEPA and the other authorities, as long as they do not violate the limits imposed by FACA. The ACHP and others provide training in how to write agreement documents under Section 106, and many of the lessons taught are applicable to agreements under other authorities as well.

7. ACHP Comments

Under Section 106, agreements about how to mitigate impacts are not required, although the regulations and the statute itself strongly encourage them. If agreement is not reached about how to mitigate impacts on historic properties, the agency must request the comments of the ACHP. These comments are rendered by the 20-member Advisory Council, not by its staff, and they go to the head of the agency. Under Section 110(l) of NHPA, the agency head must document any response to the comments, and may not delegate this responsibility to a field office, an applicant, or anyone else. This sort of high-level attention can have career implications for those farther down the agency food chain, so the great bulk of Section 106 consultations *do* result in agreements. On occasion, though, the ACHP does have to render a formal comment, which often recommends mitigation measures. The agency isn't required to follow these recommendations, but agencies often do, at least in part. This, of course, may result in the adoption of mitigation measures even without a formal agreement to do so.

8. Implementing Mitigation

As with all other environmental impacts, measures to mitigate impacts on cultural resources are no good if they're not implemented. As a result, it's very important to provide explicitly for mitigation to be done, and for progress to be monitored, in such conclusory documents as MOAs, PAs, POAs, CAs, FONSIs, and RODs. Some specific measures that are often useful include:

- Monitoring by outside parties, such as the SHPO or THPO or an Indian tribe.

- Specified terms to be included in contracts, property disposal documents, construction specifications, and project plans.

- Periodic reports to and reviews by outside parties, on specified dates.

- Periodic reports to the public, with provision for public objections to be addressed.

These kinds of measures are often stipulated in Section 106 MOAs, and can be specified in RODs, FONSIs, and other mitigation-driving documents.

Summary and Conclusion:
Integrating Cultural Resource Impact Assessment into Environmental Impact Assessment

To successfully integrate cultural resource impact prediction and assessment into EIA, agencies, applicants, and their contractors should:

1. Remember that "cultural resources" are more than just historic properties, or archeological sites.

2. Be familiar with the whole range of laws that require consideration of impacts on cultural resources.

3. Consider possible cultural resource impacts when deciding whether a given action should be treated as a categorical exclusion; such impacts may represent "extraordinary circumstances" under which an action may not be categorically excluded under CEQ's regulations.

4. Remember that the fact that an action *is* categorically excluded under an agency's NEPA procedures does *not* mean that it is categorically excluded from consideration under Section 106 and other cultural resource laws.

5. Initiate Section 106 review and other considerations of cultural resource impacts during formal or informal scoping. Remember that scoping involves more than just a public meeting. Some cultural resource

issues may not be appropriate for public disclosure, and should be identified outside the context of, and often before, public meetings.

6. Cultural resources should be identified, either specifically or by prediction of property type distributions, in the description of the affected environment, and impacts on them should be analyzed in the discussion of environmental consequences. The regulations implementing Section 106 and NAGPRA should be followed in organizing descriptive and analytical data regarding historic properties and Native American cultural items, and stakeholders should be fully involved. The *Guidelines and Principles for Social Impact Assessment* should be used for general guidance.

7. Consultation with stakeholders, including the SHPO or THPO, Indian tribes, local governments, property owners, applicants, and concerned citizens, should be continuous throughout the analysis and review process.

8. Formal consultation with the SHPO or THPO and others to define impacts on historic properties and determine how to resolve them should be undertaken after the DEIS is completed, or on the basis of initial EA work or the review of a categorically excluded action. The views of the public on any draft document should be addressed in the consultation.

9. Mitigation measures should be developed, and agreements finalized, regarding cultural resources during finalization of NEPA analyses. Agreements on mitigation measures, such as Section 106 MOAs and NAGPRA POAs, should be included in final EISs, and/or in FONSIs and RODs.

10. Measures should be adopted and committed to by the agency to ensure that mitigation actually occurs in the manner agreed upon.

Chapter 8

Cultural Resource
Management Plans

Introduction

The classic way of "putting it all together" in mainstream cultural resource management is through implementation of a "cultural resource management plan" or CRMP (cf. DoE 1995). Variants on this theme are called historic resources management plans (HRMPs), historic preservation plans (HPPs), and (by far the best, dreamed up by a group of Irishmen in the Navy) historic and archeological resource protection (HARP) plans.

CRMPs have been very faddish at various times—everybody's had to have them—but they're really applicable only if you've got a lot of actions going on in the same general area (e.g., a military base, a National Forest), so you can prescribe standard operating procedures. It *is* possible to do a CRMP of a sort for a large, non-spatially specific entity—I did one for the Army Materiel Command (King 1995)—but it comes out very processual and unspecific.

SHPOs also do plans, called State Historic Preservation Plans and specifically called for by NHPA. In my experience these tend to be neither fish nor fowl kinds of things, simultaneously trying to establish a general strategy for historic preservation in the state and trying to plan the management of the SHPO office itself. Thus the plan tries at the same time to be responsive to large statewide development pressures and social changes, and address the structure of the historic property inventory system. It doesn't always work well.

Preservation has a long and honorable history as part of urban planning. Cities like Charleston and New Orleans integrated their designated historic districts into city planning as early as the 1930s, and historic district planning became part of the reaction to Urban Renewal in the 1960s and 70s (cf. New Orleans 1968; San Francisco 1972).

Multi-jurisdictional regional plans have been tried a few times; this was something I promoted from an archeological perspective way back in the '70s (King 1971), though I then lost my way and thought that State Historic Preservation Plans would suffice (King 1977b). The one such plan I've helped put together was interesting but sank like a stone (King and Hickman 1973, 1977), and I don't know of anyone who's done much better. To plan effectively, and make a plan effective, I think you've got to have a fairly delimited piece of space to work with, and a somewhat limited number of entities operating on it, with some kind of common organizational, decision-making framework.

In the late 1970s, NPS came up with the Resource Protection Planning Process (RP3) as its preservation planning mantra. RP3 was focused on State Historic Preservation Plans, though it was supposed to be good for everything. Not surprisingly, given NPS's jurisdictions, it also focused on evaluating properties for National Register eligibility. It addressed the difficulty of judging eligibility piecemeal by promoting the use of "historic contexts"—big-picture overviews of an area's historic resources that in theory would make it possible to make rational, comparative judgements about the significance of given historic properties. You'd develop a historic context on, say, "prehistoric agriculture," or "German immigrant beer brewers," and develop enough knowledge of this context that you could judge whether this old field or that tumbled-down hop dryer was a good example of the context's historic properties.

There was a lot wrong with historic contexts, not the least being that a given property could, after all, represent several contexts—including contexts that nobody had thought of, or conceived of as contexts at all—and be eligible for the Register even though it didn't rise to the top ten list within the context to which the planner had attached it. The bridge that was a not-particularly-good example of through-truss bridges in Minnesota might be the bridge where the mayor committed suicide in 1923, or where everybody's gone to propose marriage since 1917. But the big problem with contexts was that people got so enamored of producing them that they didn't do any planning. Doing a context was great academic fun for a historian or archeologist, but it didn't necessarily lead to anything but a volume on the shelf. Most context-based "plans" aren't plans at all; they're research tomes with a few pages at the end that regurgitate Section 106.

And of course, they don't deal with cultural resources as a whole; they deal with historic properties, and, for that matter, only with those that relate to the defined contexts.

I think you can and should do strategic planning for a SHPO office or an agency cultural resource program, but you can't plan with reference to specific resource types and specific action types. You can do that only with reference to somewhat bounded pieces of land like cities and National Parks and military bases. This chapter offers some recommendations about how to do such a plan. It's derived from studies I've participated in for the Department of Defense (CEHP 1993) and the Navy (CEHP 1997).

What is a Cultural Resource Management Plan (CRMP) Good For?

The idea of a CRMP is to give an agency or a facility a tool it can use to get on with whatever it does (its mission) in a manner that's consistent with the cultural resource laws and the national policy of environmental stewardship.

So the CRMP needs to respond to the mission of the agency or facility. It's got to be realistic in terms of that mission.

The CRMP also needs to establish achievable goals, in ways that can serve as the bases for budget decisions, assigning staff, establishing performance measures, setting up contracts, and so on.

The CRMP needs to be integrated with other plans, such as operating plans, natural resource management plans, and recreation plans.

Ideally, a CRMP should address all the "cultural resources" that may be affected or managed by the entity to which the CRMP applies. If it doesn't, it should be very explicit about what it *does* address, and what it does *not*.

If the CRMP doesn't cover the full range of cultural resources, it probably shouldn't be called a CRMP; to do so is misleading. Call it what it is—an HRMP, an HPP, whatever.

It's important not to forget that the traditions of the area, including its communities and perhaps the agency or facility itself, may be important cultural resources. Respecting them can help build support for the CRMP.

The CRMP should be based on a full understanding of the applicable laws. For example, if NAGPRA applies, there are distinct limitations on what the CRMP can provide for with respect to Native American cultural items.

What Should Be In A CRMP?

Generally, the CRMP should include both *proactive* and *reactive* elements. An example of a proactive element is the adaptive use of historic buildings, or providing access to a gathering site by Native American medicine people. An example of a reactive element is a procedure for stabilizing eroding archeological sites, or a system to ensure that planned land use changes are reviewed for impacts on cultural resources.

The CRMP should include procedures—such as review procedures, or the application of standards—to minimize damage to cultural resources, and also procedures to promote their proper use. It should establish realistic goals and targets for completing specified tasks.

The CRMP should provide for ready access to pertinent information, such as survey data, pertinent standards and guidelines, and points of contact for consultation. A geographic information system (GIS) can be an ideal context for accessing such data.

If all cultural resources haven't been identified, the CRMP needs to provide for ongoing identification, coordinated with mission needs. If data aren't complete, there needs to be a procedure to ensure that this doesn't lead to decisions that unnecessarily damage cultural resources and enrage other stakeholders.

The Planning Context

The CRMP needs to include basic contextual data, such as the location of the entity to which the plan applies. A particularly important thing to consider is the mission of the entity, and the needs and constraints it establishes. The CRMP is supposed to support that mission while ensuring that good cultural resource management is done. If the mission of a hydroelectric project is to produce X amount of electricity, there is no point in designing a CRMP that requires drawdown of its reservoir to a point at which only Y amount can be produced.

It's also important to look at the management systems of whatever entity the plan applies to. If the system is highly decentralized, for example, it will be fruitless to design a CRMP that requires a centralized system. The CRMP needs to work within the management philosophy of the entity. Further, it needs to relate to the specific management structure of the entity—for example, to the processes by which planning and budgetary decisions are made.

Resource Types

The CRMP should deal with all the types of cultural resources that exist in the area to which the plan applies, or that are affected by the entity to which it applies, for instance:

- Historic properties—places eligible for the National Register of Historic Places. Consideration is required under NHPA and NEPA.

- Native American cultural items such as human remains, funerary items, sacred items, and cultural patrimony. Consideration is required under NHPA, NAGPRA, AIRFA, and NEPA.

- Archeological sites and other scientific data. Consideration is required under ADPA, ARPA, NEPA and, to some extent, NHPA, NAGPRA.

- Native American sacred sites. Consideration is required under AIRFA, Executive Order 13007.

- Cultural institutions, lifeways, culturally valued viewsheds, places of cultural association, other valued places, social institutions, socio-economics. Consideration is required under NEPA, Executive Order 12898, sometimes other authorities.

Even within the relatively narrow category "historic resource," the CRMP needs to be specific about what kinds of resources it addresses. For example:

- Historic buildings, structures, and designed landscapes, whose study is usually the province of architectural historians and landscape historians, and whose management requires historical architects and landscape architects.

- Cultural landscapes and traditional cultural properties, which usually require extensive consultation with communities, possibly with a lot of cultural diversity.

- Roads, trails, canal districts and complexes made up of multiple properties; linkages among multiple properties, which need to be considered as parts of a complex whole, not in isolation.

- Archeological sites, which contain data important to archeologists but may have other values as well.

Stakeholders

The CRMP needs to identify pertinent stakeholders, and they need to be involved both in its creation and in its implementation. The agency that wants the CRMP is obviously a stakeholder. In addition:

- Indian tribes may be very important stakeholders, with special rights under treaty and because of the government-to-government relationship that exists between them and the U.S. Government.

- Regulators such as the SHPO, the ACHP, and EPA may have important roles to play.

- Local residents are obviously stakeholders, and if they constitute a minority or low income community, their interests require special consideration under Executive Order 12898.

- Property owners naturally have stakes in what happens to their land or community, and there may be a variety of legitimate special interest groups such as land rights groups, environmental groups, and historic preservation groups.

Identifying and Resolving Conflicts

The central reason for a CRMP is to address and resolve conflicts between mission and preservation, so these should be as carefully framed as possible. Usually problems and conflicts fall into two categories:

PLANNING CONFLICTS

For some reason, our planning doesn't properly consider cultural resources. Maybe it's because of some sort of institutional failure—management just doesn't care about this sort of thing. Or maybe it's a lack of data—we don't know what we may be getting into when we plan something in this or that location, and we don't have a ready way of finding out—or even of knowing that *not* knowing is a problem.

ONGOING MANAGEMENT PROBLEMS

We may have archeological sites eroding into the reservoir. We may have a problem with vandalism, or with unauthorized artifact collecting, or plant harvesting. We may have a tribe that wants unfettered access to a piece of land to carry out subsistence fishing where we normally hold live-fire exercises And we may have clashes over cultural values—for example, between the tribe's cultural authorities who don't want to talk about deeply spiritual matters, and our planners who say "if you won't tell us where your sacred sites are, how can we manage them?"

The CRMP needs to define these conflicts and problems, as a basis for solving them.

What to Do?

This is where the rubber meets the road. The CRMP should analyze and answer questions like:

WHAT'S PRACTICAL TO DO?

Are there management system changes that will help? Are they do-able? Can we establish partnerships with other stakeholders? Should we? Would it help simply to have better stakeholder involvement in what we do? Do we need more data, more study of specific matters, before we can figure out what to do? And are there specific, short-term management actions we can take (providing access, capping the archeological site)?

WHAT'S LEGAL TO DO?

The various laws establish standards that must be met. Sometimes these are not as rigorous as people think they are, but you need to talk with your lawyers and with other knowledgeable people to determine just what can be legally done. For example, if NAGPRA applies, we can't just negotiate a reburial agreement with a tribe and go rebury bodies; we have to go through the specific steps set forth in the NAGPRA regulations for establishing title and carrying out repatriation.

Make it Useable

Make sure that your CRMP is tied in with other plans, other operating systems, other standard procedures. Make sure it's readily available to those who need it.

Make your CRMP easy to use by those who will use it. If those who will use it work on computers, the CRMP should probably be computer-based. If they work more comfortably with books, maybe it should be in hard copy (though this is not recommended over the long run). And the CRMP needs to fit within the user's accustomed system. There's no use designing something for a Macintosh if everybody is on PCs, and vice versa.

Plan for training. The CRMP will not work if people aren't trained to use it.

Plan for periodic review and updating. No plan is good forever; things change, people change, systems change.

Scoping is the Key

Just as you "scope" an Environmental Impact Statement, you need to develop a scope for your CRMP. And just as a good EIS scoping involves more than just a public meeting, so does your CRMP scoping. You need to think *yourself* about the issues the CRMP should address, and you need to coordinate your thoughts with those of others, including people and groups inside the organization, such outside regulators as the State Historic Preservation Officer and such other stakeholders as Indian tribes and local communities. You need to integrate your work with what's going on elsewhere in the organization—for example, natural resource planning and recreation planning.

What Do You Do With a CRMP?

You seldom do a CRMP just because it's good to do. The justification for funding its preparation is usually to stay out of legal trouble and get on with the mission, at reduced or at least reasonable cost in terms of money and time. It follows that you need to have a scheme in mind for making use of your CRMP.

CRMPs are often the basis for PAs under Section 106, and, in theory, could be the basis for CAs under NAGPRA. A PA may be executed before the plan is done, and set to plan standards with respect to historic properties. In such a case, the PA needs to provide for review and acceptance of the plan by the SHPO, ACHP, and other key parties. Or the PA can be done after the plan is complete, and simply endorse it: as long as we follow the plan, we're in compliance with Section 106.

Of course, even without a PA, a properly prepared plan—done in consultation with all the pertinent stakeholders and reflecting compliance with all the pertinent laws and executive orders—will also demonstrate that the agency or facility is meeting its legal obligations. This can be important to management if the agency or facility gets reviewed for environmental compliance under an internal or external environmental audit system (as required by ISO 14000), and of course it can do an agency good in court.

Summary and Conclusions: the CRMP

A CRMP can be a very useful tool for complying with the various cultural resource management legal requirements in a practical way. To do a good one, you need to plan the plan, based on solid, thoughtful scoping, with the involvement of all key internal and external stakeholders. The CRMP should deal with all kinds of cultural resources and all pertinent laws, or explain precisely which ones are not dealt with and why. Although you need to know about the resource types that have to be dealt with, defining them—à la RP3—should not be the primary focus of the plan. The plan should be sensitive to the mission of the agency or facility, and relate effectively to internal management and decision-making systems. It should serve as the basis for demonstrating compliance with pertinent laws such as Section 106 and NAGPRA, and for complying with these authorities in a cost-effective, time-effective manner.

Chapter 9

The Future

Your Future: Working in CRM

If you've dipped into this book either on your own or as part of a class, you presumably have some interest in the field of practice that's loosely called "cultural resource management." Very likely, you're wondering whether there's a future for you in the field. Let's look at some possibilities.

Jobs in Action Agencies

You may work, or be interested in working, in an agency that actually does things—funds highway construction, builds dams, assists farmers, manages land. If so, you'll most likely find yourself working in a "NEPA Shop"—the office or division or department that is responsible for project review under NEPA and some of the other authorities we've discussed in this book. You may instead be in a more specialized "cultural resource shop," that probably focuses mostly on the care and feeding of historic properties, archeological sites, and the like—sometimes both in the context of project review and in that of long-term management. Or you may be in a specialized "SIA shop" concerned with social and economic impacts, perhaps at both project and policy levels. Increasingly, there's the possibility of employment in a "Native American shop," where your concerns will include managing the government-to-government relationship with tribes and with handling treaty rights issues as well as dealing with Native American cultural resources per se.

In any of these contexts, and irrespective of the professional specialization you bring to the job, if you're a new employee you'll have some important things to learn as quickly as you can, and some attitude adjustments to make, if you're going to be happy in your work.

The major attitude adjustment is to respect the agency's mission and priorities. This may not come easy. You probably—I hope—have commitments to environmental protection, to doing right by cultural resources, and to public responsibility. You may, in fact, be a bit starry-eyed about these things. You may be a very moral, ethical archeologist or historical architect who believes in protection of "the resource" over all else. Finding yourself in the company of a bunch of engineers in a state department of transportation may be something of a shock. You may be used to thinking of the agency that's now your employer as a raper of the world, and of your colleagues as dangerous deadheads.

You've got to set those attitudes aside. Don't lose them completely, because they're probably not entirely incorrect; just keep them encapsulated, and give your agency and your colleagues a chance. Recognize that, for all its warts, your agency is doing something that the public wants, and that some substantial segment of the public thinks is in its interests. You may not like a particular policy or project—that's fine, but if you can't accept the idea that your agency overall has a worthwhile mission, you ought not to be working for it.

You need to learn your agency's internal procedures. How are decisions made? How does paperwork move? How does the budget process work? How does the agency relate to others? To Congress? To other agencies? To the public? What are the limits of your agency's power, and the scope of its concerns? Don't expect your agency to ram something down the throats of the state agencies that receive its assistance if your agency just doesn't relate to its customers that way. Think of some other way to get them to swallow it.

You ought to learn something about what your colleagues do. Particularly if you have colleagues who perform other aspects of cultural resource management, or related kinds of management, learn something about their practice. What does the SIA guy do? What are the concerns of the wildlife manager? The handicap accessibility specialist? At the very least, it will help you garner their assistance and support if you show respect for what they do, and equip yourself to help them look out for their interests.

Jobs in Review Agencies

In a review agency like the ACHP, or a SHPO's "compliance shop," you need many of the same attitudes and skills as in an action agency. In fact you need to know something about, and respect, the missions and operations of the agencies whose actions you review, as well as those of your own agency. Balanced with this, you need a very strong commitment to the public interest, and a lot of tolerance for a diversity of publics. You're going to be on the firing line, expected by people to help them represent their interests against agencies they feel are riding roughshod over them. It's a narrow line to walk, but it's imperative that you be seen by one and all as fair and unbiased.

Of course, you'll need to know the laws and regulations under which your agency operates, and you ought to know how far you can flex them and how. You should know the laws and regulations other than your own, with which your authorities interact. If you're doing Section 106 review you ought to know about NEPA and NAGPRA, and the Clean Water Act if you interact a lot with the Corps of Engineers.

And more than some others, you'll need to get familiar with the professional specializations of your colleagues. You may be an urban planner, but you're not necessarily going to be able to call on your friendly neighborhood architectural historian or archeologist when you're faced with a problem involving their specialties. You need to know something about them yourself—and know your limitations, when *to* ask for help.

Formal training in alternative dispute resolution, particularly mediation, is strongly recommended. You'll often be in the position of middleperson between an agency and an affected community or affected interests. Most of us fly by the seats of our pants in such situations, but there's a better way. Take some classes, get some hands-on guided experience, tap the expertise that's out there in the world of ADR.

Jobs in Local Government

Historic preservation specialists in local government typically are employed as staff to design review commissions, in planning agencies, in housing agencies, and occasionally in city archeology programs. Social impact specialists may be found in planning, housing, and social services agencies. Other kinds of cultural resource management jobs may be in local museums, libraries, and educational institutions. Depending on your position, you may need to know a lot about the *Secretary of the Interior's Standards for Rehabilitation* (cf. Morton et al. 1992) or federal authorities like NEPA and NHPA, or these may not be particularly important to you at all. You'll certainly have local ordinances and standards to deal with, and probably state enabling rules and the rules of various funding agencies like HUD. And if you intend to live long and prosper in your work, you'll learn your way around the local political system.

Jobs in Contracting

A cultural resource contractor, to a considerable extent, needs to know, learn, and do all of the above, in varying degrees depending on what kinds of contract work she or he does. In addition, the more you can learn about business, the better—budgets, safety and health requirements, workers' compensation, marketing, proposal writing, how to read the *Commerce Business Daily*. But it's not enough just to know—say—archeology plus business, as a lot of contractors seem to think. You need to know the laws, the rules, the regulations, the agency procedures, and the range of disciplines whose practice may be necessary to give a client full service. Contractors, more than anyone else, have to be generalists.

Jobs in Advocacy

Finally, you may be able to work in an advocacy organization that promotes some aspect of cultural resource management—in the National Trust for Historic Preservation, perhaps, or in some national, state or local environmental group. In such a job you can have the satisfaction—unique in the CRM world—of *not* having to balance conflicting interests very much; you're expected to be partisan.

But even in this kind of role, an understanding of the points of view of the agencies, organizations, and professional specialists with which and with whom you deal is important—if for no other reason than to know the enemy.

In General...

So, some general advice for those who may want to work in CRM:

Learn more than one specialty. It's fine to be the expert landscape historian, but you'd better know about some other fields of specialization if you're going to work well in an interdisciplinary team, and in an environment where your employer, client, reviewee or enemy is interested in and responsible for things other than landscapes.

Learn the laws, regulations, rules of practice. Don't accept them as God-given; if you think something's wrong with them, say so, and work to fix it, but don't scorn them as a bunch of bureaucratic fol-de-rol. They're what cause you to be paid, and you disrespect them at your peril.

Don't be a purist. If you come into CRM believing that it's a sin ever to knock down a historic building or muck up an archeological site for any reason other than research, or that human communities should never change, or that local values should always prevail, you're going to be very disillusioned. And when this happens, terrible things can happen to your soul. Some of the most crass, dishonest, disreputable people I know in CRM are those who came into the field as true believers. When they found that they couldn't make the world entirely safe for roadside commercial architecture or cultural landscapes or whatever, their belief systems fell in on themselves as into a black hole. Don't let this happen to you. Maintain perspective; understand that your piece of CRM is only one piece that has to be balanced with others, and that all of CRM is just one piece of public policy. And your business is promoting good public policy, not your own professional interests.

The Future of Cultural Resource Management

As one of my classes on some aspect of CRM winds down, I'm often asked to prognosticate about the future. Though this book is no more about the future than it is about the past, a few comments on the future may be the most graceful way to bring it to a close.

It probably reflects some limitation of mind, but I can't help thinking about CRM in dialectic terms, and I can't help being pretty obvious about the side of each dialectic on which I come down. This may be as good a way as any to organize a brief foray into the future.

Interdisciplinary or Not?

After some thirty years of practice, we still have little effective communication among even the disciplines that make up traditional historic preservation. Architectural historians and historical architects can still talk about "historic properties" when they mean "historic buildings," while archeologists remain uncomfortable about being regarded as historic preservation practitioners at all. NPS and most SHPOs continue to bifurcate their offices between "above-ground" and "below-ground" people, and things that aren't quite either—cultural landscapes, traditional cultural properties, districts whose significance doesn't lie in their architecture or archeology—are left to catch as catch can. And whichever historic preservation practitioner is assigned the "CRM" label in preparation of an EIS or EA seldom has anything to do with the people doing SIA, who tend to be economists or sociologists bedazzled with number-crunching. Is this just the way things somehow have to be? Maybe so. Would it be better to have a truly interdisciplinary practice? Maybe not. I think it would be, however, and I think that if we don't develop in this direction we'll soon become irrelevant, as broader and more effective ways of addressing the cultural environment develop in areas of practice that don't align themselves in any way with CRM.

Flexible or Inflexible Procedures?

My frequent use of the words "it depends" in this book reflects my observation and conviction that there's little that's black and white in the world of CRM practice—if there is anywhere. We need flexible, creative approaches to the management of cultural resources and impacts on them. Will we get them? I don't know, but I'm not sanguine. What do we do to identify historic properties in the State of Washafornia? A Phase I survey following the SHPO's guidelines? Why? Because that's the way we do it. How do we determine whether we're going to have disproportionate impacts on a minority population? Look at the census. Why? Because it's easy. Why can't a treasure salvor fund good shipwreck archeology? Because they're evil. Inflexibility is comfortable; nobody has to think much. Can the urge toward inflexibility be counteracted? I don't know, but history is full of lessons about what happens to social and biological entities that fail to flex.

Process or Outcome?

As I've suggested elsewhere, good process is vital, and if you're interested in balanced policy you can find great pleasure in a process that works, that's fair, that's efficient, regardless of the substantive outcome. But there's danger in the comfort that one can find in process. Not that one will stop caring about the results altogether; I don't know that that would be bad, and I also don't think it's humanly possible. The danger lies, I think, in getting so enamored of a particular process, a particular set of procedures, that we cannot or will not consider alternative ways to achieve the purposes for which the procedures were created. We can't consider the effects of the project until we've determined the eligibility of the potentially affected properties for the National Register. Why not, if we can clearly achieve the purposes of Section 106 without investing time and money in evaluation? Because the regulations are built around a sequence of steps, and we train people to follow them. We encourage people to think of them as immutable, and we select for employment those who are comfortable with immutable rules and don't care much about outcomes—or who have become too jaded to care much about anything. Can we achieve a more outcomes-oriented system without sacrificing fair process? Should we try?

Professionals and Publics

For whom do we try to deal with impacts on cultural resources? However much we may puff out our chests and pontificate about doing things "for the resource," it's a safe assumption that old buildings, archeological sites, and even living human social institutions in the abstract really don't greatly care what happens to them. It's people who care, so the question really comes down to: for which groups of people do we concern ourselves with impacts on cultural resources? Are we concerned primarily about the interests of professional specialists, or with the public in all its permutations?

Professional archeologists, historians, and others will protest that we are, after all, trying to preserve things for the future, for generations yet unborn, and are trying to take a longer view than one can expect of the contemporary self-seeking multitude. There's truth in that, I think, and it ought to be respected, but it can be carried too far.

Out on the flat plains of southern Illinois there's a little town that grew up around a surface mine. The mine tailings formed a big heap at the edge of town that people called "the Gob Pile." The Gob Pile was the only geographic relief for miles around, and it became a familiar and appreciated local landmark. People would go up to the top of the Gob Pile to look out over the world, and doubtless to have beer parties and neck and look at the stars and do all the other things that people tend to do in special places. When it came time to reclaim the old mine site, a question arose as to whether the Gob Pile might be eligible for the National Register, and hence whether its preservation would have to considered before it was pushed back into the mine. The Keeper ended up evaluating it, and found that since it really wasn't a very good representative of historic mining technology, it wasn't eligible.

Was this to the point? Was the major reason for considering impacts on the Gob Pile its potential importance to students of mining technology, or its known importance to the people who lived around it, and in whose local culture it had come to play a role?

This sort of thing happens all the time in the historic preservation side of CRM—we don't really know, we haven't really settled on, why old things may be worth saving. Certainly a place that can tell us a lot about early mining technology is worth saving in some form, if only in that of documentation, but is a place that figures in a community's sense of itself not equally worthy of consideration?

Comprehensive or Particular?

Are we moving toward the kind of comprehensive, interdisciplinary, public-oriented CRM that this book obviously espouses? Should we? I obviously think we should; indeed I think we must if we aren't to get swept off into corners and left to decay. But we don't have to. We can settle back into what we're comfortable doing—be it sociology or archeology or architectural history or landscape history or cultural anthropology—and probably be pretty happy with ourselves for quite awhile. We can sip our sherry or slurp our beers and age gracefully among our like-minded, culturally and professionally homogenous peers, debating fine points of theory and practice, occasionally expressing frustration with the fact that our academic co-practitioners don't respect us as we think they should. Absent some event that shakes us up and forces change, that's probably exactly what we'll do; it's very human.

When I was in graduate school we were all enamored of Thomas Kuhn's *Structure of Scientific Revolutions* (Kuhn 1962). Kuhn demonstrated—to our satisfaction at the time, anyway—that science is not characterized by slow, steady growth. Rather, we have long periods of "normal science" in which everybody does pretty much the same thing and doesn't greatly question their assumptions, punctuated by occasional paradigm shifts that shake people up and stimulate a burst of exploration in new directions. What we now call CRM was born out of set of paradigm shifts in the 1960s and 70s when people in the "social sciences and the environmental design arts" that Section 102(2)(A) of NEPA alludes to began to grapple with a new relationship between human society and its environment. Historic preservationists began looking beyond the preservation of landmarks and house museums, archeologists began looking beyond salvage, and anthropologists, sociologists, and other social scientists began to apply their skills and knowledge outside academia. We've all settled into the practice of normal science in the last couple of decades, I think—into a dispersed scattering of normal science practices, actually. Are we due for a paradigm shift? It would be nice to think so, but who knows?

It depends.

Bibliography

ACHP (Advisory Council on Historic Preservation)
  1988   *Preparing Agreement Documents*. Washington, D.C.

ACHP, UNR (University of Nevada, Reno), and T.F. King
  1996   Course syllabus: "Preparing Agreement Documents Under Section 106 of the
         National Historic Preservation Act."

Anzalone, Ronald
  1995   Remarks for "Public Benefit of Mitigation." Annual Meeting of the National
         Conference of State Historic Preservation Officers, Washington D.C., March 27.

Bickman, Leonard, and Debra J. Rog
  1997   *Handbook of Applied Social Research Methods*. Sage Publications, Thousand Oaks,
         Calif.

Branch, Kristi, et al.
  1983   *Guide to Social Impact Assessment*. Westview Press, Boulder, Colo.

Burdge, Rabel J., and Colleagues
  1994   *A Conceptual Approach to Social Impact Assessment*. Social Ecology Press, Madison,
         Wisc.

Cantor, Larry W.
  1996   *Environmental Impact Assessment* (Second Edition). McGraw-Hill, New York.

Carson, Rachel
  1962   *Silent Spring*. Houghton Mifflin, Cambridge, Mass.

CEHP, Inc.
  1993   "Principles of Cultural Resource Management Planning in the Department of
         Defense." Legacy Resource Management Program, Department of Defense,
         Washington, D.C.

  1994a "Cultural Resource Law and Department of Defense International Activities."
         Interim Paper, January 12.

  1994b "Cultural Resource Law and Department of Defense International Activities."
         Background Paper, March 1, Washington, D.C.

  1997   *Historic and Archeological Resource Protection Planning Guidelines*. Department of
         the Navy, NAVFACENGCOM Code 150RH, Alexandria, Va.

CEQ (Council on Environmental Quality)
  1997   "Guidelines for addressing environmental justice under NEPA." Manuscript,
         Washington, D.C.

Costantino, Cathy A., and Christina Sickles Merchant
 1995 *Designing Conflict Management Systems.* Jossey-Bass Publishers, San Francisco.

Derry, Anne, Ward E. Jandl, Carol D. Shull, and Jan Thorman
 1985 *Guidelines for Local Surveys: A Basis for Preservation Planning.* National Register
    Bulletin 24, first issued 1977, revised 1985 by Patricia L. Parker, National Park
    Service, Washington, D.C.

DoE (Department of Energy)
 1995 *Environmental Guidelines for Development of Cultural Resource Management Plans.*
    Office of Environmental Policy and Assistance, Washington, D.C.

Finsterbusch, Kurt, and C.P. Wolf
 1981 *Methodology of Social Impact Assessment.* Second Edition. Hutchinson Ross,
    Stroudsburg, Pa.

Fisher, Roger, and Scott Brown
 1988 *Getting Together: Building Relationships as We Negotiate.* Penguin Books, New
    York.

Fisher, Roger, and William Ury
 1981 *Getting to Yes.* Penguin Books, New York.

Fitch, James Marsten
 1982 *Historic Preservation: Curatorial Management of the Built World.* McGraw-Hill,
    New York.

Freudenburg, William R.
 1986 Social Impact Assessment. *Annual Review of Sociology* 12:451-478.

GSA (General Services Administration)
 1997 *NEPA Desk Guide.* Public Buildings Service, GSA, Washington, D.C.

Georgia Tech.
 1993 HBPP Building Manager's Training Course. Syllabus, Georgia Tech Continuing
    Education and General Services Administration, Atlanta, Ga.

Glass, James A.
 1990 *The Beginnings of a New National Historic Preservation Program, 1957 to 1969.*
    American Association for State and Local History, Nashville TN and National
    Conference of State Historic Preservation Officers, Washington, D.C.

Grimm, Lydia T.
 1997 Sacred Lands and the Establishment Clause: Indian Religious Practices on
    Federal Lands. *Natural Resources and Environment* 12(1):19-78, American Bar
    Association Committee on Natural Resources, Energy, and Environmental Law.

Hosmer, Charles B., Jr.
 1965 *Presence of the Past: The History of the Preservation Movement in the United States
    Before Williamsburg.* G.P. Putnam's Sons, New York.

 1981 *Preservation Comes of Age: From Williamsburg to the National Trust, 1926-49*
    (2 vols). University of Virginia Press, Charlottesville, Va.

Hutt, Sherry, Elwood W. Jones, and Martin E. McAllister
 1992 *Archeological Resource Protection.* The Preservation Press, Washington, D.C.

Interorganizational Committee on Guidelines and Principles for Social Impact Assessment
  1993 Guidelines and Principles for Social Impact Assessment. Published in various
      venues; see NOAA 1994.

ISO (International Organization for Standards)
  1995 Environmental Management Systems: 14000 Series. Released by American
      National Standards Institute, ASQC, P.O. Box 3005, Milwaukee, Wisc. 53201-
      3005.

Johnson, Ronald W., and Michael G. Schene
  1987 *Cultural Resources Management*. Robert E. Krieger Publishing, Malabar, Fla.

Judge, W. James, and Lynne Sebastian
  1988 *Quantifying the Present and Predicting the Past: Theory, Method, and Application of
      Archaeological Predictive Modeling*. Bureau of Land Management, Department of
      the Interior, Denver, Colo.

Keller, J Timothy, and Genevieve P. Keller
  1987 *How to Evaluate and Nominate Designed Historic Landscapes*. National Register
      Bulletin 18. National Register of Historic Places, National Park Service,
      Washington, D.C.

King, Thomas F.
  1971 A Conflict of Values in American Archaeology. *American Antiquity* 36:255-262.

  1977a *The Archeological Survey, Methods and Uses*. Interagency Archeological Services
      Division, National Park Service.

  1977b Resolving a Conflict of Values in American Archaeology. In *Conservation
      Archaeology: a Guide for Cultural Resource Management Studies*, ed. Michael B.
      Schiffer and George J. Gumerman. Academic Press, New York.

  1991 Looters or Lovers: Studying the Non-Archeological Uses of Archeological Sites.
      Manuscript report: CEHP, Inc. for Society for American Archaeology and
      National Park Service, Washington, D.C.

  1995 *Command-Wide Cultural Resource Management Plan*. Komatsu-Rangel Associates,
      submitted to Fort Worth District, U.S. Army Corps of Engineers, for Army
      Materiel Command, Fort Worth, Tex.

  1998 How the Archeologists Stole Culture. A Gap in American Environmental
      Impact Assessment and How to Fill It. *Environmental Impact Assessment Review*
      74:18:2:117-134, Elsevier Science Services, New York.

King, Thomas F., and Patricia P. Hickman
  1973 *The Southern Santa Clara Valley: A General Plan for Archaeology*. San Felipe
      Archaeology I, San Francisco State University A.E. Treganza Anthropology
      Museum, San Francisco.

  1977 San Felipe: Designing a General Plan for Archaeology. In *Conservation
      Archaeology: A Guide for Cultural Resource Management Studies*, ed. Michael B.
      Schiffer and George J. Gumerman. Academic Press, New York

King, Thomas F., Patricia P. Hickman, and Gary Berg
  1977 *Anthropology in Historic Preservation*. Academic Press, New York.

King, Thomas F., and Ethan Rafuse
  1994 *NEPA and the Cultural Environment: An Assessment of Effectiveness*. CEHP, Inc. for
      Council on Environmental Quality. CEHP, Inc., Washington, D.C.

Klesert, Anthony L., and Alan S. Downer
    1990   *Preservation on the Reservation: Native Americans, Native American Lands, and Archeology.* Navajo Nation Papers in Anthropology No. 26, Navajo Nation Archeology Department, Window Rock.

Kritek, Phyllis Beck
    1994   *Negotiating at an Uneven Table.* Jossey-Bass Publishers, San Francisco.

Kuhn, Thomas
    1962   *The Structure of Scientific Revolutions.* University of Chicago Press.

Lee, Antoinette J.
    1987   Discovering Old Cultures in the New World: the Role of Ethnicity. In *The American Mosaic,* ed. Robert Stipe and Antoinette J. Lee. U.S. Committee for the International Council on Monuments and Sites (US/ICOMOS), Washington, D.C.

Lipe, W.D., and A.J. Lindsay, Jr.
    1974   *Proceedings of the 1974 Cultural Resource Management Conference.* Museum of Northern Arizona Technical Series No. 14, Flagstaff, Ariz.

Loomis, Ormond H.
    1983   *Cultural Conservation. The Protection of Cultural Heritage in the United States.* American Folklife Center and National Park Service, Washington, D.C.

Lynch, Kevin
    1972   *What Time Is This Place?* MIT Press, Cambridge, Mass.

McCarthy, John P.
    1996   Who Owns These Bones? Descendant Communities and Partnerships in the Excavation and Analysis of Historic Cemetery Sites in New York and Philadelphia. *Public Archaeology Review* 4:2:3-12.

McClelland, Linda Flint, J. Timothy Keller, Genevieve P. Keller, and Robert Z. Melnick
    1990   *Guidelines for Evaluating and Documenting Rural Historic Districts.* National Register Bulletin 30, National Register of Historic Places, National Park Service, Washington, D.C.

Miller, Frederic M.
    1990   *Arranging and Describing Archives and Manuscripts.* Society of American Archivists, Chicago.

Morton, W. Brown III, Gary L. Hume, Kay D. Weeks, and H. Ward Jandl
    1992   *The Secretary of the Interior's Standards for Rehabilitation and Illustrated Guidelines for Rehabilitating Historic Buildings.* Preservation Assistance Division, National Park Service, Washington, D.C.

Murtagh, William J.
    1997   *Keeping Time: The History and Theory of Preservation in America.* Revised Edition. John Wiley and Sons, New York.

NARA (National Archives and Records Administration)
    1989   *NARA and the Disposal of Federal Records. Laws and Authorities and their Implementation.* A Report of the Committee on Authorities and Program Alternatives. Washington, D.C.

    1992   *Disposal of Federal Records.* Washington, D.C.

NOAA (National Oceanic and Atmospheric Administration)
1994 *Guidelines and Principles for Social Impact Assessment.* National Marine Fisheries Service; prepared by the Interorganizational Committee on Guidelines and Principles for Social Impact Assessment.

NPS (National Park Service)
1983 *The Secretary of the Interior's Standards for Archeology and Historic Preservation.* F8 Fed. Reg. (Federal Register) 44716-68.

1988 *Guidelines for Federal Agency Responsibilities Under Section 110 of the National Historic Preservation Act.* 53 Fed. Reg. 4727-46. Annotated and republished by ACHP as "The Section 110 Guidelines."

1990a *Keepers of the Treasures: Protecting Historic Properties and Cultural Traditions on Indian Lands.* Report on tribal preservation funding needs, submitted to Congress. Interagency Resources Division, Washington, D.C.

1990b *Abandoned Shipwreck Guidelines.* 44 Fed. Reg. 50116-45.

1992 *The Secretary of the Interior's Standards for the Treatment of Historic Properties.* Brochure, Preservation Assistance Division, Washington, D.C.

1998 *Secretary of the Interior's Standards and Guidelines for Federal Agency Historic Preservation Programs Under Section 110 of the National Historic Preservation Act.* 63 Fed Reg. 20495-20508.

NPI (National Preservation Institute)
1998 Syllabus, Section 106: An Advanced Seminar. Washington, D.C.

NRHP (National Register of Historic Places)
1990 *Guidelines for Evaluating and Documenting Traditional Cultural Properties.* National Register Bulletin 38, National Park Service, Washington, D.C.

1991 *How to Apply the National Register Criteria for Evaluation.* National Register Bulletin 15, National Park Service, Washington, D.C.

New Orleans
1968 Vieux Carre Historic District Demonstration Study. Bureau of Government Research for the City of New Orleans, New Orleans.

Odegaard, Nancy, et al.
1990 Training in Collections Care and Maintenance. In *Archaeology and Ethnography,* Vol. 1, National Institute for Conservation, Washington, D.C.

Parker, Patricia L., and Thomas F. King
1987 Intercultural Mediation at Truk International Airport. In *Anthropological Praxis: Translating Knowledge into Action,* ed. Robert M. Wulff and Shirley J. Fiske. Westview Press, Boulder, Colo.

Price, H. Marcus III
1991 *Disputing the Dead: U.S. Law on Aboriginal Remains and Grave Goods.* University of Missouri Press, Columbia, Mo.

Rapoport, Amos
1982 *The Meaning of the Built Environment: A Nonverbal Communications Approach.* Sage Publications, Beverly Hills, Calif.

Rubenstein, David, Jerry Aroesty, and Charles Thompsen
1992   *Two Shades of Green: Environmental Protection and Combat Training.* Rand National Defense Research Institute R-4220-A, Santa Monica, Calif.

Rushlow, Frederick J., and Don Kermath
1994   *Proactive Maintenance Planning for Historic Buildings.* USACERL Technical Report CRC-94/01, Construction Engineering Research Laboratories, Champaign, Ill.

San Francisco (City and County of)
1972   Urban Design Plan. Department of City Planning, City of San Francisco, San Francisco.

Sayre, Don
1996   *Inside ISO 14000: The Competitive Advantage of Environmental Management.* St. Lucie Press, Delray Beach, Fla.

Stipe, Robert, ed.
1982   *Historic Preservation in Foreign Countries.* U.S. Committee of the International Council on Monuments and Sites, Washington, D.C. (Supplement 1986).

Stipe, Robert E., and Antoinette J. Lee , eds.
1987   *The American Mosaic: Preserving a Nation's Heritage.* U.S. Committee of the International Council on Monuments and Sites, The Preservation Press, Washington, D.C.

Stoffle, Richard W., ed.
1990   *Cultural and Paleontological Effects of Siting a Low-Level Radioactive Waste Storage Facility in Michigan: Candidate Area Analysis Phase.* Institute for Social Research, University of Michigan, Ann Arbor.

Taylor, C. Nicholas, D. Hobson Bryan, and Colin C. Goodrich
1990   *Social Assessment: Theory, Process and Techniques.* Studies in Resource Management No. 7, Center for Resource Management, Lincoln University, New Zealand.

Thompson, J.G., and Gary Williams
1992   Social Assessment: Roles for Practitioners and the Need for Stronger Mandates. *Impact Assessment Bulletin* 10(3):43-56.

UNESCO (United Nations Educational, Scientific, and Cultural Organization)
1962   *Recommendation Concerning the Safeguarding of the Beauty and Character of Landscapes and Sites.* UNESCO, United Nations, New York.

1976   *Recommendation Concerning the Safeguarding and Contemporary Role of Historic Areas.* UNESCO, United Nations, New York.

1976   *Convention on the Means of Prohibiting and Preventing the Illicit Import, Export and Transfer of Ownership of Cultural Property.* UNESCO, United Nations, New York.

Ury, William
1991   *Getting Past No.* Bantam Books, New York.

U.S. Conference of Mayors
1967   *With Heritage So Rich.* Random House, New York.

Vaughn, Charlene Dwin
1996   "Five W's for Good Agreements." Manuscript, Advisory Council on Historic Preservation Education Program.

Walker, Gregg (Moderator; Oregon State University)
  1996   Public Involvement and Social Assessment: Wenatchee National Forest Fire
          Recovery Planning. Session at Sixth International Symposium on Society and
          Resource Management, Pennsylvania State University, University Park, Pa.

Warnow, Joan, et al.
  1982   *Documentation of Postwar Physics* (3 volumes). American Institute of Physics,
          New York.

Wilson, Rex L., ed.
  1987   *Rescue Archeology: Proceedings of the Second New World Conference on Rescue
          Archeology.* Southern Methodist University Press, Dallas, Tex.

Wilson, Rex L., and Gloria Loyola, eds.
  1981   *Rescue Archeology: Papers from the First New World Conference on Rescue
          Archeology.* The Preservation Press, Washington, D.C.

Wilson, Sherrill D.
  1996   Citations on the New York African Burial Ground: 1991-1996. Third Edition.
          Compiled by the Office of Public Education and Interpretation of the African
          Burial Ground, New York.

WRC/FEMA (Water Resource Council [defunct] and Federal Emergency
Management Agency [successor])
  1978   Floodplain Management: Guidelines for Implementing Executive Order 11988,
          43 FR 6030-55, Friday, Feb. 10, 1978. Further advice on EO 11988 available from
          FEMA at 500 C St. SW, WDC 20472.

Regulations Cited

18 CFR 1312:	Protection of Archeological Resources (Tennessee Valley Authority ARPA)
32 CFR 229:	Protection of Archeological Resources (Dept. of Defense ARPA)
36 CFR 60:	National Register of Historic Places. National Park Service
36 CFR 63:	Determinations of Eligibility for Inclusion in the National Register of Historic Places
36 CFR 68:	Secretary of the Interior's Standards for the Treatment of Historic Properties
36 CFR 79:	Curation of Federally-Owned and Administered Archeological Collections
36 CFR 296:	Protection of Archeological Resources (Dept. of Agriculture ARPA)
36 CFR 800:	Protection of Historic Properties. Advisory Council on Historic Preservation (Section 106 regulations)
36 CFR 1222-1238:	Federal Records Act. National Archives and Records Administration
40 CFR 1500-1508:	Regulations for Implementing the Procedural Provisions of the National Environmental Policy Act
43 CFR 7:	Protection of Archeological Resources (Dept. of Interior ARPA)
43 CFR 10:	Native American Graves Protection and Repatriation Act Regulations

Some Useful
World Wide Web Sites

Here are some World Wide Web sites that—as of 1998—can provide you with access to a wide range of reference material on CRM.

- For information on and from the ACHP, including laws, regulations, publications, and training about Section 106, and a summary of Section 106 case law: **http://www.achp.gov**

- For information, regulations, publications, and training relating to NEPA and the functions of the Council on Environmental Quality: **http://ceq.eh.doe.gov/nepa/nepanet.htm**

- For information on NPS programs in historic preservation, including the National Register, preservation standards and guidelines, and the Historic American Buildings Survey/Historic American Engineering Record, and accessible copies of many NPS publications including National Register Bulletins and various standards and guidelines: **http://www.cr.nps.gov**

- For information on NEPA-related topics, including model language for Section 106 Memoranda of Agreement and Programmatic Agreements: **http://www.gsa.gov/pbs/pt/call-in/nepa.htm**

- For access to state historic preservation laws: **http://ncsl.org/programs/arts/statehist.htm.**

- For a wide range of historic preservation laws, regulations, and related material, including legislation, court cases, and local historic district ordinances: **http://www.preservenet.cornell.edu/law/plawmain.htm.**

- For access to anthropologists involved in environmental matters and access to pertinent anthropological databases: **http://dizzy.library.arizona.edu/ej/ipe/anthenv/**

- For information on and from the National Archives and Records Administration, and access to government documents, the Federal Register, Federal laws, the Code of Federal Regulations, and records management procedures: **http://www.nara.gov/**

- For access to environmental databases: **http://moe.csa.com/routenet/** (Subscription required)

- For information on and from the National Association of Environmental Professionals: **http://www.naep.org**

- For environmental legislation, federal and state environmental agencies, organizations concerned with environmental management: **http://www.clay.net/**

- For information on the International Organization for Standards, including ISO 14000 environmental management standards: **http://www.iso.ch/welcome.html**

- For links to various archeological web pages: **http://members.tripod.com/~archonnet/net.htm**

- For information on training in cultural resource management from the National Preservation Institute: **http://www.npi.org**

- For information on training in cultural resource management from the University of Nevada, Reno: **http://www.dce.unr.edu/htm**

Appendix I

Abbreviations

ACHP:	Advisory Council on Historic Preservation
ADPA:	Archeological Data Protection Act (aka Archeological and Historic Preservation Act
ADR:	Alternative (to litigation) Dispute Resolution
AFC:	American Folklife Center
AFPA:	American Folklife Preservation Act
AIRFA:	American Indian Religious Freedom Act
APE:	Area of Potential Effect
ARPA:	Archeological Resources Protection Act
ASA:	Abandoned Shipwrecks Act
BIA:	Bureau of Indian Affairs
BLM:	Bureau of Land Management
BOC:	Bureau of the Census
BOR:	Bureau of Reclamation
CA:	Comprehensive Agreement
CATEX:	Categorical Exclusion under NEPA (Also CX or CatEx)
CBA:	Central business area or centralized business area
CDBG:	Community Development Block Grant
CEHP:	Conservation, Environment, and Historic Preservation, a Consulting Firm
CEQ:	Council on Environmental Quality
CERCLA:	Comprehensive Environmental Response, Compensation, and Liability Act
CFR:	Code of Federal Regulations
Cir:	Circuit (in legal citations)
Clovis:	Early (ca. 12,000 years ago) archeological complex
CNAE:	Conditional No Adverse Effect Determination under Section 106
CNO:	Chief of Naval Operations
COE:	Corps of Engineers (U.S. Army)
Council:	Depending on context: Advisory Council on Historic Preservation or Council on Environmental Quality
CRM:	Cultural Resource Management
CRMP:	Cultural Resource (or Resources) Management Plan
CX:	Categorical Exclusion under NEPA (also CATEX or CatEx)

DEIS:	Draft EIS
DoD:	Department of Defense
DoT:	Department of Transportation
EA:	Environmental Assessment under NEPA
EIS:	Environmental Impact Statement under NEPA
EJ:	Environmental Justice (See Executive Order 12898)
EO:	Executive Order
EPA:	Environmental Protection Agency
EQA:	Environmental Quality Advisory (in GSA)
FACA:	Federal Advisory Committees Act
Facade:	Face of a building or structure
FEIS:	Final EIS
FEMA:	Federal Emergency Management Agency
FERC:	Federal Energy Regulatory Commission
FHWA:	Federal Highway Administration
FLETC:	Federal Law Enforcement Training Center
FLPMA:	Federal Land Policy and Management Act
FNSY:	Finding of No Significant Impact under NEPA (also FONSI)
FONSI:	Finding of No Significant Impact under NEPA (also FNSI)
FPO:	Federal Preservation Officer
FR:	Federal Register: Really boring daily publication of regulations, notices, etc. by U.S. Federal Government
FRA:	Federal Records Act
GIS:	Geographic Information System
GSA:	General Services Administration
HABS:	Historic American Buildings Survey (NPS)
HAER:	Historic American Engineering Record (NPS)
HARP:	Historic and Archeological Resource Protection (Plan: Navy)
HBPP:	Historic Building Preservation Plan
HPP:	Historic Preservation Plan
HRMP:	Historic Resource (or Resources) Management Plan
HSA:	Historic Sites Act of 1935
HSR:	Historic Structures Report
HUD:	Department of Housing and Urban Development
Ironfront:	Building with front facade of cast iron
ISO:	International Standards Organization; also Greek for "balance"
kV:	Kilovolt
MFASAQHE:	Major Federal Action Significantly Affecting the Quality of the Human Environment
MFONSI:	Mitigated FONSI under NEPA
MOA:	Memorandum of Agreement
Muntin:	Divider between lights in a window
LDS:	Latter Day Saints (churches)
NAGPRA:	Native American Graves Protection and Repatriation Act
NARA:	National Archives and Records Administration

NCAI:	National Congress of American Indians
NCSHPO:	National Congress of State Historic Preservation Officers
NEPA:	National Environmental Policy Act
NFMA:	National Forest Management Act
NHL:	National Historic Landmark under Historic Sites Act
NHPA:	National Historic Preservation Act of 1966, as amended
NPI:	National Preservation Institute
NPS:	National Park Service
MOA:	Memorandum of Agreement under Section 106
NOAA:	National Oceanic and Atmospheric Administration
NOI:	Notice of Intent (to prepare an EIS)
Nuke:	Dramatically destroy, as with nuclear weapons
NPS:	National Park Service
OAHP:	Office of Archeology and Historic Preservation (defunct)
OEBGD:	Overseas Environmental Baseline Guidance Document (DoD)
OPNAVINST:	Naval Operations Instruction
PA:	Programmatic Agreement under Section 106
PAD:	Preparing Agreement Documents
PADC:	Pennsylvania Avenue Development Corporation (defunct)
PBCUA:	Public Buildings Cooperative Use Act
PC:	Personal computer
POA:	Plan of Action under NAGPRA
PMP:	Proactive Maintenance Plan (Corps of Engineers)
ppm:	Parts per million
REA:	Rural Electrification Administration (defunct)
Rehab:	Rehabilitate (a building, structure, or part thereof)
RFRA:	Religious Freedom Restoration Act
ROD:	Record of Decision
RP3:	Resource Protection Planning Process (NPS)
Scope:	What an analysis will contain. Verb: to figure out what the scope of an analysis should be.
SECNAVINST:	Secretary of the Navy Instruction
Section 106:	Section of NHPA that directs agencies to consider the effects of their actions on historic properties
SEPA:	State Environmental Policy Act (or "Little NEPA")
SHPO:	State Historic Preservation Officer
SIA:	Social Impact Assessment
SPIDR:	Society of Professionals in Dispute Resolution
TCP:	Traditional Cultural Property or Place
THPO:	Tribal Historic Preservation Officer
UNESCO:	United Nations Educational, Scientific, and Cultural Organization
USC:	United States Code
WNRC:	Washington Naval Records Center
WRC:	Water Resources Council (defunct)
WWW:	World Wide Web

Appendix II

Definitions

I've tried to define terms as we've gone along, but it may be helpful to include a somewhat comprehensive glossary here. I've put the following definitions in alphabetical order for ease of reference, with no intimation of priority.

Advisory Council on Historic Preservation (ACHP): An independent federal agency that advises the President and Congress on historic preservation matters, and oversees the review of projects under Section 106 of the National Historic Preservation Act (NHPA). The Council itself is made up of 20 members— presidential appointees, agency heads, and people named in NHPA; it is served by a staff of about 40 in Washington and Denver, who do the ACHP's real work.

Ambience: The feeling of a place—a concatenation of visual, auditory, olfactory, and, perhaps, other stimuli that convey the sense of a place to the resident or visitor.

Council on Environmental Quality (CEQ): Part of the Executive Office of the President, CEQ is a small (3-member) council served by an almost equally small staff, that advises on environmental matters, prepares studies and assessments, and oversees implementation of the National Environmental Policy Act (NEPA).

Cultural resource: This definition is belabored in Chapter 1. A cultural resource—in this book, at least—is any resource (i.e., thing that is useful for something) that is of a cultural character. Examples are social institutions, historic places, artifacts, and documents.

Cultural resource management (CRM): The management both of cultural resources and of effects on them that may result from land use and other activities of the contemporary world.

Historic property: Any district, site, building, structure or object included in or eligible for inclusion in the National Register of Historic Places (16 U.S.C. 470w[5]).

Indian tribe: Can mean different things to different people. There are federally recognized Indian tribes—those the federal government recognizes formally as sovereign entities with which it has a government-to-government relationship and for which, in many but not all cases, it holds lands in trust. Then there are Indian tribes that are not federally recognized for various reasons (because they were virtually wiped out by Euroamericans, or because their formal status was terminated during one of our spasmodic seizures of passion for the American melting pot, for example). Generally speaking, it's the federally recognized tribes that have special rights under federal law, and it's them that I've meant, in most cases, when I've used the term. Where there seemed to be utility in distinguishing between recognized and non-recognized tribes, I've tried to do so.

National Park Service (NPS): A bureau of the Department of the Interior whose primary function is to manage the National Park System. As such, it's a major federal land manager, much of whose land has cultural value to somebody or other. NPS also has external functions that relate to cultural resource management—particularly in historic preservation.

National Register of Historic Places (National Register): A list of districts, sites, buildings, structures and objects maintained by NPS, each determined by NPS to be of historic, cultural, architectural, archeological, or engineering significance at the national, state, or local level.

Preservation (or historic preservation): According to the National Historic Preservation Act, *includes identification, evaluation, recordation, documentation, curation, acquisition, protection, management, rehabilitation, restoration, stabilization, maintenance, research, interpretation, conservation, and education and training regarding the foregoing activities or any combination of the foregoing activities* (NHPA Sec. 301[8]). According to the Secretary of the Interior's Standards for the Treatment of Historic Properties (NPS 1992), preservation means *the act or process of applying measures necessary to sustain the existing form, integrity, and materials of an historic property.*

Significance: Under NHPA, the historical, cultural, archeological, architectural or engineering importance of a property. Under NEPA, the seriousness of a potential impact, measured in terms of "context" and "intensity" (discussed in Chapters 4 and 5).

Social impacts: The impacts of a project, program, or activity on:

> *...the ways in which people live, work, play, relate to one another, organize to meet their needs and generally cope as members of society. The term also includes cultural impacts involving changes to the norms, values, and beliefs*

that guide and rationalize their cognition of themselves and their society... (Interorganizational Committee 1993, NOAA 1994:1).

Social impact assessment (SIA): An assessment of the social impacts of a project, program, or activity.

Socioeconomic impact assessment: Often confused with social impact assessment. An assessment that focuses on economic and sometimes other easily quantifiable indicators of social impact.

State Historic Preservation Officer (SHPO): The state official, designated by the governor, to carry out the functions ascribed to the SHPO by the National Historic Preservation Act. SHPOs receive and administer matching grants from NPS to support their work and pass through to others. They identify historic properties and nominate them to the National Register. They maintain inventories, do plans, and consult with others about historic preservation.

Traditional cultural property or traditional cultural place (TCP): A district, site, building, structure or object that is valued by a human community for the role it plays in sustaining the community's cultural integrity. Generally a place that figures in important community traditions or in culturally important activities. May be eligible for inclusion in the National Register.

Tribal Historic Preservation Officer (THPO): The official of a federally recognized Indian tribe that oversees the tribe's historic preservation program, particularly where the tribe has been approved by NPS to carry out all or some of the functions of the SHPO within the external boundaries of its reservation.

Appendix III

Laws, Executive Orders, and Regulations

We've discussed a lot of legal tools in this book; this appendix is intended to summarize them and briefly discuss how they're dealt with—or not—by federal agencies and others.

It's convenient to divide the legal authorities up by subject—the kinds of resources or situations they apply to, so that's what I've done, beginning with the most general and proceeding toward the particular.

Authorities that Deal with All Types of Cultural Resources

The National Environmental Policy Act—NEPA—is the broadest authority of all, articulating national policy on environmental protection and requiring agencies to analyze the effects of their actions on the environment. Since the environment includes sociocultural elements, NEPA requires agencies to be concerned with their impacts on all kinds of cultural resources—as well as on the whole panoply of natural resources. This is not to say that all agencies do a very good job of considering impacts on the full range of resources—only that in theory, they should.

NEPA is probably the best understood of the legal authorities, in that most agencies have staff dedicated to NEPA compliance, there's a large body of practitioners, and there are several organizations and journals that focus on NEPA practice. NEPA is widely *misunderstood*, though—and abused—as a mere process of documentation, justifying decisions made and impacts tolerated on the environment. That's not what it's supposed to be; it's supposed to be an honest, open, analysis of impacts, leading to decisions that balance environmental protection—including cultural resource protection—with other public values.

Executive Order 12898 also deals with all kinds of resources, but in a particular socioeconomic context. This executive order deals with "environmental justice" (EJ)—preventing the levying of disproportionate adverse environmental impacts on low income and minority populations. The executive order is implemented in the context of NEPA analyses, and requires consideration of all kinds of impacts on all aspects of the environment, provided they are relevant to low income populations or minority populations. It's particularly important for CRM because it promotes active, culturally-sensitive public participation in environmental review, and because the impacts that low income and minority groups are often concerned about are impacts on social and cultural aspects of the environment.

Executive Order 12072 in theory causes the consideration of cultural resources of all kinds in the context of urban centers. This executive order directs agencies to give priority to siting their activities in central business areas (CBA). Importantly for CRM, it requires that the positive and negative cultural effects of such sitings be considered. This executive order provides a legal rationale for some social impact assessments, typically absorbed into NEPA analyses.

Historic Preservation Authorities

The National Historic Preservation Act—NHPA—is the best-known authority dealing with historic properties, including archeological resources. Actually the best known part of NHPA is Section 106, which requires agencies to consider the effects of their actions on historic properties. There are many other sections of NHPA, however, some of which have real potential impacts on federal agencies and recipients of federal assistance and permits. In general, NHPA requires agencies to identify and manage historic properties under their jurisdiction or control; to consider doing things that will advance the purposes of NHPA, and avoid, if possible, doing things contrary to its purposes; to consult and cooperate with others in carrying out historic preservation activities, and to consider the effects of their actions—including permit and assistance actions—on historic properties following a regulation issued by the ACHP (36 CFR 800). NHPA also spells out the roles and functions of the ACHP, the SHPO, and the THPO.

The Historic Sites Act (HSA) of 1935 was a seedbed from which NHPA eventually sprang. Rather narrow in its actual provisions, it was politically important because it established NPS as the government's paramount historic preservation advocate. The HSA authorized NPS to identify, register, describe, document, and acquire full or partial title to historic properties determined to be nationally significant in the interpretation and commemoration of the nation's history. It had no regulatory provisions, and didn't actually require NPS or anyone else to do much of anything. NPS promoted its passage, however, and seized the authority it gave to create what are today the National Historic Landmarks (NHL) and Historic American Buildings Survey (HABS) programs. These in turn, together with archeological elements of NPS that grew out of the River Basin Salvage programs of the 1950s and 60s, provided the organizational and theoretical frameworks within which the post-NHPA national historic preservation program grew.

Executive Order 13006 complements both NHPA and Executive Order 12072. It requires agencies to give priority consideration to using historic buildings in historic districts in CBAs. This is a rather new order, issued only in 1996, and it's not yet clear what impact it's going to have, if any.

Section 4(f) of the Department of Transportation Act prohibits any agency of the Department of Transportation (DOT)—for example, the Federal Highway Administration (FHWA), the Federal Aviation Administration (FAA), the Federal Railroad Administration (FRA), and the Coast Guard—from implementing a transportation project that uses a historic property (or a park or wildlife refuge) unless there is "no prudent and feasible alternative" to doing so and all possible planning is carried out to minimize harm. Section 4(f) has been the subject of a tremendous body of litigation, and Section 4(f) analyses— typically carried out in tandem with NEPA analyses—are a major preoccupation of DOT agencies.

The Federal tax code contains provisions—which change often, given the highly political nature of tax law—encouraging the preservation and rehabilitation of income-producing historic structures. Generally speaking, the owner of an income-producing historic structure (e.g., an historic hotel) can claim a credit against his or her federal income tax based on the costs incurred in rehabilitating the structure in accordance with standards issued by NPS (the *Secretary of the Interior's Standards for Rehabilitation*). Every session of Congress sees new battles over the shape of these provisions—notably over how actively the claimant of a credit must participate in the rehabilitation project upon which the claim is based, and over extending the credit to non-income producing residential structures.

Executive Order 11593, issued by President Richard Nixon in 1972, directed federal agencies to nominate all historic properties under their jurisdiction or control to the National Register of Historic Places by mid-1974. More importantly, it directed them to treat properties eligible for the Register as though they were already included, and it directed NPS to publish guidance as to how such determinations were to be made. Since nobody met the deadline for nominations, and since the Order's provisions have all been absorbed by amendment into NHPA itself in some way or other, EO 11593 today is a sort of historical oddity, but it was very important in its time.

Archeological Authorities

The Antiquities Act of 1906, the nation's earliest historic preservation law, prohibits the unauthorized excavation, removal, or defacement of "objects of antiquity" on public lands. It also authorizes the president to withdraw land from multiple use status for purposes of creating national monuments—a rather controversial provision since 1997, when President Clinton used it to create the gigantic Stairstep-Escalante National Monument in Utah. The prohibition on removal of "objects of antiquity" was declared "fatally vague" by courts in the 1970s, leading to enactment of...

The Archeological Resources Protection Act (ARPA) prohibits the unauthorized excavation, removal, or damage of "archeological resources" on federal and Indian lands. "Archeological resource" is comprehensively defined to include archeological sites, structural remains, artifacts, bones, debris— everything including the kitchen sink, provided it's at least 100 years old. ARPA provides stiff penalties for violators, and spells out permit requirements which are elaborated upon in uniform regulations issued jointly by the Departments of the Interior, Agriculture and Defense and the Tennessee Valley Authority. Interior's regulations apply to all agencies that are not Agriculture or Defense, except for TVA.

The Archeological Data Preservation Act of 1974, a.k.a. the "Moss-Bennett Act" after its authors, and the "Archeological and Historic Preservation Act," amended the Reservoir Salvage Act of 1960, which authorized NPS to fund salvage archeology in Corps of Engineers reservoirs. The 1974 act applied to all agencies and all kinds of projects, directing the agencies themselves to pay attention to their impacts on archeological, historical, and scientific data. It also directed them either to fund the recovery of such data themselves or to assist NPS in doing so, and authorized transfer of up to 1% of the cost of a project to NPS to defray its expenses.

The Abandoned Shipwrecks Act (ASA) deals with a particular class of archeological site—the shipwreck. Designed to remove shipwrecks from the purview of the maritime courts, which were perceived to be too sympathetic to commercial salvors, ASA asserts U.S. ownership of all abandoned wrecks in its waters, and then transfers control of them to the states. NPS issued guidelines for implementing ASA, but these are advisory only; the states call the shots on shipwreck management—except with regard to commissioned naval vessels, which enjoy sovereign immunity from the statute.

Native American Cultural Resource Authorities

In a way, the archeological authorities are Native American cultural resource authorities as well, since all archeological resources over about 500 years old in the United States are of Native American origin. But there are several legal authorities that deal more explicitly with Native American resources—and with a broader range of resources than just archeological sites.

The American Indian Religious Freedom Act—AIRFA—is a joint resolution of Congress declaring that the U.S. government will protect the inherent rights of Indian tribes to the free exercise of their traditional religions. Generally, AIRFA has been taken to require agencies to consult with tribes—but not necessarily accede to their requests—when any action is contemplated that might affect the practice of traditional religions. Note that the "resource" involved here is the practice of religion itself. The places and physical paraphernalia needed for religious practice are among the elements to be considered, but AIRFA deals with the broader, less tangible resource of religious practice itself.

Executive Order 13007, another fairly new Bill Clinton executive order, deals with "Indian sacred sites" on federal and Indian land. It calls on agencies to do what they can to avoid physical damage to such sites, and to avoid keeping tribal religious practitioners from having access to them. This executive order contains a number of potentially troublesome definitions, but, to their credit, the agencies do not seem to be confused by them. Although this executive order is concerned with physical places, it's important to note that a "sacred site" need not be an historic property; the scope of Executive Order 13007 is different from that of NHPA.

The Native American Graves Protection and Repatriation Act—NAGPRA— is one of the more complicated and directive of the Native American cultural resource authorities. In a small nutshell that doesn't begin to do justice to its complexity, NAGPRA requires that federal agencies and museums that have received federal funds repatriate Native American ancestral human remains and cultural items to tribes that can show genetic or cultural affiliation with such remains and items. It also regulates excavation of such remains and items on federal and Indian land, and provides for a minimum 30-day hold on earthmoving activities that cause the inadvertent discovery of such remains and items. NPS regulations, applicable to all agencies, are at 43 CFR 10.

Historical Documents Authorities

The Federal Records Act (FRA), and its very extensive implementing regulations, deal with how federal agencies are to manage their records—largely for the purpose of ensuring that historically important records aren't lost. Agencies are required to establish and implement their own FRA records retention and disposal procedures, approved by the National Archives and Records Administration (NARA), and to have personnel assigned to ensure that records are properly managed in accordance with such procedures. FRA is about the only cultural resource authority for which violation is punishable by fines and prison sentences, though this does not seem to deter many agencies— including, amusingly enough, NPS and the ACHP—from routinely ignoring it.

Land Management Authorities

Finally, most major land management agencies have some kind of "organic" legislation that establishes policy direction for the way they manage the land and resources under their charge, including cultural resources. Examples are, the National Forest Management Act (NFMA), which governs the Forest Service, and the Federal Land Policy and Management Act (FLPMA), which governs the Bureau of Land Management. Agency organic laws contain important direction to agencies about how they are to carry out their management activities, and usually contain helpful procedures by which concerned members of the public can appeal agency decisions up the chain of command.

Appendix IV

Model Section 106
Memorandum of Agreement

Note: Besides illustrating the basic form and typical content of an MOA, this wholly hypothetical model tries to show how a Section 106 MOA could be prepared on a project at an early stage in planning, when multiple alternatives are under consideration—improving coordination with NEPA and ensuring that effects are considered while there is still something to do about them. Such early planning necessarily requires dealing with historic properties at a more conceptual level than most historic practitioners are comfortable with, so an MOA of this kind may not be—probably will not be—widely acceptable. If nothing else, however, this appendix does illustrate generally what an MOA looks like, and the administrative stipulations are pretty standard. Reports and appendices referenced herein are identified for illustrative purposes only and are not actually included. For standard, downloadable MOA stipulations and formats, see **http://www.gsa.gov/pbs/pt/call-in/nepa.htm**.

**MEMORANDUM OF AGREEMENT
AMONG THE NATIONAL BUILDING SERVICE,
THE NORTH NORWICH STATE HISTORIC PRESERVATION OFFICER,
AND THE ADVISORY COUNCIL ON HISTORIC PRESERVATION
REGARDING CONSTRUCTION OF THE
GOVERNMENT LOGISTICS INVESTIGATION BUREAU
REGIONAL LABORATORY**

WHEREAS the National Building Service (NBS) proposes to provide a new regional laboratory for the Government Logistics Investigation Bureau (GLIB) in the City of Featherberg; and

WHEREAS NBS has agreed to assume lead installation/activity status in review of the proposed laboratory project (laboratory) under Section 106 of the National

Historic Preservation Act as amended (16 U.S.C. 470) on behalf of itself and GLIB, as represented in the document entitled "Memorandum of Understanding, Featherberg Laboratory," executed by representatives of GLIB and NBS and dated March 15, 2002; and

WHEREAS NBS is giving primary consideration to three optional sites for the laboratory (plus a no-project alternative) in its analysis of environmental impacts under the National Environmental Policy Act (NEPA) and its implementing regulations (40 CFR 1500-1508): the Parking Structure Site, the Burned Block Site, and the Weatherbeat Warehouse Site, as described in the document entitled "Preliminary Identification of Feasible Alternatives, Featherberg Laboratory" by Kungbutaie Consultants, Ltd. (Kungbutaie), dated April 1, 2002 (Preliminary ID Report); and

WHEREAS NBS has established the laboratory's area of potential effects, as defined at 36 CFR § 800.2(c), to be:

- For the Parking Structure Site, the construction site, the utility and road rights-of-way to the site, and the vacant land within approximately 1/4 mile of the site, where induced development may occur, plus the upper slopes of Grassy Knob where visual effects may occur, all as shown in the Preliminary ID Report at Figure III.4;

- For the Burned Block Site, the construction site and the neighborhoods bordering the site on all sides for approximately eight (8) blocks, where visual and social effects may be expected, as shown in the Preliminary ID Report at Figure III.5;

- For the Weatherbeat Warehouse Site, the Weatherbeat Warehouse, which would be renovated to serve as the main Laboratory building, plus the proposed new construction sites, plus the complex of early twentieth century warehouses of which the Weatherbeat Warehouse is a part, as shown in the Preliminary ID Report at Figure III.6;

- For the No Project Alternative, the site of the existing Laboratory at 793 Mudd Street and the land between the Laboratory and the Bigslow River, as shown in the illustration of the existing toxic waste plume in the Preliminary ID Report at Figure I.3; and

WHEREAS NBS has determined that the laboratory may have effects on districts, sites, buildings, structures, and/or objects eligible for inclusion in the National Register of Historic Places (historic properties) if any of the above alternatives is pursued, and

WHEREAS NBS has conducted background studies, preliminary field investigations, and consultation with the parties listed in Appendix I, "Parties Consulted During Scoping, Featherberg Laboratory," prepared by Kungbutaie and dated February 14, 2002, on the basis of which it has developed predictions about the distribution and character of historic properties subject to effect by the various alternatives, as presented in the Preliminary ID Report at Chapter V; and

WHEREAS possible historic properties in the areas of potential effects include, but are not limited to, Grassy Knob, the Red Rooster Neighborhood, the warehouse complex of which the Weatherbeat Warehouse is a part, and several possible archeological sites, as discussed in the Preliminary ID report at Chapter V;

WHEREAS NBS has consulted with the North Norwich State Historic Preservation Officer (SHPO) and the Advisory Council on Historic Preservation (Council) in accordance with Section 106 of the National Historic Preservation Act, 16 U.S.C. § 470 (NHPA), and its implementing regulations (36 CFR Part 800) to resolve the potential adverse effects of the laboratory on historic properties; and

WHEREAS pursuant to Section 101(d)(6)(B) of NHPA, the American Indian Religious Freedom Act, Executive Order 13007, and the Native American Graves Protection and Repatriation Act (NAGPRA), NBS has invited the Wimok Indian Tribe (Tribe) to participate in the consultation and to concur in this Memorandum of Agreement (MOA); and

WHEREAS NBS, the SHPO and the Council have also invited GLIB, the City of Featherberg, the Bigslow River Planning Authority, the Featherberg Association for Architectural Heritage (FAAH), the Featherberg Archeological Society (FAS), and the Red Rooster Neighborhood Commission (Red Rooster) to participate in the consultation and to concur in this MOA; and

WHEREAS NBS intends to use the provisions of this MOA to address applicable requirements of NHPA Section 110(a)(1), the Archeological Data Preservation Act (16 U.S.C. 469-469c: ADPA), and Executive Orders 13006 and 13007, and has represented this intention in a separate document entitled "Memorandum to the File: Featherberg Laboratory Compliance with Historic Preservation Requirements" dated April 1, 2002;

NOW, THEREFORE, NBS, the North Norwich SHPO, and the Council agree that should NBS elect to proceed with the laboratory using any of the alternatives listed above, NBS will ensure that the following stipulations are implemented, in order to take into account the effect of the laboratory on historic properties.

Stipulations

I. Priority Consideration. *Pursuant to Executive Order 13006, NBS shall give priority of consideration to the adaptive use of the Weatherbeat Warehouse for the Laboratory.* Should NBS not consider the Weatherbeat Warehouse its preferred alternative, NBS will consult with and explain its rationale to the parties to this MOA prior to issuance of its draft Environmental Impact Statement (DEIS), and fully justify its decision in the DEIS.

II. Weatherbeat Warehouse. *Should NBS consider the Weatherbeat Warehouse its preferred alternative, NBS shall ensure that the following stipulations are implemented:*

    A. Review of Documents. No demolition or site preparation work shall be permitted until the following documents have been reviewed by the City, NBS, and SHPO.

        1. Demolition drawings or equivalent information indicating all known or anticipated historic fabric on the site, and detailing how such fabric will be treated during demolition and site preparation.

        2. A complete interim report on all archeological investigations carried out as of the date of the submittal including a plan of action for treating archeological resources (if any) that may be disturbed by demolition or site preparation, and where archeological data recovery is conducted, a report on completion of the fieldwork component of such data recovery.

    B. Use of Approved Documents. All demolition and site preparation shall be guided by documents approved in accordance with this Memorandum of Agreement (MOA).

    C. Interim Protection. NBS shall ensure that the Weatherbeat Warehouse is properly secured and protected from vandalism, fire, and weather damage during the period it is unoccupied, following the guidelines set forth in Preservation Brief #31, Mothballing Historic Buildings (Department of the Interior, National Park Service, 1993) until it is rehabilitated.

III. Parking Structure Site. *Should NBS consider the Parking Structure Site its preferred alternative, NBS shall ensure that the following stipulations are implemented:*

    A. Archeology

        1. NBS will ensure that the construction site, the utility and road rights-of-way, and any other areas subject to physical disturbance by the laborator are subjected to intensive archeological study in accordance with a study

plan developed in consultation with the SHPO, the Tribe, and FAS, and submitted in draft to the SHPO, Tribe, and FAS for at least thirty (30) days review and comment. The study shall include, as needed, further background research and subsurface field testing, and shall explicitly address the potential existence of the archeological remains of an ancestral Wimok village site and the 19th century Six Corners neighborhood, as outlined in the Preliminary ID Report, Chapter V. Fieldwork and analysis shall be conducted in consultation with, and to the extent they so desire with active participation by, the Tribe and FAS.

2. Should the study indicate the existence of archeological resources, NBS will review the potential significance of such resources in consultation with the SHPO, the Tribe, and FAS, to determine whether they are significant enough to justify expenditure of funds on their preservation. Depending on the outcome of this review, NBS may elect to design the project to preserve resources in place, to conduct archeological data recovery to recover significant data from such resources, or to document such resources through archeological monitoring during construction, subject to the terms of a Plan of Action to be developed by NBS pursuant to the regulations implementing NAGPRA (43 CFR 10). NBS shall afford the SHPO, Tribe, and FAS at least thirty (30) days to review and comment on, or object to, its decision about treatment of archeological resources.

3. Any plan to avoid impacts on archeological resources shall meet the requirements of the "Standards for Avoidance," set forth in "Technical Standards: Featherberg Laboratory Historic Preservation" (Kungbutaie 6/3/02), appended hereto as Appendix I.

4. Any archeological data recovery plan shall meet the "Standards for Archeological Data Recovery, Featherberg Laboratory" set forth in Appendix I.

5. Having determined a course of action pursuant to Stipulation III.A.2, and subject to dispute resolution under Stipulation VI.E, NBS will implement the selected course of action.

B. Growth Inducement

1. NBS will conduct background archeological studies and sample field investigation on the vacant land within 1/4 mile of the construction site, in consultation with the Tribe, SHPO, City, and FAS, to determine the likelihood that archeological resources are present and if so to define their approximate extent. NBS shall develop the scope of work for such studies and investigation in consultation with the Tribe, SHPO, City, and FAS.

2. Should the study indicate that significant archeological resources may be present, NBS will consult with the City, the Tribe, the SHPO and FAS to determine what steps the City may take to protect such resources from development that may occur as a result of the laboratory, and will encourage the City to take such steps.

C. Visual Impacts

1. NBS will consult with the Tribe concerning the possible visual impacts of the laboratory on traditional cultural use of Grassy Knob, and will seek agreement with the Tribe regarding measures to mitigate any such impacts, subject to Stipulation VI.E.

2. Should NBS's agreement with the Tribe, or any supporting documents, reveal the nature of the Tribe's use of Grassy Knob, such that releasing such information could affect such use, NBS will endeavor to withhold such information from public release in accordance with NHPA Section 304.

3. Impact mitigation measures may include, but are not limited to:

a) Controls on the design of the laboratory buildings, including siting, massing, color, and placement on the land;

b) Controls on the season in which construction occurs;

c) Vegetative barriers;

d) Compensatory actions such as purchase of easements to guarantee future tribal access to Grassy Knob.

D. Parking Structure Demolition. In consultation with FAS, NBS will ensure that demolition of the existing parking structure on the site is monitored to test the local tradition that the body of Jimmy Hoffa is embedded in one of the supporting concrete pylons.

IV. Burned Block Site. *Should NBS consider the Burned Block Site its preferred alternative, NBS shall ensure that the following stipulations are implemented:*

A. Archeology

1. Coordinated with the identification of toxic and hazardous wastes (if any) associated with the burned out residential block on the construction site, NBS will ensure that the site is subjected to intensive archeological study

in accordance with a study plan developed in consultation with the SHPO, the City, the Tribe, and FAS, and submitted in draft to the SHPO, City, Tribe and FAS for at least thirty (30) days review and comment. The study shall include, as needed, further background research and subsurface field testing, and shall explicitly address the potential existence of the archeological remains of the mid-19th century Muntinmasher's Window Factory, as outlined in the Preliminary ID Report, Chapter V, as well as the archeological significance, if any, of the burned out residential block. Fieldwork and analysis shall be conducted in consultation with, and to the extent they so desire with active participation by, the City, Tribe and FAS.

2. Should the study indicate the existence of archeological resources, NBS will review the potential significance of such resources in consultation with the SHPO, the City, the Tribe, and FAS, to determine whether they are significant enough to justify expenditure of funds on their preservation. Depending on the outcome of this review, NBS may elect to design the project to preserve resources in place, to conduct archeological data recovery to recover significant data from such resources, or to document such resources through archeological monitoring during construction, subject to the terms of a Plan of Action to be developed by NBS pursuant to the regulations implementing NAGPRA (43 CFR 10). NBS shall afford the SHPO, City, Tribe, and FAS at least thirty (30) days to review and comment on, or object to, its decision about treatment of archeological resources.

3. Any plan to avoid impacts on archeological resources shall meet the requirements of the "Standards for Avoidance," set forth in "Technical Standards: Featherberg Laboratory Historic Preservation" (Kungbutaie 6/3/02), appended hereto as Appendix I.

4. Any archeological data recovery plan shall meet the "Standards for Archeological Data Recovery, Featherberg Laboratory" set forth in Appendix I.

5. Having determined a course of action pursuant to Stipulation IV.A.2, and subject to dispute resolution under Stipulation VI.E, NBS will implement the selected course of action.

B. Visual and Social Effects

1. NBS will analyze the laboratory's possible visual and social (including economic) effects on the Red Rooster neighborhood and the other older residences within the area of potential effect, in consultation with the City,

Red Rooster, and residents of the area. NBS will ask Red Rooster and the City to assist NBS in consulting with residents, including those who are not members of Red Rooster. In accordance with Executive Order 12898, consultation will be designed to accommodate the special needs of the Hispanic and Orthodox Jewish residents of the Red Rooster neighborhood and surrounding areas, as well as the needs of Red Rooster's numerous disabled residents.

2. Subject to Stipulation VI.E, NBS will seek agreement with the City, Red Rooster, and other concerned residents regarding means of mitigating any adverse visual or social (including economic) effects on the Red Rooster neighborhood and surrounding residential neighborhoods.

3. Measures selected may include, but are not limited to:

   a) Controls on the design of the laboratory buildings, including siting, massing, color, scale, and fenestration, to harmonize with the character of surrounding older residential structures, taking into account the guidelines for new construction in the *Secretary of the Interior's Standards for Rehabilitation and Guidelines for Rehabilitating Historic Buildings* (National Park Service 1992: hereinafter "Rehabilitation Standards").

   b) Implementing a program to educate laboratory employees about the unique cultural and architectural features of the neighborhoods surrounding the site, and encouraging respect for such features by anyone planning to relocate to the neighborhoods.

   c) Encouraging businesses and homeowners to conduct any new construction or rehabilitation in a manner consistent with the Rehabilitation Standards.

   d) Creation of a revolving fund to assist local businesspeople and homeowners in maintaining their properties.

   e) Purchase of development rights.

   f) City property tax controls to minimize financial impacts on local businesses and homeowners.

V. Existing Laboratory Site. *Whichever alternative NBS selects as its preferred alternative, NBS will provide all data in its possession pertinent to the historic preservation implications of the "no project" alternative to GLIB for use in GLIB's compliance with environmental and historic preservation authorities in the remediation of toxic wastes at the existing Laboratory site.*

VI. Administration

A. Review of Submittals. Whenever any party to this MOA is given the opportunity to review documents prepared pursuant to the terms of this MOA, that party shall have thirty (30) calendar days to conduct such review. Failure of a reviewing party to provide comments in accordance with this stipulation may be taken to indicate approval of the pertinent document by the reviewing party.

B. Professional Supervision. NBS shall ensure that all activities regarding treatment of historic buildings carried out pursuant to this MOA are carried out by or under the direct supervision of a person or persons meeting at a minimum the Secretary of the Interior's Professional Qualifications Standards for Historic Architecture (48 FR 44739), and that all activities regarding archeology carried out pursuant to this MOA are carried out by or under the direct supervision of a person or persons meeting at a minimum the Secretary of the Interior's Professional Qualifications Standards for Archeology (48 FR 44739). However, nothing in this stipulation may be interpreted to bar NBS or any agent or contractor of NBS from utilizing the properly supervised services of employees and volunteers who do not meet the above standards.

C. Alterations to Project Documents. NBS shall not alter any plan, scope of services, or other document that has been reviewed and commented on pursuant to this MOA, except to finalize documents commented on in draft, without first affording the other parties to this MOA the opportunity to review the proposed change and determine whether it shall require that this MOA be amended. If one or more of the parties determines that an amendment is needed, the parties to this MOA shall consult in accordance with 36 CFR 800.5(e) to consider such an amendment.

D. Annual Report and Review

1. On or before December 5 of each year until NBS, the Council, and the SHPO agree in writing that the terms of this MOA have been fulfilled, NBS shall prepare and provide an annual report to the parties to this MOA, detailing how the applicable terms of this MOA are being implemented.

2. NBS shall ensure that the annual report is made available for public inspection, that potentially interested members of the public are made aware of its availability, and that interested members of the public are invited to provide comments to the Council and SHPO as well as to NBS.

3. The SHPO and Council shall review the annual report and provide comments to NBS. Other parties to this MOA may review and comment on the annual report at their discretion.

4. At the request of any party to this MOA, a meeting or meetings shall be held to facilitate review and comment, to resolve questions, or to resolve adverse comments.

5. Based on this review, NBS, the SHPO, and the Council shall determine whether this MOA shall continue in force, be amended, or be terminated.

E. Resolving Objections

1. Should any party to this MOA object to any action carried out or proposed with respect to development of the Laboratory or implementation of this MOA, NBS shall consult with the objecting party to resolve the objection. If after initiating such consultation NBS determines that the objection cannot be resolved through consultation, NBS shall forward all documentation relevant to the objection to the Council, including NBS's proposed response to the objection. Within thirty (30) days after receipt of all pertinent documentation, the Council shall exercise one of the following options:

   a) Advise NBS that the Council concurs in NBS's proposed final decision, whereupon NBS will respond to the objection accordingly;

   b) Provide NBS with recommendations, which NBS shall take into account in reaching a final decision regarding its response to the objection; or

   c) Notify NBS that the objection will be referred for comment pursuant to 36 CFR § 800.6(b), and proceed to refer the objection and comment. The resulting comment shall be taken into account by NBS in accordance with 36 CFR § 800.6(c)(2) and § 110(l) of NHPA.

2. Should the Council not exercise one of the above options within thirty (30) days after receipt of all pertinent documentation, NBS may assume the Council's concurrence in its proposed response to the objection.

3. NBS shall take into account any Council recommendation or comment provided in accordance with this stipulation with reference only to the subject of the objection; NBS's responsibility to ensure that all responsibilities under this MOA that are not the subjects of the objection are carried out shall remain unchanged.

4. At any time during implementation of the measures stipulated in this MOA, should an objection pertaining to this MOA be raised by a member of the public, NBS shall notify the parties to this MOA and take the objection into account, consulting with the objector and, should the objector so request, with any of the parties to this MOA to resolve the objection.

F. Amendments. Any party to this MOA may propose to NBS that the MOA be amended, whereupon NBS shall consult with the other parties to this MOA to consider such an amendment. 36 CFR § 800.5(e) shall govern the execution of any such amendment.

G. Termination

1. If NBS determines that it cannot ensure implementation of the terms of this MOA, or if the SHPO or Council determines that the MOA is not being properly implemented, NBS, the SHPO, or the Council may propose to the other parties to this MOA that it be terminated.

2. The party proposing to terminate this MOA shall so notify all parties to this MOA, explaining the reasons for termination and affording them at least thirty (30) days to consult and seek alternatives to termination.

3. Should such consultation fail and the MOA be terminated, NBS shall either:

   a) Consult in accordance with 36 CFR § 800.5(e) to develop a new MOA; or

   b) Request the comments of the Council pursuant to 36 CFR § 800.5(e)(6).

4. If the terms of this MOA have not been implemented by January 1, 2005, this MOA shall be considered null and void, and NBS, if it chooses to continue with its participation in the development, shall re-initiate its review in accordance with 36 CFR 800.

Execution of this MOA and implementation of its terms evidence that NBS has afforded the Council an opportunity to comment on development of the Laboratory, and that NBS has taken into account the effects of the Laboratory on historic properties.

NATIONAL BUILDING SERVICE

By:_____ Date:_____

NORTH NORWICH STATE HISTORIC PRESERVATION OFFICER

By:_____ Date:_____

ADVISORY COUNCIL ON HISTORIC PRESERVATION

By:_____ Date:_____

CONCUR:

GOVERNMENT LOGISTICS INVESTIGATION BUREAU

By:_____ Date:_____

CITY OF FEATHERBERG

By:_____ Date:_____

WIMOK INDIAN TRIBE

By:_____ Date:_____

BIGSLOW RIVER PLANNING AUTHORITY

By:_____ Date:_____

FEATHERBERG ASSOCIATION FOR ARCHITECTURAL HERITAGE

By:_____ Date:_____

FEATHERBERG ARCHEOLOGICAL SOCIETY

By:_____ Date:_____

RED ROOSTER NEIGHBORHOOD COMMISSION

By:_____ Date:_____

Appendix V

Model NAGPRA
Plan of Action

Following is a wholly hypothetical POA on a wholly fictitious project across the aboriginal lands of a number of fictitious tribes. The measures stipulated in it are just as hypothetical as the project and participants. The model is terribly complicated, though I've tried to make it as straightforward as possible. It's made more complex by the fact that it requires a number of special appendices, which I've not drafted for obvious reasons, but that are referred to in the body of the plan.

The model comports as closely as I could make it to the specific requirements of the NAGPRA regulations. It illustrates just how complicated it can be to prepare a POA that actually meets the regulatory requirements.

PLAN OF ACTION FOR THE TREATMENT OF
NATIVE AMERICAN CULTURAL ITEMS
DURING CONSTRUCTION OF THE LIGHTGAS PIPELINE
WITHIN THE STATE OF UTAZONA

I. Background

A. Pursuant to 43 CFR 10.5(a), the Bureau of Land Management (BLM), assisted by the Lightgas Transportation Company (LTC), has determined that:

1. There are no known lineal descendants of specific Native Americans whose remains or cultural items are likely to be disturbed by construction of the Lightgas Pipeline (pipeline);

2. The three alternative routes for the pipeline within the State of Utazona cross the aboriginal lands of the following Indian tribes:

a) Alternative A: Yavajo and Malagansett;
b) Alternative B: Loomatilla, Tunipa, and Yavajo; and
c) Alternative C: Loomatilla and Malagansett.

3. Each of the four above-listed tribes is likely to be culturally affiliated with any human remains, funerary objects, sacred objects, or objects of cultural patrimony discovered within its aboriginal lands in connection with construction of the pipeline in Utazona. In addition, the Chippesaw, whose ancestors are said to have occupied eastern Utazona prior to the coming of the Tunipa, may be culturally affiliated with Native American cultural items from eastern Utazona.

4. The Southern Skyute have a demonstrated cultural relationship with human remains and other cultural items associated with their passage across Utazona in 1879 along the "Trail of Hardship," which crosses the Alternative A and C rights of way near the City of Flatrock.

B. Pursuant to 43 CFR 10.3(c)(1) and 43 CFR 10.5(b)(1), BLM notified the governments of the six above-listed tribes (the tribes) of the plans for the pipeline, providing them with the information required by 43 CFR 10.3(c)(1), and proposed consultation.

C. Pursuant to 43 CFR 10.3(b)(2) and 43 CFR 10.5(b)(2) and (3), BLM and LTC consulted with the tribes and their traditional religious leaders, providing them with the information required by 43 CFR 10.5(c) and requesting the information required by 43 CFR 10.5(d).

D. Pursuant to 43 CFR 10.3(b)(4), proof of BLM's and LTC's consultation with tribes is provided in Appendix C-7 ("Native American Consultation") of the draft Environmental Impact Statement dated July 31, 1996, and entitled "Draft Environmental Impact Statement: Lightgas Pipeline."

E. Based on BLM's program of identification and consultation, and pursuant to 43 CFR 10.5(e), BLM and LTC have developed the Plan of Action set forth in Section II.

F. Pursuant to 43 CFR 10.3(c)(3), BLM and LTC have coordinated consultation with tribes and development of the Plan of Action with review of the pipeline under Section 106 of the National Historic Preservation Act, and propose that the following Plan of Action shall become a part of the Memorandum of Agreement (MOA) being developed pursuant to Section 106 of the National Historic Preservation Act and its implementing regulations (36 CFR 800).

II. Plan of Action

BLM will ensure that the following Plan of Action (POA) is implemented:

A. Pursuant to 43 CFR 10.3(b)(1), LTC will contract for all excavation and treatment of Native American cultural items, as defined below, to be carried out by or under the direct supervision of holders of permits issued in accordance with the requirements of the Archeological Resources Protection Act (ARPA) (16 U.S.C. 470aa et seq.) and its implementing regulations. Such a permit may take the form of a contract, provided BLM certifies that the terms of such contract meet the requirements of ARPA and its implementing regulations. BLM employees certified by BLM to meet the professional standards set forth in ARPA's implementing regulations shall also be understood to hold ARPA permits when engaged in their professional duties.

B. Pursuant to 43 CFR 10.3(b)(3), BLM and LTC will ensure that disposition of any Native American cultural items is as specified in paragraph J below.

C. Based on BLM's and LPG's consultation with tribes, and pursuant to 43 CFR 10.5(e)(1), BLM and LTC shall consider the following as Native American cultural items:

1. Human remains.

2. Associated funerary objects, which shall be understood to mean objects placed intentionally with human remains and still physically associated in space with such remains. The location of objects within the grave fill or in immediate proximity to human remains shall be understood to evidence intentional placement with human remains.

3. Unassociated funerary objects, which shall be understood to mean objects intentionally placed with human remains but whose association has been disturbed through vandalism, erosion, plowing, rodent action, and other ground-disturbing phenomena. Types of objects typically placed intentionally with human remains in Yavajo, Malagansett, Loomatilla, Tunipa, Chippesaw, and Southern Skyute cultural practice are listed in the report entitled "Typical Funerary Objects, Sacred Objects, and Cultural Patrimony of the Yavajo, Malagansett, Loomatilla, Tunipa, Chippesaw, and Southern Skyute," prepared by Backdirt Consultants, Inc. in consultation with the tribes and dated June 1, 1996 (Appendix A).

4. Sacred objects, which shall be understood to include those classes of objects identified by Yavajo, Malagansett, Loomatilla, Tunipa, Chippesaw, and Southern Skyute religious leaders as needed in the practice of traditional Yavajo, Malagansett, Loomatilla, Tunipa, Chippesaw, and/or Southern Skyute religions by their present-day adherents. Such classes of objects are identified in Appendix A.

5. Objects of cultural patrimony, which shall be understood to include those classes of items having ongoing historical, traditional, or cultural importance central to the Yavajo, Malagansett, Loomatilla, Tunipa, Chippesaw, and/or Southern Skyute tribes, as distinct from items that could be owned and alienated by individual tribal members. Such classes of objects are identified in Appendix A.

D. BLM shall determine custody of Native American cultural items as follows:

1. Should Alternative A, which crosses the Loomatilla Reservation, be selected for construction of the Pipeline, the Loomatilla tribe shall have custody of any Native American cultural items found within the external boundaries of that reservation. No other tribal lands are crossed by any of the alternatives.

2. For Native American cultural items found beyond the boundaries of the Loomatilla Reservation, BLM will determine custody based on the findings of the report entitled "Cultural Affiliation with Lands along the Alternative Routes of the Proposed Lightgas Pipeline," prepared by Backdirt Consultants, Inc. in consultation with the tribes and dated May 1, 1996 (Appendix B).

E. BLM and LTC shall treat, care for, and handle Native American cultural items as follows:

1. Treatment, care, and handling of Native American cultural items found during archeological data recovery at specific, pre-identified sites shall be in accordance with the data recovery plan for the specific site, as prepared, reviewed, and finalized in accordance with the Memorandum of Agreement (MOA) executed by BLM, the Utazona State Historic Preservation Officer, and the Advisory Council on Historic Preservation after consultation with the tribes pursuant to Section 106 of the National Historic Preservation Act, subject to paragraph II.H.

2. Native American cultural items found during archeological monitoring shall be treated, cared for, and handled as follows:

a) All pipeline-related ground disturbance shall be monitored by an archeological monitoring team employed by LTC and accepted by BLM after consultation with the tribes.

b) Should an object that in the opinion of the archeological monitoring team might be a Native American cultural item be found during the course of monitoring, LTC shall halt work that might disturb the item or items until the following procedures have been implemented:

(1) The archeological monitoring team shall inspect the possible Native American cultural item and record it in place to the extent feasible employing standard archeological recordation methods, subject to paragraph II.H. If the team determines that the object is not a Native American cultural item, it shall so certify in writing, and construction may continue in the vicinity of the object, subject to the terms of the MOA where an object of historical significance is found that is not a Native American Cultural Item.

(2) Where the archeological monitoring team certifies that the object is a Native American cultural item, LTC shall reroute construction to the extent feasible to leave the item or items in place and unharmed. The items shall be recorded in place by the monitoring team, and LTC will cover them with earth under the monitoring team's supervision, to protect them in place.

(3) Where rerouting is not feasible, the monitoring team shall remove the item or items to a safe location for study and preparation for reburial or repatriation, employing standard archeological field study and recordation procedures. LTC may resume construction in the vicinity as soon as the archeological monitoring team certifies that the item or items have been properly and safely removed.

(4) LTC will provide for recordation and analysis of items removed in accordance with Paragraph II.F.2.

F. BLM and LTC shall ensure that archeological recording and analysis of Native American cultural items is carried out as follows:

1. LTC shall record and analyze any Native American cultural items found during archeological data recovery at specific, pre-identified sites in accordance with the data recovery plan for the specific site, as prepared, reviewed, and finalized in accordance with the Memorandum of Agreement (MOA) executed by BLM, the Utazona State Historic Preservation Officer, and the Advisory Council on Historic Preservation after consultation with the tribes pursuant to Section 106 of the National Historic Preservation Act, subject to paragraph II.H.

2. LTC shall record and analyze any Native American cultural items found during archeological monitoring following the procedures set forth in the document entitled "Archeological Monitoring Plan, Lightgas Pipeline," prepared by Backdirt Consultants, Inc. in consultation with the tribes and dated May 20, 1996 (Appendix C).

3. In no case shall LTC allow analysis of Native American cultural items to extend beyond one year after the date such items are recovered, without the express written concurrence of BLM and the tribe(s) affiliated with such items. Analysis of material other than Native American cultural items may extend over a longer period of time.

G. BLM and LTC shall maintain continuous contact with the tribes throughout the conduct of archeological data recovery and monitoring, as follows:

1. As the U.S. Government's formal government-to-government contact with the tribe, BLM shall request the governing body of each tribe to designate an official point of contact (POC) to maintain ongoing contact with LTC.

2. LTC shall contact the POC during planning for any data recovery or monitoring on lands with which such tribe is affiliated, advise the POC of the work schedule, and invite the POC to participate in or monitor the work.

3. Through the POC, LTC shall offer employment to tribal members on all archeological data recovery projects and monitoring teams, and shall make special efforts to employ tribal members in work carried out on lands with which each tribe is affiliated.

4. Upon the identification of a possible Native American cultural item during data recovery or monitoring, LTC shall notify the POC, and invite the POC to observe and advise during the treatment and handling of the item.

5. LTC may, at its discretion, compensate or reimburse the POC for the POC's assistance.

6. LTC shall provide the tribes with written reports on all work accomplished.

H. BLM and LTC shall provide each tribe with reasonable opportunities to conduct traditional treatment of Native American cultural items during their recovery, analysis, treatment and handling. Should a tribe request to conduct ceremonies or other traditional activities with respect to a Native American cultural item or items, BLM and LTC will accommodate such request to the maximum extent allowable by considerations of health, safety, environmental protection, and the project schedule. BLM and LTC shall ensure that all Native American cultural items found during archeological data recovery and archeological monitoring are treated with respect, and that the following specific provisions are observed:

1. Sacred objects with which the Malagansett are affiliated shall not be washed or otherwise cleaned.

2. No person under the age of eighteen (18) years shall be permitted to view or handle any sacred object with which the Chippesaw are affiliated.

3. Human remains and funerary objects with which the Yavajo are affiliated shall be reburied by non-Yavajo persons, or by Yavajo persons who specifically volunteer to do so, as close to their location of recovery as is consistent with their continued safety.

4. Human remains with which the Loomatilla are affiliated shall be delivered unwashed and without analysis beyond the determination of age, sex, and major physical abnormalities and traumas to the Loomatilla Elder's Council for appropriate treatment.

I. BLM and LTC shall ensure that reports are prepared, meeting contemporary archeological standards, on each pre-planned data recovery project and on the archeological monitoring program on the lands with which each tribe is affiliated. In consultation with the tribes, BLM and LTC will ensure that these reports are designed to minimize the likelihood that they can be used to facilitate the excavation or vandalism of any Native American cultural item without the express permission of the affiliated tribe(s). LTC shall distribute reports to the tribes and to any parties specified in the MOA.

J. Except in the case of items disposed of in accordance with paragraphs H.3 and H.4, BLM and LTC shall ensure that Native American cultural items are disposed of in the following manner:

1. Upon the completion of analysis, LTC shall deliver all Native American cultural items to BLM. LTC shall ensure that all such items are appropriately labelled to designate the tribe with which each is affiliated. LTC may deliver items to BLM in lots as analysis is completed.

2. Within one week after receiving a lot of Native American cultural items, BLM shall contact the affiliated tribe through its POC, and arrange a time, place, and means of transferring the items to the tribe. BLM shall then proceed to transfer the items to the tribe, documenting the date, time, and place of such transfer and a description of the items transferred.

APPROVED:

_____

STATE DIRECTOR, BUREAU OF LAND MANAGEMENT

Index

A

Abandoned Shipwrecks Act (ASA), 203, 272

Advisory Council on Historic Preservation (ACHP), 15, 20, 25, 126, 128, 229, 265, 272

Action agencies, CRM jobs in, 241-242

Admiralty law 202-203

Archeological Data Preservation Act (ADPA), 138, 201

Alternative dispute resolution (ADR) 119

Advocacy, CRM jobs in, 243-234

African Burial Ground, New York City, 7 8, 57, 127

Agency-specific laws, 214

Agua Caliente Band of Cahuilla Indians, 98

Albuquerque, NM, 99

American Folklife Center, 19, 25

American Folklife Preservation Act, 19, 175

American Indians Against Desecration, 22

American Indian Movement, 22

American Indian Religious Freedom Act (AIRFA), 19, 156-159, 161-162, 272-273

Antiquities Act, 13

Anzalone, Ronald, 133-134

Arbitration, 119

Archeological and Historic Preservation Act of 1974, 199-200, 272

Archeological Data Preservation Act (ADPA), 199-200, 272

Archeological Resource Protection Act (ARPA), 20, 131, 197-199

Archeology: origins of dominance of CRM, 17-18

Army Materiel Command, 233

Artifacts, archeological, 201-202

Artifacts, non-archeological, 207-208

Assistance agency roles, 27

B

Barton, Clara, 208-209

Bickman, Leonard, and Debra Rog, 223

Birthplaces, Graves, and National Register of Historic Places, 81

Boone, Daniel, 138

Bowie State University, 120

Branch, Kristi, 175

Bremerton, Washington, 104

Brokering, 120

Building, historic, definition, 181

Burdge, Rabel J, and Colleagues, 5, 176

Bureau of Census, 169

C

Cahokia, 105-106

Cahuilla Indians, 98

Cantor, Larry W., 5, 36, 219

Cape Canaveral, 86

Carson, Rachel, 16

Carter, Jimmy, 20, 179-180

CEHP, Inc., 5, 215, 234

Cell-phone antennae, 105

Cemeteries and National Register of Historic Places, 81

Central Business Area (CBA), 179-181, 270

Certified Local Government program, 22

About The Author

Thomas F. King was a teen-aged pothunter. Interested in archeology by age 5, he dug into his first prehistoric site at age 14. By the time he completed undergraduate work in anthropology at San Francisco State University, he was supporting himself and his family as a field archeologist, working on "salvage archeology" projects—digging sites that were about to be destroyed by highways and reservoirs. King continued his archeological studies at UCLA and received his PhD from the University of California at Riverside. His career includes working as a consultant in historic preservation, as an archeologist with the National Park Service, with the "State" Historic Preservation Officer of the Trust Territory of the Pacific Islands, and with the ACHP. He brings to his writings and teachings a substantial knowledge of archeology; a more general acquaintance with architectural history, historical architecture, and planning; experience in writing and implementing laws, regulations, and guidelines; and an appreciation for the concerns of indigenous and other minority communities and groups. This book is drawn from the many short courses in historic preservation and cultural resource management that he has taught.

King can be contacted at TFKing106@aol.com.